CLIVE BARKER'S A-Z OF HORROR

COMPILED BY STEPHEN JONES

BBC Books

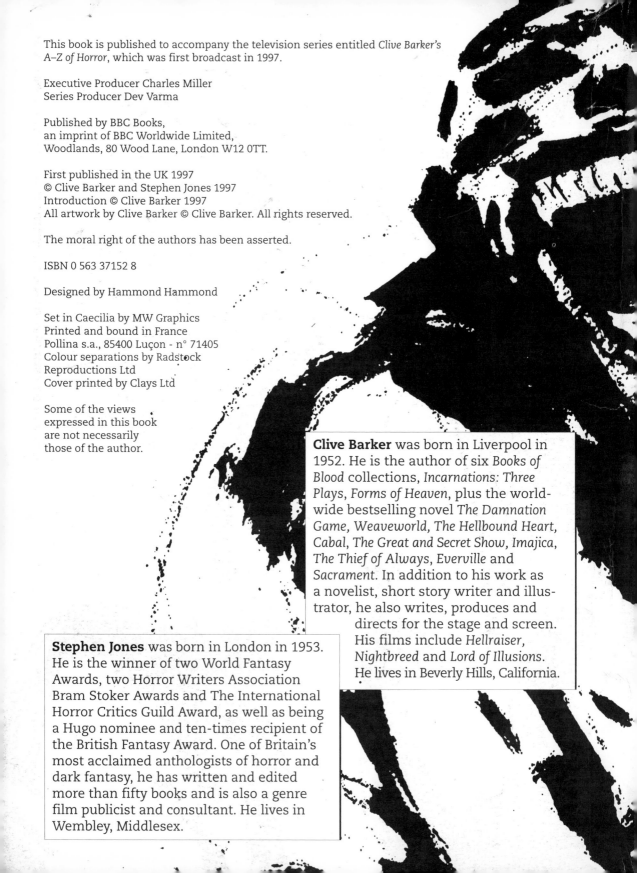

This book is published to accompany the television series entitled *Clive Barker's A–Z of Horror*, which was first broadcast in 1997.

Executive Producer Charles Miller
Series Producer Dev Varma

Published by BBC Books,
an imprint of BBC Worldwide Limited,
Woodlands, 80 Wood Lane, London W12 0TT.

First published in the UK 1997
© Clive Barker and Stephen Jones 1997
Introduction © Clive Barker 1997
All artwork by Clive Barker © Clive Barker. All rights reserved.

The moral right of the authors has been asserted.

ISBN 0 563 37152 8

Designed by Hammond Hammond

Set in Caecilia by MW Graphics
Printed and bound in France
Pollina s.a., 85400 Luçon - n° 71405
Colour separations by Radstock
Reproductions Ltd
Cover printed by Clays Ltd

Clive Barker was born in Liverpool in 1952. He is the author of six *Books of Blood* collections, *Incarnations: Three Plays*, *Forms of Heaven*, plus the world-wide bestselling novel *The Damnation Game*, *Weaveworld*, *The Hellbound Heart*, *Cabal*, *The Great and Secret Show*, *Imajica*, *The Thief of Always*, *Everville* and *Sacrament*. In addition to his work as a novelist, short story writer and illustrator, he also writes, produces and directs for the stage and screen. His films include *Hellraiser*, *Nightbreed* and *Lord of Illusions*. He lives in Beverly Hills, California.

Stephen Jones was born in London in 1953. He is the winner of two World Fantasy Awards, two Horror Writers Association Bram Stoker Awards and The International Horror Critics Guild Award, as well as being a Hugo nominee and ten-times recipient of the British Fantasy Award. One of Britain's most acclaimed anthologists of horror and dark fantasy, he has written and edited more than fifty books and is also a genre film publicist and consultant. He lives in Wembley, Middlesex.

CLIVE
BARKER'S
A-Z OF
HORROR

Acknowledgements

Special thanks to Clive Barker, Emma Tait, Julian Flanders, Sheila Ableman, Dev Varma, Viv Adelman, David Barraclough, Harlan Ellison, Michael A. Morrison, Marcel Burel, Stan Nicholls, Randy Broecker, Mandy Slater, Ramsey Campbell, Linda Fairbairn, Sarah Cartwright, Jane Willey, Robb Humphreys, Peter Atkins, Mike Wathen, Steve Roe, Tracey Smith and, especially, Kim Newman, for their help and support.

Grateful acknowledgement is also made to the many publications and individuals whose quotes are used to supplement the main text throughout this book, including Kathy Acker, Robert Bloch, William Castle, Lon Chaney Sr, David Cronenberg, Peter Cushing, August Derleth, Robert Englund, Riccardo Freda, John Wayne Gacy, William Gibson, Reverend Billy Graham, James Herbert, Clare Higgins, Alfred Hitchcock, Boris Karloff, Stephen King, Elsa Lanchester, Timothy Leary, Fritz Leiber, H.P. Lovecraft, Antonio Margheriti, Richard Matheson, Dan O'Bannon, Dorothy Parker, Edgar Allan Poe, Vincent Price, Chuck Russell, Quentin Tarantino, Lisa Tuttle, Dennis Wheatley and Gahan Wilson.

we fear death and dismemberment, we fear pain, insanity and loss, we even fear sexuality, and it's only by addressing these fears that we avoid living in a state of constant trepidation. Horror can speak of such things in a way that a more realistic or naturalistic genre can't.

Horror is a leap of faith and imagination in a world where the subconscious holds dominion; a call to enter a territory where no image or act is so damnable it cannot be explored, kissed and courted; finally – why whisper it? – embraced.

Clive Barker

Bibliographic Sources

I am indebted to the following books and periodicals for the supplementary quotes and information used in this volume:

The Aurum Film Encyclopaedia: Horror (Aurum Press, 1993) edited by Phil Hardy.

Behind the Mask: The Secrets of Hollywood's Monster Makers (Titan Books, 1994) by Mark Salisbury and Alan Hedgecock.

The BFI Companion to Horror (British Film Institute/Cassell Group, 1996) edited by Kim Newman.

Cinefantastique (Frederick S. Clark, Publisher & Editor).

Clive Barker's Shadows in Eden (Underwood-Miller, 1991) edited by Stephen Jones.

Cronenberg on Cronenberg (Faber and Faber, 1992) edited by Chris Rodley.

The Crow (Kitchen Sink Press, 1994) by J. O'Barr.

The Crow: The Movie (Titan Books, 1995) by Jeff Conner & Robert Zuckerman.

Danse Macabre (Macdonald, 1981) by Stephen King.

The Dark Side (Allan Bryce, Editor).

Deviant: The Shocking True Story of the Original 'Psycho' (New English Library, 1989) by Harold Schechter.

Expressions of Dread, Issue 3, Winter 1993/94 (Spencer Lamm, Editor in Chief).

Fangoria (Anthony Timpone, Editor).

Filmfax (Michael Stein, Editor/Publisher).

The Films of Peter Lorre (The Citadel Press, 1982) by Stephen D. Youngkin, James Bigwood and Raymond G. Cabana, Jr.

The Films of Roger Corman: Brilliance on a Budget (Arco Publishing, 1982) by Ed Naha.

The Frankenscience Monster (Ace Publishing, 1969) by Forrest J Ackerman.

From Hell (Mad Love Publishing/Kitchen Sink Press, 1994/95) by Alan Moore and Eddie Campbell.

From Hell: The Compleat Scripts (Borderlands Press/SpiderBaby Grafix, 1994) by Alan Moore.

Funeral Party, No. 1, 1995 (David Fox, Marlene Leach, Michael Rorro, Shade Rupe, Editors).

Grand Guignol (Editions Henri Veyrier, 1979) by François Rivière and Gabrielle Wittkop.

Graven Images: The Best Horror, Fantasy, and Science Fiction Film Art from the Collection of Ronald V. Borst (Grove Press, 1992) edited by Ronald V. Borst, Keith Burns and Leith Adams.

Harlan Ellison's Watching (Underwood-Miller, 1989) by Harlan Ellison.

The Haunted Realm: Ghosts, Witches and Other Strange Tales (Webb & Bower/Michael Joseph, 1987) by Simon Marsden.

The Hellraiser Chronicles (Titan Books, 1992) edited by Stephen Jones.

The Horror People (Macdonald and Jane's, 1976) by John Brosnan.

H.P. Lovecraft's Book of Horror (Robinson Publishing, 1994) edited by Stephen Jones and Dave Carson.

Horror: 100 Best Books (New English Library, 1992) edited by Stephen Jones and Kim Newman.

The Illustrated Dinosaur Movie Guide (Titan Books, 1993) by Stephen Jones.

The Illustrated Edgar Allan Poe (Jupiter Books, 1976) edited by Roy Gasson.

The Illustrated Frankenstein Movie Guide (Titan Books, 1993) by Stephen Jones.

The Illustrated Werewolf Movie Guide (Titan Books, 1996) by Stephen Jones.

James Herbert by Horror Haunted (New English Library, 1992) edited by Stephen Jones.

Lon of 1000 Faces! (Morrison, Raven-Hill Company, 1983) by Forrest J Ackerman.

Million, No.1, January/February 1991 (David Pringle, Editor & Publisher).

Nightmare Movies (Harmony Books, 1988) by Kim Newman.

Once Around the Bloch (Tor Books, 1993) by Robert Bloch.

The Penguin Encyclopaedia of Horror and the Supernatural (Viking, 1986) edited by Jack Sullivan.

Sci-Fi Entertainment (Edward Flixman, Editor).

Scream Queens: Heroines of the Horrors (Collier Books, 1978) by Calvin Thomas Beck.

Shivers (David Miller, Editor).

Shock Xpress (Stefan Jaworzyn, Editor).

Speakeasy (Stuart Green, Editor).

Species Design (Morpheus International, 1995) by H.R. Giger.

Tabula Rasa (David Carroll and Kyla Ward, Editors).

The Vampire Book: The Encyclopædia of the Undead (Visible Ink Press, 1994) by J. Gordon Melton.

Video Watchdog (Tim and Donna Lucas, Editors).

Who's Who in Horror and Fantasy Fiction (Elm Tree Books, 1977) by Mike Ashley.

The publishers would like to acknowledge the following for permission to reproduce copyright material:

'**Children of the Corn**' in **Nightshift** (Doubleday, 1978) by Stephen King.

Drawing Blood (Delacorte Press, 1993) by Poppy Z. Brite.

It (Viking, 1986) by Stephen King.

Life Among the Savages (Farrar, Straus & Young, 1953) by Shirley Jackson.

'**Precious**' in **Dark Voices 5** (Pan Books, 1993) by Roberta Lannes.

Psycho (Transworld, 1959) by Robert Bloch.

'**The Call of Cthulhu**' in **Weird Tales** (February, 1928) by H.P. Lovecraft.

'**The Chimney**' in **Whispers** (Doubleday, 1977) by Ramsey Campbell.

The Devil Rides Out (Hutchinson, 1935) by Dennis Wheatley.

The Haunting of Hill House (Viking Press, 1959) by Shirley Jackson.

The Lottery (Farrar, Straus & Young, 1949) by Shirley Jackson.

'**The Madonna**' in **Books of Blood Volume 5** (Sphere, 1984) by Clive Barker.

The Secret Life of Laszlo, Count Dracula (Hyperion, 1994) by Roderick Anscombe.

'**The Small Assassin**' in **Dark Carnival** (Arkham House, 1947) by Ray Bradbury.

'**The Whisperer in Darkness**' in **Weird Tales** (August, 1931) by H.P. Lovecraft.

They Used Dark Forces (Hutchinson, 1964) by Dennis Wheatley.

Uncharted Seas (Hutchinson, 1938) by Dennis Wheatley.

We Have Always Lived in the Castle (Viking, 1962) by Shirley Jackson.

CONTENTS

An encyclopaedia dealing with the subject of horror is, in a sense, a delirious paradox. Most horror, whether it's real or fictitious, literary or cinematic, deals with the eruption of chaos into human existence (or else the revelation of its constant, unseen presence), while an arrangement like 'A is for American Psycho, Z is for Zombie', implies order: a neat examination of the whole grim business, laid out for our easy consumption. Between these covers, the title suggests, is all you need to know, a handy guide to the atrocities everyone should be familiar with in case they come up over cocktails. Oh, the insights you'll be able to proffer; the droll asides on mortuary practice; the off-hand remarks on the sociological significance of killer clowns.

Of course, this *isn't* all you need to know; not by a long way. The title of this book is a convenience. Perhaps it's a comfort, too, implying as it does a schematic for the encapsulation of terror. But the matter at hand can never be summarized in a book or a television series. The truth is far more complex. As soon as we begin to delve into the nature of horror, or attempt to list its manifestations in our culture, the sheer scale of the beast becomes apparent.

Horror is everywhere. It's in fairy tales and the evening headlines, it's in street corner gossip and the incontrovertible facts of history. It's in playground ditties (*Ring-a-ring o' roses* is a sweet little plague song); it's in the doctor's surgery ('I've some bad news, I'm afraid...'); it's on the altar, bleeding for our sins ('Forgive them, Father, for they know not what they do'). It is so much a part of our lives (and deaths) that a hundred volumes could not fully detail its presence.

This isn't to say we should give up on the endeavour. After all, don't we make everything in our lives – art, love, children – in the certainty that what we create will be flawed? Why not an encyclopaedia? Let's make the lists anyway knowing they're arbitrary. Let's pretend – at least for a little while – that we consider the subject authoritatively covered. Let's even ask a few questions of ourselves, as though there might be some kind of answer to be had.

We must inevitably begin with the root question: what is horror? We can all point to its presence. It's in black-jacketed books and lurid movie posters. It's in police reports from murder sites and tearful recollections from battlefields. It's in our nightmares. It's in our secret ambitions. But is there any common thread of subject matter that connects all these manifestations? Maybe. Perhaps the body and its vulnerability. Perhaps the mind and its brittleness. Perhaps love and its absence.

What becomes apparent, however, the more closely we study the issue, is how misleading the term actually is, describing as it does a response rather than a subject. Horror elicits far more complex responses than gasps and giddiness. It can shame us into recognizing our own capacity for cruelty; it can arouse us, making plain the connection between death and sexual feeling; it can inspire our imaginations, removing us to places where our most sacred taboos may be challenged and overturned. If this encyclopaedia, whether on the page or on the screen, simply serves to alert the viewer or the reader to the intricacies of all this, then it will have provided no small service.

Do I believe it will make converts of the blinkered commentators who think that horror – particularly if it takes the form of popular entertainment – is sick or likely to degrade fine minds? No, I'm afraid not. I was, at the beginning of my career, a passionate believer in

16

the need to convince people to re-evaluate horror, particularly in its literary form. After all, I argued, the best of science-fiction novels and spy thrillers are now viewed as literature, why should the same respect not be paid to a fictional form that uses supernatural conceits to debate and illuminate the dark side of our personal planets? Much of the work in the genre is, of course, sheer sensationalism, but then there are a thousand disposable hackworks for every book by John Carré or Frank Herbert. Shouldn't we judge a genre by its finest members not by its runts? That was the

core of my position. But over the years I've largely given up on the debate. People will come to the point-of-view in their own time or not at all.

(Of course, there's the 'guilty pleasure' aspect of all this: that while I love well-turned phrases and great cinema, I also have a sentimental fondness for the literary or cinematic equivalent of *Titus Andronicus*. Indeed, there are times when the sheer artlessness of a Z-grade zombie flick can tellingly reveal the root of the genre's fascination in a fashion that a more sophisticated piece of work may conceal.)

Here – while we're talking about horror's appeal – may be an appropriate spot to discuss its enduring popularity. I have no new answers to the puzzle, only the strengthening sense that, as our century advances and the casual cruelty of our world becomes ever more visible through the medium of television, we seem to take comfort in fantastications of that cruelty; fictions in which we may savour the very subjects that distress us in the real world. Does it empower us to do so; give us a sense of control over forces that, in truth, threaten to over-whelm us? Or are we simply warming ourselves at the blaze that's burning our culture down? I suspect a little of both.

Bathing for a time in the red rivers of violence and retribution that feed the heart of this fiction may indeed wash away some part of our insanity; discharging our anger by indulging our private monsters. But if it doesn't – if we're simply making ourselves all the crazier by inflaming these appetites – then I humbly suggest that it's the way of the world and perhaps our culture, in its fall from faith and certainty, *needs* to go through a dark night of the soul, in which the atrocities of street and battlefront, and those conjured by storytellers, become one seamless nightmare...

Only this seems certain: the subject is part of our psyche from

childhood, enshrined in innumerable tales as a force that helps us understand the primal battle of our natures. The abomination, whether it comes in the form of a fairy tale dragon, a serial killer, a piece of special effects or a crazed terrorist, is a necessary part of the human story. It defines what the best in us despises; and reminds us how close to it we come in our most forbidden thoughts.

There are countless interpretations of this enigma, and – as I stated at the beginning – this book can offer only a few chosen more from personal taste than out of any truly encyclopaedic ambition. There's much here that fascinates me: the history of Grand Guignol, the work of Messerschmidt, tales of lynch-mobs and vampires and the End of the World. But it's just a beginning; a collage of facts and ruminations, notes and witticisms from an extraordinary cross section of sources, which might be extended in any one of a thousand different directions, if a researcher chose to explore a little further. It can never be definitive.

Think of it, perhaps, as footnotes to the grand encyclopaedia that we are each of us amassing as we pass through our lives. That book will contain a number of entries under *bliss*, I hope, and *love*. But there will almost inevitably be a whole host of entries under *horror*. If these footnotes help illuminate the moments of dread and despair that inevitably come into our lives, however careful or sheltered an existence we lead, then it has found a fine purpose. And if such a high-flown intention offends you, try reading the book in the bath. You'll find upon emerging that after a certain age – say, eighteen – the mirror may remind you how much we need the comfort of another's misery.

Clive Barker

A For American Psycho

A

Opposite: Ed Gein is arrested in 1957.

IN THE WINTER OF 1957, police on the trail of a missing woman were led to a Wisconsin farmhouse by the sighting of a pick-up van near the Plainfield hardware store run by the missing 58-year-old widow. What they found there stunned the local community. As the facts of the case seeped into the American consciousness, they became the stuff of myth – four classic horror movies over three decades drew on the atrocities in that small town to reflect the nightmares of their own age.

And each movie went a little deeper into the death, the ritual and the insanity...

'You know, America was probably very naïve at that time and very unsuspecting,' says Roy Rowan, who covered the investigation for *Life* magazine. 'And suddenly I think this changed people's attitudes. They suddenly realized that maybe you shouldn't trust the person next door. People knew about horrors and they had seen all kinds of Frankenstein and Dracula movies, but that was a different world. This was our world. This was small town America, where things like that just didn't happen.

'Plainfield was a typical American farm community. A small place consisting of very conservative people who were not accustomed to having a horrible crime like this committed in their midst.'

Police investigators believed that a sales receipt for a gallon of anti-freeze found at the hardware store pointed to a suspect who was alleged to have shot Mrs Bernice Worden with a .22 calibre rifle from her own store. The victim's body was subsequently discovered by Sheriff Arthur Schley hanging by its heels on the farm of 51-year-old Edward Gein. Her heart was found in a coffee can on a stove in the house.

Virgil 'Buck' Batterman was the Deputy Sheriff of Waushara County at the time. 'I went out to the house with the sheriff. It was dark; we all had flashlights. The sheriff took the shed, I went into the kitchen, and Deputy Fritz went into the living room. Then the sheriff called out that he had found her hanging in the shed.

'Of course, seeing her there without a head and cut open like you would a deer, it would make anybody sick, but Deputy Fritz did get sick and went outside and sat in his squad car. He didn't come back into the house after that.'

Dan Hanley, a reporter for the *Milwaukee Journal*, remembers arriving at the scene: 'I came up the drive and went around the back where Mrs Worden had been found in the shed. From a reporting standpoint there was a problem with this story in that the things that were

found were so horrible and so grizzly that we couldn't write about them.'

Roy Rowan first heard about the discovery on a news flash on the radio: 'I remember thinking when we got to this house, would Mrs Worden still be hanging from the rafters? What caught my attention right away in this story was the fact that it was the opening of the deer season, and here was an innocent woman, the owner of a hardware store, that had been murdered and then dressed out like a deer. This to me was just revolting. It was a stark, terrible image in my mind.'

Georgia Foster remembers hearing about the murder on the ten o'clock news, and asked her neighbour if she knew anything about it. 'She said, yes, that it was Mrs Worden that was killed and she said, "You'll never guess who they picked up." And I said, "Well, who was that?" She said, "Eddie Gein." Neither one of us could believe

Opposite: The interior of Ed Gein's home.
Left: The exterior of Gein's farmhouse.

that he would hurt anybody. We just knew Eddie wouldn't hurt a fly. So I went home and locked my door for the first time in years.'

'I knew him pretty well all my life,' says another neighbour, Bob Hill, 'probably from the time I was six years old. I don't know of anybody else that was real close to Eddie like I had been. He was a lonely man. He was quiet and withdrawn. Some people thought he was a hermit, I guess.'

Just a few hours after he had butchered Mrs Worden, Ed Gein agreed to drive the then sixteen-year-old Bob Hill into town. The boy's parents even invited Gein in for supper afterwards. 'So we were in the house eating

A supper that night,' recalls Hill, 'and my brother-in-law came in from deer hunting and he wanted to know what all the commotion was going on in town. There were a lot of squad cars and red lights flashing and that sort of thing.

'So I asked Ed, "Well, let's go to town and see what's happening." And he said, "Well, yeah, that'll be fine." So we got in the car, and he had it started up and running, and then another car pulled up on the road and it was a county squad car. A police officer came over to our car and Ed opened his window, and the officer says, "Are you Ed Gein? Well, I'd like to talk to you." They took him off to Waushara right then and there, and that was actually the last time that I'd ever see him.'

Among the filth and squalor of Ed Gein's house, the police discovered a bizarre collection of preserved body parts and human skulls and skeletons. There were nine death masks covered with human skin, strips of skin had been used to cover chairs, and a bowl was fashioned out of a skull. In all, Gein had collected the parts from

> ' "I brought Mother back home with me. That was the exciting part, you see – going out to the cemetery at night and digging up the grave. She'd been shut up in that coffin for such a long time that at first I thought she really *was* dead. But she wasn't, of course. She couldn't be." '
>
> FROM PSYCHO BY ROBERT BLOCH

"THE DARK BROTHERS" by HAROLD LAWLOR

SEPTEMBER

Weird Tales

15¢

Ray Bradbury

Seabury Quinn

THE SKULL OF THE MARQUIS DE SADE

Robert Bloch

THRILL-PACKED TALES OF SCIENCE AND FANTASY!

fantastic

ADVENTURE

JULY 25¢

STILL 132 PAGES

The DEAD DON'T DIE! By ROBERT BLOCH

COULD A LONE GIRL FIGHT AGAINST THE HORROR OF THESE LIVING DEAD?

BOOKS BY ROBERT BLOCH (1917–1994)

NOVELS: *The Scarf* (1947), *Spiderweb* (1954), *The Kidnaper* (1954), *The Will to Kill* (1954), *Shooting Star* (1958), *Psycho* (1959), *The Dead Beat* (1960), *Firebug* (1961), *Terror* (1962), *The Couch* (1962), *Ladies Day/This Crowded Earth* (1968), *The Star Stalker* (1968), *The Todd Dossier* (as Collier Young, 1969), *Sneak Preview* (1971), *It's All in Your Mind* (1971), *Night-World* (1972), *American Gothic* (1974), *Reunion with Tomorrow* (1978), *Strange Eons* (1978), *There is a Serpent in Eden* (1979), *Psycho II* (1982), *Twilight Zone The Movie* (1983), *The Night of the Ripper* (1984), *Unholy Trinity (The Scarf/The Dead Beat/The Couch*, 1986), *Screams (The Will to Kill/Firebug/The Star Stalker*, 1989), *Lori* (1989), *Psycho House* (1990), *The Jekyll Legacy* (with Andre Norton, 1990).

COLLECTIONS: *Sea-Kissed* (1945), *The Opener of the Way* (1945), *Terror in the Night and Other Stories* (1958), *Pleasant Dreams* (1960), *Blood Runs Cold* (1961), *Nightmares* (1961), *Yours Truly Jack the Ripper: Tales of Horror (aka The House of the Hatchet*, 1962), *More Nightmares* (1962), *Atoms and Evil* (1962), *Horror-7 (aka Torture Garden*, 1963), *Bogey Men* (1963), *Tales in a Jugular Vein* (1965), *The Skull of the Marquis de Sade and Other Stories* (1965), *Chamber of Horrors* (1966), *The Living Demons* (1967), *The Night-Walker* (1967), *Dragons and Nightmares* (1969), *Bloch and Bradbury (aka Fever Dream and Other Fantasies*, with Ray Bradbury, 1969), *Fear Today Gone Tomorrow* (1971), *The King of Terrors* (1977), *Cold Chills* (1977), *The Best of Robert Bloch* (1977), *Out of the Mouth of Graves* (1979), *Such Stuff as Screams Are Made Of* (1979), *Mysteries of the Worm* (1979), *Midnight Pleasures* (1987), *Lost in Time and Space with Lefty Feep* (1987), *The Selected Stories of Robert Bloch* (1987), *Fear and Trembling* (1989), *The Early Fears* (1994), *Robert Bloch: Appreciations of the Master* (1995).

the bodies of fifteen middle-aged women.

He had killed two of them and the rest were taken from graves he had violated. Although the forensic experts had been involved in numerous homicide investigations, they had never seen anything like what the police had discovered at the Gein farm.

As journalist Dan Hanley remembers: 'They'd reach into a box and they would pull out a string and it would look like it was a necklace. But it turned out to be a necklace made of nipples. The upholstered furniture was

'We went in just as Janet Leigh's sister is descending into the apple cellar at the end of *Psycho*. She's going down the stairs and we know that Mama – or rather we don't know that Mama Bates is at the bottom of the stairs, in fact. So the first four or five minutes of any horror movie I ever saw was her going down into the apple cellar, Mrs Bates turning around, her knocking the light – all that stuff – and then Norman comes to the door dressed as Mummy and I thought, "Shit! Is it all like this?"'

Clive Barker

'We see that the Werewolf myth does indeed run through a great many modern horror novels and movies. Perhaps the best example of all is Alfred Hitchcock's film *Psycho*, although in all deference to the master, the idea was there for the taking in Robert Bloch's novel.'

Stephen King

Opposite: Anthony
Perkins, still crazy in
Psycho III.

'It still works – every
brooding, manipula-
tive scene. I even
liked the pseudo-
psychological expla-
nation of Norman
Bates' condition at
the end of the
picture: the voice of
reason attempting to
make sense of insan-
ity and failing to do
anything but make
Norman more
mysterious. That's
why I dislike the
Psycho sequels. Not
because they're badly
made (they're not),
but because
Norman's mystery
is eroded when the
plot makes him a
short-order cook.'

Clive Barker

made from body parts. They just couldn't believe what they were coming across.'

On 6 January 1958, Ed Gein was found innocent by reason of insanity, on a single count of murder. He was committed to the Central State Hospital in Waupun for an indeterminate term. 'From the opinions of various experts,' said Circuit Judge Herbert A. Bunde, 'I think it is adequate for me to say that it does not appear that he will ever be at liberty again. Perhaps that is a desirable conclusion.'

In 1974, Gein asked for a sanity hearing, but his peti-tion for freedom was turned down by Circuit Judge Robert Gollmar. At the hearing, authorities testified that Gein was never a problem. He worked as a carpenter, mason and hospital attendant, but he reacted poorly to the other inmates. 'They treat you pretty good there,' he told the press.

According to Harold Schechter, a Professor of English at Queens College, New York, and author of *Deviant: The Shocking True Story of the Original 'Psycho'*, a biography of Ed Gein: 'The really significant thing about Gein is that, in a sense, he Americanized horror. Before Gein and the films that sprang from the obsession with this case, the monsters that populated horror films were always for-eign in some way. They either came from Transylvania, or Egypt, or from outer space. With Gein you really get the beginning of a very specifically American kind of horror.

'Gein was a real-life ghoul. He dug up the corpses of middle-aged women, hauled them back to the murk of his remote ramshackle farmhouse and there dissected them. He turned their flesh into furniture, turned their skulls into soup bowls. Skinned their faces, stuffed them with paper, and hung them on the bedroom walls like hunting trophies. Even today, when serial killing has become, if not epidemic, then certainly more common-place than it used to be, these are crimes that still seem unprecedented in their ghastliness.'

A year after the police discovered the Wisconsin house of horrors, a 41-year-old writer of pulp magazine stories sat down to write a novel in which a seemingly normal and ordinary small-town resident led a dual life as a psychotic murderer, unsuspected by his neighbours. The author was Robert Bloch (1917–1994), and the title of his book was *Psycho*.

'I based my story on the *situation* rather than on any person, living or dead, involved in the Gein affair,' Bloch later recalled. 'Indeed, I knew very little of the details concerning the case and virtually nothing about Gein himself at the time. It was only some years later that I

PSYCHO

USA, 1960. Dir: Alfred Hitchcock. With: Anthony Perkins, Vera Miles, John Gavin, Martin Balsam, John McIntire, Janet Leigh. Paramount. B&W.

One of the most famous horror films ever made, based on the novel by Robert Bloch. Best remembered for its Hitchcockian set-pieces (the murder of Marion Crane [Leigh] in the shower, the killing of Milton Arbogast [Balsam] at the top of the stairs). Perkins gives a marvellously subdued performance as the insane Norman Bates. The shock discovery of Norman's mummified mother is overshadowed by the final scene of Norman talking in both his own and his mother's voices. During its original release, patrons were not allowed into the movie theatre after the screening had begun. Great music score by Bernard Herrmann. S.J.

Sequels: *Psycho II* (Dir: Richard Franklin, 1983); *Psycho III* (Dir: Anthony Perkins, 1986); *Bates Motel* (Dir: Richard Rothstein, TV 1987); *Psycho IV The Beginning* (Dir: Mick Garris, TV 1990).

discovered how closely the imaginary character I'd created resembled the real Ed Gein both in overt act and apparent motivation.

'But at the time I decided to write a novel based on the notion that the man next door may be a monster, unsuspected even in the gossip-ridden microcosm of small-town life. In order to become a successful serial murderer in a close-knit rural society, a man must adopt a reclusive existence: operating a motel on the outskirts of town seemed a solution. So I invented Norman Bates. I built him a motel and I installed a shower in it for him.'

Shortly after *Psycho* was published in 1959, Bloch's agent was approached by someone from the talent agency MCA with an offer to buy the book for the movies. It was a blind offer – the buyer's name wasn't mentioned,

just a flat fee of $5000. Bloch refused and told his agent to hold out for more. A few days later MCA came back with an increased bid of $9500, which the author accepted.

'My agent got ten per cent, my publishers took fifteen, the tax people skimmed off their share of the loot, and I ended up with about $6250. Hitchcock got *Psycho*, and the rest is history.'

When director Alfred Hitchcock was erroneously told that Bloch wasn't available to write the screenplay, the assignment went to radio writer Joseph Stefano.

'It was a very strange and seemingly good time in the country,' recalls Stefano, 'but it wasn't a good time at all.

'Psycho made me neither rich nor famous, but it gradually invested me with a small amount of notoriety.'
Robert Bloch

Most of us knew that. But if you think about where we were before *Psycho* and where we were after *Psycho*, it's almost as if *Psycho* was the robin that tells you winter is here – and it sure as hell came.

'It was a bigger movie than anybody thought it was going to be, including me. It became important, and I think a lot of the talk about how terrible and shocking it was was because we didn't necessarily want to talk about how important all this was. A boy attracted to his mother. A boy who won't bury his mother. I mean, terrible ideas are in that movie and they had to be made palatable.'

Above: Alfred Hitchcock directs Janet Leigh, behind-the-scenes on *Psycho*.

DERANGED

Canada, 1974. Dir: Jeff Gillen and Alan Ormsby. With: Roberts Blossom, Marion Waldman, Cosette Lee, Micki Moore, Robert Warner, Pat Orr. American International/Karr International. Colour.

Based on the same source material as *Psycho* (1960) and *The Texas Chainsaw Massacre* (1974), this low budget chiller benefits from Blossom's wonderfully deranged performance as Wisconsin murderer and necrophile Ezra Cobb, who keeps a bunch of mummified bodies (created by Tom Savini) around his house. 'Absolutely True' announces the opening title, and just to prove it, Leslie Carlson pretends to be a reporter who keeps interrupting the narrative with his on-camera observations. Some scenes were cut for British release. *S.J.*

Opposite: The wonderful Roberts Blossom looking totally *Deranged*.

Gein's psychiatrist, Dr George Arndt, explains that, 'Mr Gein's mother was a very domineering woman and he listened to her because Mother was the dominant theme in his life. And when Mother died and he could not raise her from the dead as he'd hoped he could, he then wanted to find replacements. If he couldn't have his mother when she was deceased, then he'd have to have a mother substitute.'

'It was psychiatrists that said that he was so in love with his mother, that was why he had to rob those graves and bring parts of women back to remind him of his mother,' says Virgil Batterman. 'But that's psychiatrists...'

Dr Arndt also points out that, 'Mr Gein in his younger years had been exposed to animals being slaughtered. His parents ran a grocery store and a meat market, and he was told never to go back in that one area there. One time he did see Mother with a bloody apron on, and that made a lasting impression on him.'

Following the success of *Psycho* (1960), countless other films about psychologically disturbed killers reached the movie screen. In 1974, the Canadian film *Deranged* depicted many of the events of the Gein case. However, it was another film made the same year, *The Texas Chainsaw Massacre,* that would capture the public's imagination.

'I read *The Texas Chainsaw Massacre* as a fairy tale which has a great deal to do with the Vietnam War anxieties among the young,' says Gein's biographer Harold Schechter. 'It seems to be a vision of America transformed into this vast killing machine that you know is feeding off its own young.'

'My relatives that lived in a town close to Ed Gein told me these terrible stories,' explains *Texas Chainsaw* director Tobe Hooper, 'these tales of human skin lampshades and furniture. I grew up with that like a horror story you tell around a camp-fire. I didn't even know about Ed Gein, I just knew about something that happened that was horrendous. But the image really stuck.

'I was thinking to create a house of ultimate horror. A house that said and smelled and tasted of death. I had to dress and redress that house many times to get the look I wanted. Like someone could just roll their sleeves up and dip their hands into death itself.

'Things are scary. The news is scary, the times are scary. We were young and naïve back then and we didn't

'When I discovered that Ed Gein really did some of these things, that he actually used meat hooks and was a cannibal, it truly surprised me'
Tobe Hooper (above)

THE TEXAS CHAINSAW MASSACRE

USA, 1974. Dir: Tobe Hooper. With: Marilyn Burns, Allen Danziger, Paul A. Partain, William Vail, Teri McMinn, Gunnar Hansen. Vortex/Henkel/Hooper Productions. Colour.

Co-scripted, produced and directed by Hooper, this powerful shocker was originally banned in Britain and only released with a local London certificate. Loosely based on the real-life exploits of Wisconsin psycho Ed Gein, the amateurish performances are overcome by the film's relentless depiction of a group of teenagers being subjected to death and degradation by a bunch of backwoods crazies, including the memorable Leatherface (Hansen). Surprisingly, not as gory as it is reputed to be, with some nice touches of the supernatural. Narrated by John Larroquette. The first sequel was also banned in Britain. *S.J.*

Sequels: *The Texas Chainsaw Massacre 2* (Dir: Tobe Hooper, 1986); *Leatherface The Texas Chainsaw Massacre 3* (Dir: Jeff Burr, 1989); *The Return of the Texas Chainsaw Massacre* (Dir: Kim Henkel, 1994).

Right: Leatherface in *The Texas Chainsaw Massacre.*

AFTER A DECADE
OF SILENCE...
THE BUZZZ
IS BACK.

THE
**TEXAS
CHAINSAW
MASSACRE
PART
2**

'Sometimes it's good
to be in the hands of
a maniac (just so
long as it's in art, not
life), and what Tobe
Hooper did with this
film was signal to his
audience that he
didn't give a shit for
their finer feelings.
The picture therefore
becomes an assault.
Its narrative is mini-
mal; its visuals are
grittily real. To com-
plete the achieve-
ment, Hooper created
Leatherface and his
family – characters
whose relentless,
ironic, obsessive
malevolence is
uniquely modern.
Most monsters of the
past had moments of
regret or fear: these
beasts know neither.'

Clive Barker

THE SILENCE OF THE LAMBS

USA, 1991. Dir: Jonathan Demme. With: Jodie Foster,
Anthony Hopkins, Scott Glenn, Ted Levine, Anthony Heald,
Diane Baker. Orion Pictures. Colour.

Very classy horror thriller, based on the bestselling novel by
Thomas Harris, and a prequel to the underrated *Manhunter*
(1986). Foster stars as a rookie FBI agent who must use the
knowledge of imprisoned psychotic psychiatrist Dr Hannibal Lector (an Oscar-winning performance by Hopkins as
'Hannibal the Cannibal') to track down Gein-like serial
killer Buffalo Bill (Levine), so named because he skins his
kidnapped victims. With Charles Napier, Roger Corman and
Chris Isaak. This huge box office hit also won Academy
Awards for Best Picture, Actress (Foster), Director and
Adapted Screenplay (Ted Tally). *S.J.*

know where all of this was heading. But now horror is
taking a different shape.

'Today it seems there's a glorification of serial killers.
My advice to film-makers is to be very cautious, because
when the first *Texas Chainsaw* was made the power of
film wasn't yet realized, nor the cause and effect on
values.'

According to Harold Schechter, 'What you see in that
film is really a version of a very old and widely distrib-
uted kind of folk story about taboo rooms or houses that
you are forbidden from entering. But of course people do
enter and what they discover there is a room full of dismembered corpses and they themselves are then killed
and dismembered. So the facts of the Gein case became
assimilated in this kind of story. It's as though there is
some kind of archaic level of our minds that makes sense
of these horrors in terms of these stories.'

Senile and suffering from cancer, Ed Gein died on 26
July 1984, of respiratory failure, in the Mendota Mental
Health Institute in Madison, one of the Wisconsin insti-
tutions for the incurably insane that had been his home
for nearly thirty years. He was 78 years old.

'There's a quality of wonder about our relationship to
Gein,' continues Schechter. 'It's as though one of those
figures that haunts the very darkest places of our minds
has suddenly appeared in bright daylight, stepped out
into the real world. Like we are encountering a supernatural monster, made flesh.

'The bad do what the good only dream. I think that
sums up the fascination, not only with Ed Gein but with
horror in general.'

B for Beelzebub

B

THE BEST (OR WORST) thing about being human is that the story doesn't necessarily end with us. Horror believes *absolutely* in strange, unknowable dark gods and demons. Agents of chaos who must never be forgotten, or domesticated, or mocked – because, in the end, they are that dark part of ourselves which we fear to embrace. And, as anyone who has laughed at a demon will tell you, when they show *their* teeth, they can be vicious beyond all our imaginings...

When the film *The Exorcist* was released in 1973, the devil had been dormant for some while. For most people, satanic forces had been confined to Samantha's cute relatives in TV's *Bewitched*. What writer William Peter Blatty and director William Friedkin understood is that dark gods do exist – *very* dark gods indeed.

The inspiration for the original novel dates back to when Blatty was at Georgetown University, Washington. There he read local newspaper accounts of an exorcism involving a fourteen-year-old boy in Mount Rainier, Maryland, in 1949. In 1970 the author, who had once considered becoming a Jesuit and entering the priesthood, began researching incidents of possession and demonology, ultimately basing his book on an earlier exorcism carried out in Earling, Iowa, in 1928, as well as the Mount Rainier episode and various historical cases, dating back to the Bible.

The book almost immediately caused controversy when it was published by Harper and Row in 1971,

Right and opposite: Memorable moments from *The Exorcist*.

remaining for fifty-five consecutive weeks in the best-seller charts, and Blatty sold the film rights to Warner Bros. for a reported $641,000. The film began shooting on 14 August 1972, in a hospital on Welfare Island, New York. Sixteen months and $10 million later it opened in twenty key American cities on Boxing Day 1973. Neither producer/screenwriter Blatty nor director Friedkin were prepared for the repercussions.

'It's what we would call today a docu-drama,' explains Friedkin. 'For a great deal of it is based on whatever we could discover about the original case. The novel that Bill Blatty wrote is based on a possible true case of demonic possession. There are more things in heaven and earth than we can understand or appreciate or explain. And I still think that is true of *The Exorcist*.'

The film soon broke attendance records in most movie theatres, and people stood in line for more than

'Friedkin's film of *The Exorcist* appeared and became a social phenomenon in itself. Lines stretched around the block in every major city where it played, and even in towns which normally rolled up their sidewalks promptly at 7.30, midnight shows were scheduled.'

Stephen King

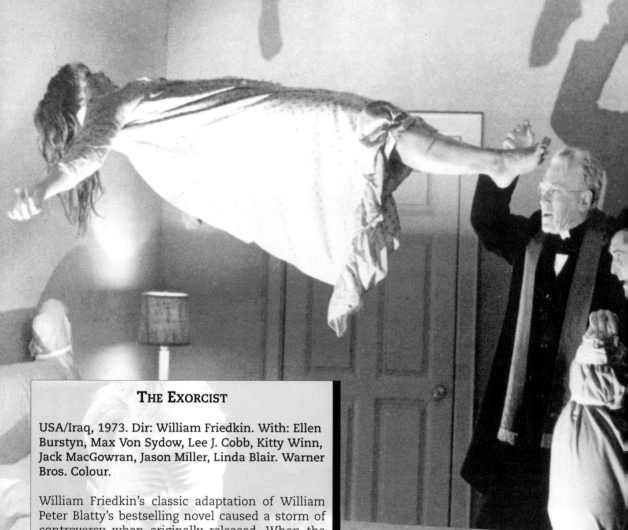

THE EXORCIST

USA/Iraq, 1973. Dir: William Friedkin. With: Ellen Burstyn, Max Von Sydow, Lee J. Cobb, Kitty Winn, Jack MacGowran, Jason Miller, Linda Blair. Warner Bros. Colour.

William Friedkin's classic adaptation of William Peter Blatty's bestselling novel caused a storm of controversy when originally released. When the body of an apparently normal twelve-year-old girl (Blair) is dominated by an ancient demon, only an aged exorcist (Von Sydow) and a priest who questions his own faith (Miller) have the power to stand against it. The opening desert scenes are nicely atmospheric, but only with the climactic possession/exorcism does the film truly achieve its potential as one of the most frightening horror movies ever made. The shooting was reportedly plagued with problems (actor MacGowran died during production), the British censor subsequently cut the scene of Regan masturbating with a crucifix and, despite ten nominations, the film only won Oscars for Best Screenplay and Best Sound. Impressive make-up effects created by Dick Smith. *S.J.*

Sequels: *Exorcist II The Heretic* (Dir: John Boorman, 1977); *The Exorcist III* (Dir: William Peter Blatty, 1990).

four hours to see it. In Washington DC, the USA District Attorney's office overruled the rating from the MPAA and banned anyone under seventeen from seeing the film, while in Boston it received an 'X' rating.

John Kerins was in the audience on the opening night of *The Exorcist*. 'Here you had this naïve, good little child that is taken over by the devil,' he recalls. 'Here you had in the audience this teenage kid from Brooklyn, New York, who had done some pretty bad things in his life. And I was thinking, if this could happen to her, then it certainly could happen to me.

'One of the women two rows behind me literally fainted. She screamed and fainted. They must have been prepared for this because people came rushing in from the back of the theatre, picked this woman up and took her right out.'

Across America, people left screenings in a distressed condition. Heart attacks and at least one miscarriage were reported, while in Berkeley, California, a man attacked the screen attempting to kill the demon. The number of people seeking psychiatric help increased, church attendance began to rise dramatically, and violence broke out at many screenings.

'I just never anticipated the dementia that grew up around the experience of reading the book or seeing the film,' recalls author Blatty. 'And the closest I've been able to come to explaining it is that there is a deep-seated belief in the core of many people that a malevolent and intelligent force of evil personified does exist.'

Referring back to the original case that *The Exorcist* is predominantly based on, the Reverend Thomas Bermingham, S.J., who acted as one of several technical advisors on the film, as well as appearing in a small role, remembers: 'It was a true possession, by which I mean very specifically that Satan had taken over the body of that child and controlled her movements and her voice.'

'After the release of the film,' says Blatty, 'I remember that Billy Graham stated in a sermon that there was a power in the film itself that could not be quantified, could not be identified. There was an "X" factor in that film that was evil and dangerous.'

'The second time I saw the film was in Rome,' says the Reverend Bermingham, 'with all these bishops and a cardinal or two. They were enraptured by it, and they would be very critical of anything they didn't believe in.'

Blatty agrees: 'The Pope did make a statement shortly after the release of *The Exorcist* reaffirming the Church's position on the existence of Satan as a supreme and intelligent force of evil. I'm sure that had something to do with *The Exorcist*.'

Academy Award-winning character actress Mercedes McCambridge is a little more sceptical about some of the reports of mass hysteria that greeted the film when it was initially released: 'The people who said they had to go into therapy, that they had to go to their confessor, had to run and hide, or take medication, or vomit explosively – I think they brought those neuroses into the theatre with them. They didn't pick them up from the screen. The special effects couldn't do that unless the receptivity was there.'

Opposite: Attempting to drive out the demon in *The Exorcist*.

'I made the film because it was a good story. I never thought of what psychological effect it would have on anyone.'

William Friedkin

'When *The Exorcist* first came out, people were saying it will ruin your life if you see this movie. How all these people saw it and killed themselves right afterwards, or were put into insane asylums. The *National Enquirer* was just filled with stories like, "I Saw *The Exorcist* and Shot Myself!" or "I Saw *The Exorcist* and Gave Up God!" There was a reason why it was blowing people's minds. If you just made it, it would blow people's minds today in pretty much the same way.'

Quentin Tarantino

'I would be opening myself up to satanic forces. I think we are dealing with a very dangerous and very strange situation. I don't believe believers can be possessed by the Devil.'

Reverend Billy Graham
on *The Exorcist*

'There were more crimes committed in the name of the Bible than were ever committed because somebody watched *The Exorcist* too many times.'

Robert Englund

42

McCambridge, whose movie credits include *All the King's Men* (1950), *Giant* (1956) and *Suddenly, Last Summer* (1960), provided the voice of the demon, Pazuzu, that possessed twelve-year-old Regan (Linda Blair) in *The Exorcist*. 'My agent called and said that there was a Hollywood director who wanted to call me. And I said, "What do they want with me?" And he said, "Well, Mr Friedkin believes" – and these were his words – "that you're the only person on the face of the earth who could do justice to the part of the demon." Well, it was a double-edged sword: I didn't want to play any devil – I'm an Irish Catholic – but on the other hand, if I was the only one in the world who could do it...

'My duty was to fall in love and understand and have compassion for the fallen Prince of Heaven. I had to become an entity, not just a voice. It drives me crazy when people say, "You were the voice in *The Exorcist*." I tried very hard to create a character, a demon – Lucifer.'

McCambridge originally claimed that director Friedkin

promised her a screen credit and then reneged on the deal. When she issued a lawsuit, claiming that, 'If there was any horror in the exorcism, it was me!', Warner Bros' legal department quickly gave her the acknowledgement she wanted. The director pointed out that her contract did not call for a credit and that the demon's voice was created through a variety of techniques. However, he did admit that the actress went to extreme measures to record her dialogue:

'She said, "I haven't had a drink for twenty-five years, and I've been off cigarettes for ten years,"' he recalls, '"but if you let me drink some whiskey and if I start smoking, then you will find weird things happening with my voice." And she said, "Let me put some raw eggs down my throat with the whiskey and cigarettes. Let me have my priest here, and let's see what happens." Then she said, "Why don't you tie me to the chair, and why don't you put me through some kind of physical torture as well?" Which we did.'

'They tore a sheet up and they restrained me,' adds McCambridge, 'my hands, my knees, my feet, my neck.'

'I did a number of things in addition to the demon voice just to grab the audience's attention at certain places,' continues Friedkin. 'They had conducted an exorcism in Rome, in the Vatican, and they made a very crude recording of it. All of a sudden, across this tape would come these blood-curdling screams of agony that were coming out of something that did not sound human. So I mixed that into the soundtrack as well.'

Ron Nagle, who helped create the special sound

Above and opposite: *The Exorcist*.

'**The** Exorcist, **by the way, is definitely a horror movie. You can't possibly call it anything else. I haven't seen it and I have no desire to see it. I don't say that I disapprove of it, it's just that I have no particular desire to see the possession of a very young child, with her using that kind of language and doing those sort of things.**'

Christopher Lee

43

effects for the film, picks up the story: 'There were certain key sounds that worked subliminally,' he explains. 'When they occurred, you would know that something else was going to be happening, that you were supposed to feel a certain thing.

'All these sounds were augmented and layered with combinations of sound. Nothing was literal. If you just have a bed shaking and you mike it, that's not enough. I went out with a tape recorder to every screwy place I could think of. I went to the slaughterhouse where they were killing pigs. These pigs knew they were going to get it, so their fear was real. I got a lot of stuff that way.

'Although for a great deal of the film the soundtrack was loud and clangy and disturbing, I would also take it down to a whisper, and then very often I would go to absolutely dead silence. That contrast kind of enhanced the idea of light and dark, good and evil.'

Above: William Friedkin (left) confers with William Peter Blatty, behind-the-scenes on *The Exorcist*. Below: Mercedes McCambridge at the premiere.

'With Mercedes McCambridge doing sterling work on the demon's hoarsely mocking voice, the film does build up a fair tension.'

Monthly Film Bulletin,
April 1974

One of the most disturbing aspects of the demon's voice was the string of profanities that emanated from the possessed Regan's lips. 'So many people would say, "Oh how could you possibly talk like that?"' recalls McCambridge. '"I mean, some of the language you used in that film…" Well, come on, that was the Devil not Billy Graham. He talked like the Devil would talk.

'It's one of the influences in my life,' she continues, 'that teaches me the broad canvas that every human being is. I am half demonic as Satan never was. If it's in me, it's in everybody. No one is without it. It is alarming sometimes to think of that. I believe I can live with the Devil in me, but I'm not sure I can live with the people who want to control the Devil in me…'

'Somebody told me that a horror magazine ran a contest for the forty scariest movies of all time,' recalls actress Ellen Burstyn, who portrayed Regan's mother in the film. 'And the results of the contest were that the first thirty-nine places were *The Exorcist*!

'I think it's the scariest movie because it is not so far-fetched,' she continues. 'It does seem within the realm of possibility. It is like something rising up from the dark sea inside – it's a very old fear.'

'I have no doubt that *The Exorcist* moved people very, very profoundly,' says William Friedkin. 'There is always an attempt to try and label and defuse the impact of something that moves us deeply. Very few people really want to accept the stuff that is going on there as a kind of unknowable phenomenon. It's easier to call it a horror film.'

C for Chaos

C

IN THE 1930s, THE Old Gods enjoyed their Golden Age, courtesy of one Howard Phillips Lovecraft (1890–1937). His works, clotted, paranoid mythologies about the clash between man and the supernatural, are dense and difficult but, for anyone interested in horror, completely indispensable.

Despite his untimely death, Lovecraft remains one of the most important and influential authors of supernatural fiction. A lifelong resident of Providence, Rhode Island, he remained a studious antiquarian for most of his life.

Below: Providence resident H.P. Lovecraft.

Poor health as a young boy led him to read voluminously, and the stories of Edgar Allan Poe, Lord Dunsany and Arthur Machen inspired his own writing. Although he was never prolific, Lovecraft's fiction, revisions for other authors, poems and essays received popular acclaim in the amateur press and through such pulp magazines as *Weird Tales* and *Astounding Stories.*

In 1939 two young fans, August Derleth and Donald Wandrei, established their own imprint, Arkham House, to publish a posthumous collection, *The Outsider and Others,* and eventually bring all of Lovecraft's work back into print. During the decades since his death, H.P. Lovecraft has become acknowledged as a master of modern horror and a mainstream American writer second only to his own literary hero, Edgar Allan Poe. Meanwhile, his relatively small body of work continues to influence countless imitators and has formed the

PROVIDENCE

Where bay and river tranquil blend,
And leafy hillsides rise,
The spires of Providence ascend
Against the ancient skies.

And in the narrow winding ways
That climb o'er slope and crest,
The magic of forgotten days
May still be found to rest.

A fanlight's gleam, a knocker's blow,
A glimpse of Georgian brick –
The sights and sounds of long ago
Where fancies cluster thick.

A flight of steps with iron rail,
A belfry looming tall,
A slender steeple, carved and pale,
A moss-grown garden wall.

A hidden churchyard's crumbling proofs
Of man's mortality,
A rotting wharf where gambrel roofs
Keep watch above the sea.

Square and parade, whose walls have towered
Full fifteen decades long
By cobbled ways 'mid trees embowered,
And slighted by the throng.

Stone bridges spanning languid streams,
Houses perched on the hill,
And courts where mysteries and dreams
The brooding spirit fill.

Steep alley steps by vines concealed,
Where small-paned windows glow
At twilight on a bit of field
That chance has left below.

My Providence! What airy hosts
Turn still thy gilded vanes;
What winds of elf that with grey ghosts
People thine ancient lanes!

The chimes of evening as of old
Above thy valleys sound,
While thy stern fathers 'neath the mould
Make blest thy sacred ground.

H.P. LOVECRAFT, MAY 1927

basis of a worldwide industry of books, games and movies inspired by his concepts.

Brian Yuzna produced *Re-Animator* (1985), one of the most successful movie adaptations of the author's work, and he took over the directorial reins for its sequel, *Bride of Re-Animator* (1989), and co-produced and co-directed the Lovecraftian anthology movie, *Necronomicon* (1993). 'As a film-maker I've often gone to Lovecraft to get inspiration,' he reveals, 'and when you read Lovecraft I would defy you to tell me exactly what the story is about. It's very elusive, but the feelings of dread and horror are always there, and very palpably so.

'Visiting Providence, albeit fifty years later, really makes you feel like you're getting another dimension on his stories; Providence itself almost takes on a different cast. His stories were inspired by that town.'

In a 1923 letter to one of his numerous correspondents, Lovecraft colourfully described in his antiquated style a walking tour he had recently undertaken of colonial Providence: 'Not a stone's throw from the travell'd business section, tuckt quietly in behind Broad and

> 'Lovecraft opened the way for me, as he had done for others before me – Robert Bloch, Fritz Leiber and Ray Bradbury among them. The reader would do well to remember that it is his shadow, so long and so gaunt, and his eyes, so dark and puritanical, which overlie almost all of the important horror fiction that has come since.'
>
> Stephen King

Weybosset Streets, lurk the beginnings of a squalid Colonial labyrinth in which I mov'd as an utter stranger, each moment wondering whether I were in truth in my native town or in some leprous distorted witch-Salem of fever or nightmare... This antient and pestilential reticulation of crumbling cottages and decaying doorways was like nothing I had ever beheld save in a dream... rotting Dorick columns rested on worn stone steps out of which rusted footscrapes rose like malignant fungi. Dirty small-pan'd windows leer'd malevolently on all sides, and sometimes glasslessly, from gouged sockets. There was a fog, and out of it and into it again mov'd dark monstrous diseas'd shapes.'

Providence writer and local historian Henry L.P. Beckworth Jr, whose study, *Lovecraft's Providence and Adjacent Parts*, was published in 1979, claims to share a distant relationship with Lovecraft: 'We all go back to the same family,' he explains. 'You're talking three hundred years of people who lived here. Everybody in Providence probably reads his stories, but they're not going to talk about it much and, in a sense, he's almost a social embarrassment.'

That is a view that Michael Price of the John Hay Library, Brown University, agrees with: 'When I was growing up, I learned about Lovecraft from people who knew him. It was kind of an underground thing. He wasn't considered a respectable writer, but in the genre he was considered to be one of the best. He was also a local boy who made good – a peculiar local boy who made good, but a local boy nonetheless.'

For Lovecraft, the library in Providence was a special place because of its connection with that other great American fantasist, Edgar Allan Poe. 'Poe visited the library on a number of occasions,' says Michael Price. 'I think one of the attractions the library held for Lovecraft was the fact that Poe had physically been there, and that his spirit in some sense still lingered.'

'I believe that Poe's fiction is more important than his verse,' Lovecraft wrote in 1921. 'The verse attains marvellous heights, but the tales are above all heights – fragments of cosmic perfection beyond the universe of dimensions. As a critic he leads all other Americans, and only in humour did he fail. Of course, I may be prejudiced; since my own aesthetic perception is admittedly narrow, and inclined toward those particular fields in which Poe worked.'

Lovecraft's own troubled life and his deep identification with Poe – another writer who died prematurely before reaching his full potential – has resulted in many people over the years attempting to psychoanalyse both

H.P. LOVECRAFT IN THE MOVIES

The Haunted Palace (Dir: Roger Corman, 1963), *Monster of Terror* (aka *Die, Monster, Die!*; Dir: Daniel Haller, 1965), *The Shuttered Room* (Dir: David Greene, 1966), *Curse of the Crimson Altar* (aka *The Crimson Cult*; Dir: Vernon Sewell, 1968), *The Dunwich Horror* (Dir: Daniel Haller, 1969), *Equinox* (Dir: Mark McGee and Jack Woods, 1969), *The Beyond* (aka *E Tu Vivrai nel Terrore...L'Aldila/Seven Doors to Death*; Dir: Lucio Fulci, 1981), *Re-Animator* (Dir: Stuart Gordon, 1985), *From Beyond* (Dir: Stuart Gordon, 1986), *The Curse* (Dir: David Keith, 1987), *Pulse Pounders* (Dir: Charles Band, 1988, unfinished), *The Unnamable* (Dir: Jean-Paul Ouellette, 1988), *Bride of Re-Animator* (aka *Re-Animator 2*; Dir: Brian Yuzna, 1989), *Transylvania Twist* (Dir: Jim Wynorski, 1989), *Cast a Deadly Spell* (Dir: Martin Campbell, TV, 1991), *The Resurrected* (Dir: Dan O'Bannon, 1991), *Cthulhu Mansion* (aka *Black Magic Mansion*; Dir: J.P. Simon, 1992), *The Unnamable Returns* (aka *The Unnamable II: The Statement of Randolph Carter*; Dir: Jean-Paul Ouellette, 1992), *Beyond the Wall of Sleep* (Dir: Hervé Hachuel, 1993), *Necronomicon* (Dir: Brian Yuzna, Christophe Gans and Shu Kaneko, 1993), *In the Mouth of Madness* (Dir: John Carpenter, 1994), *Lurking Fear* (Dir: C. Courtney Joyner, 1994), *Castle Freak* (Dir: Stuart Gordon, 1995).

the author and his influential body of work.

'He was an odd man with obsessional hatreds,' reveals Brian Yuzna, 'which included all forms of alcohol, seafood, dogs and motion pictures.'

In his 1975 book, *Lovecraft: A Biography*, author L. Sprague De Camp concluded that 'he was a man who, as a result of congenital tendencies (his schizoid personality), compounded by an abnormal upbringing, was long delayed in maturation. He showed adolescent bumptiousness, prejudices, dogmatism and affectations, and adolescent timidity towards new human contacts and relationships, in his thirties, more than a decade after he had ceased to be an adolescent. In some respects, such as the sexual and the monetary, he never did mature.'

'Both of Lovecraft's parents died in an insane asylum,' explains local psychiatrist Dr Eileen McNamara. 'His father at the age of thirty-two. His mother began to hallucinate and died in the same hospital about twenty

'The first book of Lovecraft's I read made me into a writer. I read it in a single malingering day off school, and for a year or more I thought H.P. Lovecraft was not merely the greatest horror writer of all time, but the greatest writer I had ever read.'

Ramsey Campbell

'The oldest and strongest emotion of mankind is fear, and the oldest and strongest kind of fear is fear of the unknown.'

H.P. Lovecraft

C

BOOKS BY H.P. LOVECRAFT (1890–1937)

The Shadow over Innsmouth (1936), The Notes & Commonplace Book Employed by the Late H.P. Lovecraft (1938), The Outsider and Others (1939), Beyond the Wall of Sleep (1943), The Weird Shadow over Innsmouth and Other Stories of the Supernatural (1944), Marginalia (1944), The Lurker at the Threshold (with August Derleth, 1945), Supernatural Horror in Literature (1945), The Best Supernatural Stories of H.P. Lovecraft (1945), The Dunwich Horror (1945), The Dunwich Horror and Other Weird Tales (1945), The Lurking Fear and Other Stories (1947), Something about Cats and Other Pieces (1949), The Haunter of the Dark and Other Tales of Horror (1951), The Case of Charles Dexter Ward (1952), The Dream-Quest of Unknown Kadath (1956), The Survivor and Others (with August Derleth, 1957), Cry Horror (1958), The Shuttered Room and Other Pieces (with Divers Hands, 1959), The Shunned House (1928/1961), Dreams and Fancies (1962), The Dunwich Horror and Others (1963), Collected Poems (1963), Autobiography of a Nonentity (1963), At the Mountains and Other Novels (1964), The Lurking Fear and Other Stories (1964), Dagon and Other Macabre Tales (1965), Selected Letters I-V (1965-1976), The Dark Brotherhood and Other Pieces (with Divers Hands, 1966), 3 Tales of Horror (1967), Tales of the Cthulhu Mythos (with Others, 1969), The Horror in the Museum and Other Revisions (1970), Fungi from Yuggoth and Other Poems (1971), The Shadow over Innsmouth and Other Stories of Horror (1971), The Watchers Out of Time (with August Derleth, 1974), To Quebec and the Stars (1976), Tales of the Cthulhu Mythos (with Divers Hands, 1990).

MARGINALI_
By H. P. LOVECRAFT

DAGON

& other MACABRE tales · H.P. Lovecraft

years later. As soon as his mother died, Lovecraft wrote a story called "Beyond the Wall of Sleep", where he is a psychiatrist in an insane asylum. As a psychiatrist he finds a degenerate man (his term) that he communicates with by attaching a special machine to his head, and discovers inside him is a noble soul from beyond the universe fighting noble causes.

'I really think this is a story about Lovecraft's father and his wish for him. His father died from syphilis, and I think Lovecraft was trying to say, "My father isn't a degenerate patient, my father is a noble being and I want to be with him again." That's what I think that story is about.

'I think that he was always worried that the illness that made his father and mother go mad might finally affect him.'

'The death of my mother on May 24 gave me an extreme nervous shock,' Lovecraft wrote to friends in 1921. 'Psychologically I am conscious of a vastly increased aimlessness and inability to be interested in events; a phenomenon due partly to the fact that much of my former interest in things lay in discussing them with my mother and securing her views and approval... My mother was, in all probability, the only person who thoroughly understood me.'

'He never spent a night away from home until he was thirty-two,' reveals Dr McNamara. 'His mother hovered over him and doted over her only child, although she told him that he was very ugly, and also told him that he was a little girl up until about

S·F· THEATRE OF LIVERPOOL

"THE CASE OF CHARLES DEXTER WARD"

X3 POSTERS · 407-7811

I·C·A CAMILLA
AN OPERA BY SAUNDERS
FROM THE BOOK BY H.P.
DIR. BY KEN CAMPBELL LOVECRAFT
SET DESIGNED BY MAVIS TAYLOR
PRINTED BY THE BUTLER!

APRIL 11 ↓ 29

'There had been eons when other Things ruled on the earth, and They had had great cities. Remains of Them were still to be found as Cyclopean stones on islands in the Pacific. They all died vast epochs of time before man came, but there were arts which could revive Them when the stars had come round again to the right positions in the cycle of eternity. They had, indeed, come themselves from the stars, and brought their images with Them.'

FROM 'THE CALL OF CTHULHU'
BY H.P. LOVECRAFT

'He was, in reality, a kind, considerate, courteous man, generous to a fault with his time and talent. Since his death more than half a century ago Lovecraft and his work have been both revered and reviled.'

Robert Bloch

51

'What Lovecraft did have, which I think is very influential across the genre, is this extraordinary imagination. He was very po-faced (sorry, pun not quite intended) about the whole thing but he did really believe, or seemed to believe, in the stuff, and his conviction carries you through the stories which otherwise I tend to find somewhat preposterous. He does give you the impression he means all of this stuff.'

Clive Barker

the age of six. She dressed him up as a little girl, and he grew up with this crippling self-identity.'

Many of H.P. Lovecraft's tales are set in the fear-haunted towns of an imaginary area of Massachusetts or in the cosmic vistas that exist in dimensions beyond space and time. A number of these loosely-connected stories have become identified as 'The Cthulhu Mythos', named after one of his extra-terrestrial deities.

According to Brian Yuzna, 'What is really interesting is how a lot of Lovecraft's stories deal with the spheres "beyond". To understand Lovecraft you really have to understand that that boy was looking up into the sky, and there's a kind of horror out there. He seems to have given up the religious-oriented horror of the previous centuries and embraced the idea of a mankind that has somehow been abandoned by its gods, and the horror of Lovecraft is the horror of being inconsequential in the universe.'

'In Lovecraft's view it was absurd to believe that the universe was centred on human beings or that we had any real valid place or meaning,' explains author, critic and long-time Providence resident Les Daniels. 'This was just a gigantic chaos, a meaningless madness in which we were a tiny speck of no significance at all.

'He created fusion between science fiction and horror, which was unique, especially in the 1920s when he was working. He created the idea that the monstrous forces that were considered demons by primitive religions were actually extraterrestrials or inter-dimensional creatures. So that was a sort of cosmic horror which was different from the old supernatural horror, which was going out of vogue; and in doing this he gave a new life to the horror story.'

'We know that he got most of his ideas from his dream materials,' reveals Dr McNamara. 'He was a prodigious letter writer and document keeper. He wrote down his colourful, complex vivid dreams in detail and he filled his stories from this dream material. In these stories there are women who are raped by demons from outer space and give birth to monsters. Women are pretty much uniformly portrayed as treacherous, dominating or dangerous figures.'

'Of course, I am unfamiliar with amatory phenomena save through cursory reading,' admitted Lovecraft in a 1919 correspondence. 'I always assumed that one waited till he encountered some nymph who seemed radically different to him from the rest of her sex, and without whom he felt he could no longer exist. Then, I fancied, he commenced to lay siege to her heart in businesslike fashion, not desisting till either he won her for life, or was blighted by rejection. Of seeking affection for affection's sake – without any one special fair creature in mind – I was quite ignorant!'

Lovecraft's lack of experience didn't stop him from courting in the local graveyard, as Bart St Armand, a lecturer in English Literature at Brown University, explains: 'He was fascinated by the idea that Benefit Street once ran through the graveyard, and that the graveyard was moved, leaving some of the bodies scattered in some of the cellar holes. That's the origin of one of his most famous tales, "The Shunned House", where one of the bodies has not been moved, but unfortunately it moves by itself.

'There is a favourite tomb for Providence residents, whether they are above the ground or below it. It is a place where Lovecraft courted, where Poe courted. There is evidence that he took his one sweetheart, Sonia Greene, there and showed her his favourite spot. He would talk about Poe's life. He might read a poem by Poe.'

On 3 March 1924, Lovecraft married Sonia Haft Greene, a woman seven years his senior. 'He said nothing could please him better,' she later wrote. 'Sarah Helen Whitman was older than Poe, and that Poe might have met with better fortune had he married her.'

However, within less than two years the marriage was in trouble, with the couple living separate lives. Sonia began urging Lovecraft to divorce her and, on 25 March 1929, he signed a preliminary decree on the grounds of desertion.

For the remainder of his life, Lovecraft made his home in his beloved Providence, but still managed to travel extensively as he eked out a living producing occasional short stories or ghostwriting other people's manuscripts.

'Providence – founded in 1636 – is perhaps the most Colonial & English of American cities, since the solid and generous nature of its early structures has discouraged replacement,' he wrote to author and artist Clark Ashton Smith in 1924. 'Providence's own realization of its Georgian quaintness is relatively recent. I was a pioneer in a kind of exultation that the bulk of my solidly commercial fellow-townsmen are just beginning to share…

'I have never had much inclination to depend on people for amusement. To me all mankind seems too local and transitory an incident in the cosmos to take at

Above: Lovecraft's wife, Sonia Haft Greene, *circa* 1921.

'These Great Old Ones were not composed altogether of flesh and blood. They had shape, but that shape was not made of matter. When the stars were right, They could plunge from world to world through the sky; but when the stars were wrong, They could not live. But although They no longer lived, They could never really die. They all lay in stone houses in Their great city of R'lyeh, preserved by the spells of mighty Cthulhu for a glorious resurrection when the stars and the earth might once more be ready for them.'

FROM 'THE CALL OF CTHULHU' BY H.P. LOVECRAFT

'That is not dead which can eternal lie, and in strange aeons even death may die.'
From 'The Nameless City' by H.P. Lovecraft

A few years ago in Dunwich

a half-witted girl bore illegitimate twins.

One of them was almost human!

H. P. LOVECRAFT'S CLASSIC TALE OF TERROR AND THE SUPERNATURAL!

the Dunwich Horror

SANDRA DEE
DEAN STOCKWELL
ED BEGLEY · LLOYD BOCHNER
DONNA BACCALA AND SAM JAFFE
JOANNA MOORE JORDAN

JAMES H. NICHOLSON and SAMUEL Z. ARKOFF · CURTIS LEE HANSON, HENRY ROSENBAUM & RONALD SILKOSKY
ROGER CORMAN · DANIEL HALLER · Based on a story by H. P. LOVECRAFT · AN AMERICAN INTERNATIONAL PICTURE
COLOR BY MOVIELAB

'Children will always be afraid of the dark and men with minds sensitive to hereditary impulse will always tremble at the thought of the hidden and fathomless worlds of strange life which may pulsate in the gulfs beyond the stars, or press down upon our own globe in unholy dimensions which only the dead and the moonstruck can glimpse.'

H.P. Lovecraft

all seriously. I am more interested in scenes – landscapes and architecture – I have a very real affection for the old town with its ancient steeples and belfries, hills and corners, courts and lanes, all reminding me of that eighteenth century and that Old England which I love so well.'

H.P. Lovecraft died from cancer early on the morning of 15 March 1937, at the Jane Brown Memorial Hospital. He was buried in the family plot in the Swan Point Cemetery, where his name was inscribed alongside those of his parents. Four people attended the funeral service.

'Everything I loved had been dead for two centuries,' he wrote in 1916. 'I am never a part of anything around me – in everything I am an outsider... But pray do not think, gentlemen, that I am an utterly forlorn and misanthropick creature... Despite my solitary life, I have found infinite joy in books and writing, and am by far too much interested in the affairs of the world to quit the scene before Nature shall claim me... A sense of humour has helped me to endure existence; in fact, when all else fails, I never fail to extract a sarcastic smile from the contemplation of my own empty and egotistical career...!'

D For Devil Rides Out

D

WHETHER IT'S A COUNTRY, a neighbourhood, an old dark house, or your own body, horror thrives on environments. We all crave boundaries – those carefully contrived markers that reassure us that our bodies or minds are safe from invasion. But what if those boundaries can be breached or, worse still, what if they're not keeping the horror outside, but just giving it a safe haven, in here, with us...

Classic British horror has an unwritten rule: aristocrats should suffer mightily against the forces of darkness, but it is always the servants who should mop up the blood. No British author understood this better than Dennis Wheatley (1897–1977), servant of the Queen and enemy of the Devil.

Wheatley always maintained that he obtained the material for his novels about black magic from books and from a meeting, in the 1930s, with the occultist, Aleister Crowley. 'The literature of occultism is so immense that any conscientious writer can obtain from it abundant material,' he explained. 'I have spared no pains to secure accuracy of detail from existing accounts when describing magical rites or formulas for protection against evil, and these have been verified in conversation with certain persons, sought out for that purpose, who are actual practitioners of the Art.

'I desire to state that I, personally, have never assisted at, or participated in, any ceremony connected with magic – black or white,' he added. 'But I can tell a story, yes, I can tell a story.'

That he certainly could. Dennis Wheatley was born in London on 8 January 1897, into a family of wine merchants. He entered the business after his education and became the sole owner when his father died in 1926. From 1941 to 1944 he was a wing commander on Sir Winston

THE DEVIL RIDES OUT
(USA: THE DEVIL'S BRIDE)

UK, 1967. Dir: Terence Fisher. With: Christopher Lee, Charles Gray, Nike Arrighi, Leon Greene, Patrick Mower, Gwen Ffrangcon-Davies. Hammer Films. Colour.

Entertaining adaptation of Dennis Wheatley's classic novel, scripted by Richard Matheson. Lee makes a perfect Duc de Richleau, battling to rescue his friend Simon Aron (Mower) from a black magic coven controlled by High Priest Mocata (a suitably villainous Gray). Fisher's direction moves the plot along at a swift pace, and there are some memorable set-pieces: the apparition of the demon with hypnotic eyes; the breaking-up of the coven and the banishment of the Devil/goat; and the climactic attack by the Angel of Death. However, the supporting cast is surprisingly weak for Hammer, and the special effects (particularly an unconvincing giant spider) are not as good as they should be. *S.J.*

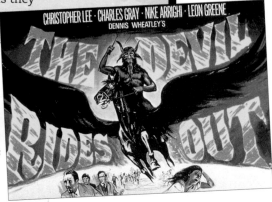

CHRISTOPHER LEE · CHARLES GRAY · NIKE ARRIGHI · LEON GREENE
DENNIS WHEATLEY'S
THE DEVIL RIDES OUT

Churchill's Joint Planning Staff of the War Cabinet.

He began writing in the early 1930s and his first novel, *The Forbidden Territory* (1933), became very success- ful. He continued to write in a number of genres, including espionage thrillers, historical romances, science fiction and lost worlds, but he is best remembered today for his books about black magic and the occult. It is said that during one forty-eight hour period, Wheatley smoked 250 cigarettes, drank five magnums of champagne, and still managed to write 20,000 words.

Despite a terrible snobbery inherent in much of his work, Wheatley was one of the most prolific and suc- cessful writers this century.

According to author and journalist Stan Nicholls, 'At

'Even as he spoke, the manifestation took on a clearer shape; the hands, held forward almost in an attitude of prayer but turned downward, became transformed into two great cloven hoofs. Above rose the monstrous bearded head of a gigantic goat, appearing to be at least three times the size of any other which they had seen. The two slit-eyes, slanting inwards and down, gave out a red baleful light. Long pointed ears cocked upwards from the sides of the shaggy head, and from the bald, horrible, unnatural bony skull, which was caught by the light of the candles, four enormous curved horns spread out – sideways and up.'
FROM *THE DEVIL RIDES OUT* BY DENNIS WHEATLEY

Above: Dennis Wheatley.

D the height of his popularity, which probably reached a peak around 1960, it is said that Dennis Wheatley had in print anywhere between forty and fifty million copies of his books in twenty-seven languages. Some of his books went through literally scores of printings in a year.

'Wheatley's books contained, across their range, a certain recipe – what these days we would call a formula. The recipe contained flying saucers, satanists, stocking tops, Nazis, Communists, stocking tops, car chases, fist fights, dashing heroes and stocking tops.'

> 'Suddenly Sabine threw the bedclothes back and, for a moment lay fully revealed through her transparent nightie... Gregory felt his heart begin to pound and his mouth go dry. Hard put to it to keep his face expressionless, he wondered how long he would be able to resist temptation if she continued to display herself to him like this. Uneasily he recalled having told her that it was six months since he had been wounded and only another month or so was needed for his complete recovery...'
>
> FROM *THEY USED DARK FORCES* BY DENNIS WHEATLEY

For many of Wheatley's adolescent readers, the appeal of his books was undoubtedly a combination of titillating sex and horror. However, there was also a certain 'Englishness' to his characters, who seemed to exist in a Britain that had never lost its Empire.

'You could say that part of the formula for Wheatley's occult novels,' continues Nicholls, 'indeed his novels as a whole, was this idea that you could somehow mechanistically confront the forces of chaos and disorder with the forces of order. It is almost militaristic. In fact, it's said that he had a very hardcore following among people who were in the military, or ex-military, and it is possible to read his text in that sense – one organizes one's life in order to push back the boundaries of darkness.

'From the beginning I have been incredibly lucky. Yet it is not luck alone that has enabled me to fly year after year to beauty spots all over the world, enjoy the most expensive food and knock back bumpers of champagne.'
Dennis Wheatley

'In the world of Dennis Wheatley, nowhere else outside these shores really exists. Foreigners should remain foreigners. If they intrude at all into our green little sphere, they tend to do so as villains. As moral degenerates. As the instigators of dark and terrible religions.'

Actor Christopher Lee, who starred in two films based on Wheatley's books, sees another side to the author's work: 'I genuinely believe that he wrote these books not just to make money and be a successful author, but they were also sort of morality plays – like some of the films I appeared in many years ago, where good always triumphs over evil.'

'Prince of Thriller-writers.'
Times Literary Supplement

'I found ample evidence,' said Wheatley, 'that black magic is still practised in London, and other cities, at the present day. Should any of my readers incline to a serious study of the subject, and thus come into contact with a man or woman of Power, I feel that it is only right to urge them, most strongly, to refrain from being drawn into the practice of the Secret Art in any way. My own observations have led me to an absolute conviction that to do so would bring them into dangers of a very real and concrete nature.'

SELECTED BOOKS BY DENNIS WHEATLEY
(1897–1977)

NOVELS: *The Forbidden Territory* (1933), *Such Power Is Dangerous* (1933), *Black August* (1934), *The Fabulous Valley* (1934), *The Devil Rides Out* (1934), *They Found Atlantis* (1936), *The Secret War* (1937), *Uncharted Seas* (1938), *Sixty Days to Live* (1939), *Strange Conflict* (1941), *The Man Who Missed the War* (1945), *The Haunting of Toby Jugg* (1948), *The Second Seal* (1950), *Star of Ill-Omen* (1952), *Worlds Far from Here* (*They Found Atlantis/ Uncharted Seas/The Man Who Missed the War*, 1952), *To the Devil – A Daughter* (1953), *The Island Where Time Stands Still* (1954), *The Ka of Gifford Hillary* (1956), *The Satanist* (1960), *They Used Dark Forces* (1964), *The White Witch of the South Seas* (1968), *Gateway to Hell* (1970), *The Irish Witch* (1973).

COLLECTIONS: *Gunmen, Gallants and Ghosts* (1943).

'Christopher Lee took the part of the Duc de Richleau and played the role magnificently. Another factor which led to the great success of the film was that the scriptwriter stuck, as far as film technique permitted, to the story.'

Dennis Wheatley

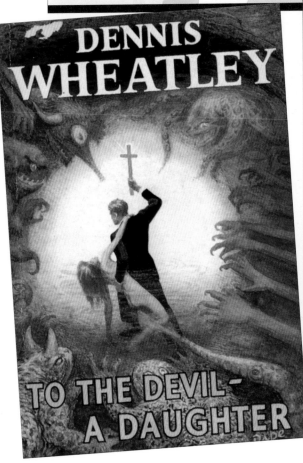

Although Wheatley had only been published for less than three years, in 1935 he was invited to edit the landmark anthology *A Century of Horror,* which eventually ran to more than a thousand pages. In his introduction, he set out to explain the attraction of supernatural horror fiction: 'Such experiences are infinitely more horrific then anything we can be called on to face in the mundane world we know so well, and there is a very great deal of evidence to show that, given certain conditions, strange forces and evil powers from a world unknown, unknowable, can materialize in our atmosphere and strike stark ungovernable terror into the soul of man.'

Stan Nicholls recalls that his first meeting with Dennis Wheatley 'really did epitomize a clash of cultures. You've got to remember this was 1972. His Chelsea flat was a kind of metaphor for the fiction he was associated with – plushly furnished, but in a style perhaps more suited to the 1930s. It had elaborate wall-hangings, sound-muffling deep-pile carpets, and weighty candelabra. It reminded me of a Hammer movie set.

'He was a man of a certain age, with slicked-back hair, wearing his smoking jacket, confronted by someone barely out of his teens, with hair long enough

> '"Only der strong guys is goin' to make der grade dis trip, Bass. I's sorry fer der dames an' der feller who got smacked down by dat oar, and der ole puss here with der dicky leg, but dey ain't got no chance nohow. Der grub dey's eatin' would keep us tough fellers goin' another day or maybe two. Six folks less in dis boat 'ud give us an extra thirty per cent chance o' gettin' some place or bein' picked up alive; so der six weakest folks is jus' unfortunate. Dey got to liquidate or be liquidated, like dem Russian Communist guys say – see?"'
>
> FROM *UNCHARTED SEAS* BY DENNIS WHEATLEY

'The greatest adventure-writer of our time.'

Daily Mail

SEE!
BLOOD-BEASTS battling over female flesh!
TORTURE PITS for forbidden lovers!
SACRIFICE to giant jaw-snapping mollusks!
ESCAPE from floating death ship!
HELPLESS BEAUTIES attacked by crazed kelp-monsters!
FIERY DESTRUCTION of the Lost Continent!

A Living Hell That Time Forgot!

THE LOST CONTINENT

UK, 1968. Dir: Michael Carreras. With: Eric Porter, Hildegard Knef, Suzanna Leigh, Tony Beckley, Nigel Stock, Neil McCallum. Seven Arts-Hammer Films. Colour.

Studio-bound adaptation of Dennis Wheatley's novel *Uncharted Seas.* When a tramp steamer ends up among decaying galleons in the legendary Sargasso Sea, the motley collection of passengers discover a cargo full of dangerous explosives, the threat of flesh-eating seaweed and giant monsters, plus survivors of a demented branch of the Spanish Inquisition! Enjoyable Hammer hokum, started by Leslie Norman (*X the Unknown,* 1956), who was replaced by producer/director Carreras. With Jimmy Hanley, James Cossins, Dana Gillespie, Victor Madden, Michael Ripper and songs by The Peddlers. *S.J.*

TO THE DEVIL A DAUGHTER
(USA: CHILD OF SATAN)

UK/West Germany, 1976. Dir: Peter Sykes. With: Richard Widmark, Christopher Lee, Honor Blackman, Denholm Elliott, Nastassja Kinski, Anthony Valentine. Hammer Films/Terra Filmkunst. Colour.

The last of Hammer's original cycle of horror films is a well-made supernatural thriller based on the novel by Dennis Wheatley. The script by Christopher Wicking and John Peacock is muddled at times, but director Sykes keeps the plot moving along, helped by some fine performances and a nice use of London locations. Occult author John Verney (Widmark) confronts defrocked priest Father Michael (Lee), who is attempting to bring the demon Azaroth to earth through the soul of a young nun (sixteen-year-old Kinski). The movie obviously had a few production problems, perhaps best indicated by the abrupt ending in which Lee's satanic minion is defeated by being hit on the head with a rock. S.J.

to sit on, wearing black from head to foot, Cuban heels and dark glasses. The interesting thing is that, at that particular time, the odd character was Wheatley, not me. Because as the tide was going out on him, my tide was coming in.'

During his heyday, there is no doubt that Dennis Wheatley was the Stephen King or James Herbert of his day, selling millions of copies of his books worldwide. Towards the end of his career, he used the knowledge he had collected over the years to write a reference book about the black arts, *The Devil and All His Works* (1971), and in 1973, Sphere Books launched an ambitious series of reprints, to include fiction and non-fiction, under the title *The Dennis Wheatley Library of the Occult*. The original concept called for 450 volumes drawing upon Wheatley's extensive knowledge of the fantastic and paranormal. In the end, less than fifty titles were published.

Nicholls was editorial consultant on the project and he recalls: 'I was given an enormous list of writers, along with Wheatley's slightly eccentric versions of the titles of their books. I checked copyrights, located actual copies of the books to print from, and compiled biographies of the authors, which formed the basis of the introductions Wheatley was to write.

'The paradoxical thing about Wheatley was that, privately, he was a considerable expert on the occult and supernatural fiction; whereas his novels were considered misrepresentative and cheaply sensational by many people with an interest in the subject matter.

'He was a man of strong and entrenched opinions,

Above: *To the Devil a Daughter*.

'The best thing of its kind since *Dracula*.'
James Hilton on *The Devil Rides Out* in the *Daily Telegraph*

61

Right: Posed exploitation still from *The Devil Rides Out*.

'Hammer also made my *Uncharted Seas*, re-christening it *Lost Continent*. But the story was entirely altered, with the result that it was less successful.'

Dennis Wheatley

'My life both in private and public has been one of extraordinary good fortune and I am deeply grateful to all those who have shared my joys and wished me well. But "The Party's Over Now".'

Dennis Wheatley

and saw himself as very much a part of the Establishment. He seemed to know everybody, and his conversation was littered with references to literary personalities, politicians, famous socialites and various monarchs. My impression was that his views had been indelibly stamped on him in his younger days, when most of the map was still coloured British red.'

Dennis Wheatley died on 10 November 1977. The funeral service was conducted by Cyril 'Bobby' Eastaugh, retired Lord Bishop of Peterborough, at Putney Crematorium. In accordance with his express wishes, Wheatley's ashes were buried at Brookwood Cemetery, and are marked by a small tombstone, inscribed: 'Dennis Wheatley 8.1.97–10.11.77 "Prince of Thriller Writers" RIP'.

Today, most of his volumes have disappeared from publishers' backlists and bookstores. His work has been eclipsed by a more visceral approach to horror, and his fiction now appears somewhat dated, containing sexist and parochial imagery that would be unacceptable to most modern readers of the genre.

'In a way,' says Christopher Lee, 'it's a very good thing that he is not alive to see what has happened today – in my opinion, the virtual breakdown of discipline in this country and in many others.'

'I'm not in the least afraid of death,' Wheatley once said. 'I truly believe in survival after death.' Sadly, time has proved – for his books, at least – that he was wrong...

E For Escape

E

I N AMERICA, THE CLICHÉ goes, people are much more mobile. In the United States there are suburbs. The day director John Carpenter moved to the suburbs, horror acquired a new sub-genre…

'After World War II, suburbia came into being because there was a giant push to normalcy,' explains Carpenter. 'That normalcy was the issue – let's all get normal again. Normalcy can be destructive to the imagination, to creativity, to the intellect, to the soul. The only way we grow as people is through confronting our dark side because, if all you want is the quiet and the safety, then you are giving up on reality.

'A lot of horror films in the past were set in a haunted house or some dark environment to begin with, so that you're immediately alerted to the fact that, oh, this is going to be scary. Well, the harder thing to do then is to take a horror movie and put it into a suburban atmosphere, with a nice little row of houses and beautiful manicured lawns and some place that you assume is very safe. Because if horror can get there, it can get anywhere.

'Suburbia is supposed to be safe. Your house is supposed to be a sanctuary. Nowadays, maybe because of conditions beyond our control, there is no sanctuary. And

HALLOWEEN

USA, 1978. Dir: John Carpenter. With: Donald Pleasence, Jamie Lee Curtis, Nancy Loomis, P.J. Soles, Will Sandin, Charles Cyphers. Compass International. Colour.

This is one of the most successful low-budget horror films ever made and it spawned a whole sub-genre of (mostly inferior) stalk 'n' slash imitations in the late 1970s and 1980s. Set in a small Illinois town, where babysitter Laurie (Curtis) is menaced by a masked killer who returns home after fifteen years in a mental asylum. Director Carpenter stages the brutal (but bloodless) killings unrelentingly, and his psychopathic protagonist, Michael Myers, is finally revealed as a supernatural menace during the gripping climax when he keeps miraculously returning from the dead. With clips from *Forbidden Planet* (1956) and *The Thing from Another World* (1951) on TV. The television version, supervised by Carpenter, varies slightly from the theatrical print. S.J.

Sequels: *Halloween II* (Dir: Rick Rosenthal, 1981); *Halloween III Season of the Witch* (Dir: Tommy Lee Wallace, 1982); *Halloween 4 The Return of Michael Myers* (Dir: Dwight H. Little, 1988); *Halloween 5* (Dir: Dominique Othenin-Girard, 1989); *Halloween 6 The Curse of Michael Myers* (Dir: Joe Chappelle, 1995).

I think that is in the audience's mind. So a film-maker, if he plays with that, can create fear. Lots of fear.'

Debra Hill, who produced and co-wrote *Halloween* (1978) with Carpenter, agrees. 'I think John wanted to use that kind of suburban neighbourhood because of the feeling of being trapped in a house that looked so beautiful, with its manicured lawns. It looked like the kind of place that you would want to have your children playing in, and the idea was that there was *something* lurking behind those trees. All these identical houses across the street from each other created this kind of claustrophobic effect and a feeling that something was wrong.'

'You shoot small-town America from an angle that gives it a sense of doom,' continues Carpenter. 'Using wide-angle lenses also helps. And if you use the tracking shot, do it very slowly and methodically, be very authoritative about it, then the audience feels there is something strange there.'

Originally based on a concept entitled *The Babysitter Murders,* John Carpenter's *Halloween* was made for just $320,000. Since then it has amassed a worldwide gross well in excess of $50 million, making it the highest proportional return on a feature film investment in movie history.

The film opens on Halloween night 1963, in the small town of Haddonfield, Illinois. Six-year-old Michael Myers watches his older sister and her boyfriend through a window of their house. When the boyfriend leaves, he takes a butcher's knife from the kitchen drawer and, wearing a blank-faced Halloween mask, follows his sister upstairs to her bedroom and brutally murders her.

Exactly fifteen years later, Michael Myers escapes from the Illinois State Mental Hospital and returns to Haddonfield. Pursued by Dr Sam Loomis (Donald Pleasence), whose care he was under, Myers stalks and systematically kills teenage babysitters and their boyfriends, slowly getting closer to heroine Laurie Strode (Jamie Lee Curtis) and her two young charges.

For much of *Halloween,* Carpenter keeps his audience off-balance by using some clever technical sleight of hand, including a Steadicam camera for the murderer's point-of-view: 'You have a gyroscopic mount on an operator,' he explains, 'and he can run and move, and that kind of gives you a dreamy, floating quality.

'Then you can use the night-time to make anything claustrophobic, because what you have is the character that is lit and beyond them is darkness. And if you are

E

'It is human nature to be fascinated by the horrible, the forbidden. We seek it out and we challenge it. The horror film is unique because it is a shared involvement; the audience feels common emotions. Ultimately, it's a test of ourselves: "Can I stand what I'm about to see? Will I make it through this?" Of course, deep down, they know they're safe and the experience gives the audience a tremendous release of tension and anxiety.'

John Carpenter

Above: Debra Hill and John Carpenter.

SELECTED FILMS OF JOHN CARPENTER
(b 1948)

The Resurrection of Bronco Billy (short, 1970), *Dark Star* (1973), *Assault on Precinct 13* (1976), *Halloween* (1978), *The Eyes of Laura Mars* (screenplay, 1978), *Someone's Watching Me!* (TV, 1978), *Elvis* (TV, 1979), *The Fog* (1979), *Escape from New York* (1981), *Halloween II* (producer/co-screenplay, 1981), *The Thing* (1982), *Christine* (1983), *Starman* (1984), *The Philadelphia Experiment* (screenplay, 1984), *Black Moon Rising* (co-screenplay, 1986), *Big Trouble in Little China* (1986), *Prince of Darkness* (1987), *They Live* (1988), *El Diablo* (co-screenplay, TV, 1990), *Blood River* (1991), *Memoirs of an Invisible Man* (1992), *Body Bags* (co-directed with Tobe Hooper, TV, 1993), *In the Mouth of Madness* (1994), *Village of the Damned* (1995), *Escape from L.A.* (1996), *Vampires* (1997).

inside a room, you can use the edges of the room as literally the edges of the frame. Because, by closing in on the character, the audience never knows where the escape route is.

'I've always thought that my movies are characterized in some ways by this obsession with people being trapped,' he continues. 'People being trapped either by their character or their environment or their situation. You can be trapped in a car – you can be driving across giant spaces and still be trapped inside your car. You can be trapped in a house, usually trapped by forces of evil on the outside.'

Cathy Braidhill is a crime reporter for the *Pasadena Star,* and her beat covers many of the city's seemingly perfect suburban areas. 'You'd be really surprised about what goes on over here,' she says. 'They had these guys taking dead people and cutting up the parts. Selling the brains and the hearts and lungs to a medical supply firm. They made tons and tons of money off of that and lied to people about what was going on.

'When I first started out in journalism, the first

Opposite: A cut above the average – *Halloween.*

'Movies don't make people kill. It's life that does it.'

John Carpenter

67

E

'Debra Hill and I were forced into making the two *Halloween* sequels for financial and business reasons. There was going to be a tremendous lawsuit if we didn't, and our business manager said, "If you don't do this, you're stupid." So we did it, and the idea was to give young directors a chance to make their first film and maybe want different stories. Well, we found out that the audience didn't want different stories. *Halloween II* was similar to the first one but *Halloween III* was not. What they wanted was just the same old thing over and over again.'

John Carpenter

Above: *Halloween.*

person that I became vividly aware of was Richard Beaumaris, who later became known as 'The Night-stalker'. He was a fellow who went around and bludgeoned people in their beds. Came upon them in the middle of the night, or people awoke to find him standing over them. And I think that case, more than any other case in suburbia, really wrecked the experience for people.'

'We were all very, very comfortable for a lot of years,' says Carpenter. 'Nowadays people are very frightened and they don't want to look underneath any more.

'There was a famous case in New York where this lady was being killed and no one helped. She was screaming and they closed their windows to it. In general there's an apathy that has taken over the country now. It was not quite as strong back in 1978 when I made *Halloween* but it was still there at that point. Now when you run and scream for help, people tend not to want to get involved. And that's a very terrifying thing.'

'In *Halloween*,' says Debra Hill, 'Jamie Lee Curtis's character runs for help but the neighbour ignores her and turns out the light. I think that epitomizes what happens in suburban neighbourhoods where people are either afraid or in denial that something bad is happening.

'And the role of Donald Pleasence's character was basically to come to this town and say, there's something going on; you have to do something. You can't just keep the door shut, you can't just keep the windows closed.'

'I remember trick or treating,' says reporter Cathy Braidhill. 'I remember going out for Halloween. Now you don't dare take your kids trick or treating. You may do it in a controlled, contained environment so that nobody can possibly touch your child these days.'

'It seems to me,' adds Debra Hill, 'that the lines between reality and fantasy in horror pictures about suburbia have really blurred because these neighbourhoods really *aren't* safe any longer.'

'Nowadays, violence is so commonplace,' agrees Carpenter. 'It seems so random; it happens all around us, in every place. People seem to be seeking reassurance in the movies. I suppose that the time is over for the kind of movie that *Halloween* is. It's time to move on, to tell other stories.'

F For Flesh

F

IN THE PANTHEON OF horror monsters, no collection would be complete without the Alien. This extraordinary creature and the world it inhabits are the creation of an artist who produces landscapes every bit as memorable as Bosch or Brueghel, walking dream territories of sinews and liquid and things with teeth. Wandering through them, you know exactly where you are – in that place where no one hears you scream...

Swiss surrealist H.R. Giger is still perhaps best known for his book *H.R. Giger's Necronomicon,* a collection of early paintings loosely inspired by the work of H.P. Lovecraft, and his designs for Ridley Scott's classic 1979 science fiction/horror film, *Alien.*

Giger was originally only asked to create the three phases of the film's alien monster – the Face Hugger, the Chest Burster and the Big Alien, but he also ended up designing the surface of the planetoid, the exterior and interior of the derelict spacecraft and its dead pilot, the Space Jockey.

The original design called for a much bigger Face Hugger, which would use its muscular tail to spring out of one of the alien eggs (Giger describes them as 'organic footballs') and attach itself to the face of Kane, played by actor John Hurt. But director Ridley Scott wanted something smaller, so Giger called upon his artistic training:

'At school I worked as an industrial designer, so everything must have a function,' he recalls. 'The Face Hugger was determined through its function. You have to show that. I was thinking that something that jumps out and then holds onto someone's face needs fingers or hands. Normally, if someone is sitting on your face you can't breathe through your nose, so you automatically open your mouth. Then the monster goes down. So it looked a little bit like a crab or a spider. I like long fingers, so it had these long fingers, then two hands and a spiral tail. That was it. The hands hold onto Kane's face and the tail wraps around his neck.'

ALIEN

UK, 1979. Dir: Ridley Scott. With: Tom Skerritt, Sigourney Weaver, John Hurt, Ian Holm, Veronica Cartwright, Harry Dean Stanton. Twentieth Century Fox. Colour.

Scripted by Dan O'Bannon, *Alien* basically takes the plots of several old science-fiction movies *(It! The Terror from Beyond Space* [1958], *Planet of the Vampires* [1965] etc) and wraps them up in a surface gloss, thanks to director Scott's incredibly detailed visual sense. The seven crew members of the commercial spacecraft *Nostromo* are awakened from a long-term sleep and ordered to investigate signals from a nearby planetoid. Once on the surface, they discover the wreck of an alien spaceship and, upon returning to their own craft, unknowingly bring on board a very deadly lifeform... H.R. Giger's (much imitated) alien designs are genuinely bizarre, and there is a pounding soundtrack and excellent Oscar-winning special effects. Major sequences were cut before release and some of the shock moments were slightly trimmed after previews. Hurt replaced Jon Finch when the latter was taken ill during filming. *S.J.*

Sequels: *Aliens* (Dir: James Cameron, 1986), *Alien³* (Dir: David Fincher, 1992), *Alien Ressurection* (Dir: Jean-Pierre Jeunet, 1997).

Opposite: H.R. Giger.

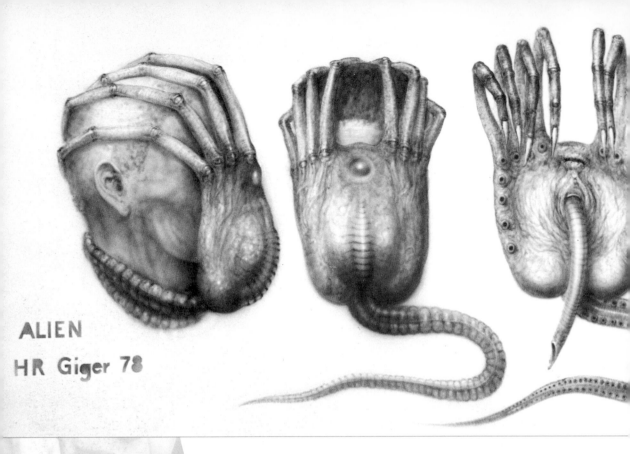

ALIEN
HR Giger 78

Top: Giger's original design for the Face Hugger in *Alien*.

Although his Chest Burster was put together by a team of technicians, Giger sculpted and constructed the Face Hugger and the Big Alien himself. 'The Alien is the star of the movie,' he maintains. 'As I do with all my work, I made the creature look biomechanical. Starting with the plaster core, I worked with Plasticine, rubber, bones, ribbed tubes and different mechanical stuff like wires.

'Ridley Scott gave me a lot of freedom. He and I would discuss the story, and sometimes use my book as a guide, and then I knew where I had to go. If you make a horror movie, then the monster must convince people. Mostly it doesn't. Only the head of the Alien was good. For me it was my first big film and I was not very familiar with these things. I learned a lot.'

Since his Oscar-winning involvement with *Alien*, his distinctive biomechanical imagery has influenced numerous movies and TV shows, and Giger is not always flattered by these uncredited imitations.

'There are a lot of American film-makers who copy my work,' he says. 'I'm not being compensated and my name is never mentioned. If at least that would happen then I could be content with the thought of having inspired something. For me, most horror films are too stupid and too boring and too badly made. I like films that are a little different. You can create something horrible but if it's filmed badly then it doesn't create any emotion in people.'

Giger's first involvement with movies came in 1969, when he created an extraterrestrial dog and humanoid alien for F.M. Murer's forty-five minute short entitled *Swiss Made*, filmed in 35mm. Two years later he co-directed *Passagen* (aka *Passages*) as an experiment in documentary film-making. However, his dealings with Hollywood have mostly been frustrating experiences for the artist.

'We have no special effects artists for the film industry in Switzerland. One must be a dedicated fanatic, and I seem to be about the only one of the kind here who is working with the Hollywood film industry. That makes me quite critical and sometimes a bit sour.

'The problem is to find someone who can realize my designs exactly as I had intended,' he laments. 'I have never been satisfied with what film-makers have done with my work in the past.'

After the two versions of *Dune* he worked on (for Alejandro Jodorowsky in 1975 and Ridley Scott in 1979) were abandoned, other projects such as *The Tourist* (1982) and *The Mirror* and *Dead Star* (both for director Bill Malone) also never made it to the screen.

In 1985, Giger was commissioned by MGM to create various horror scenes for the film *Poltergeist II The Other Side* (1986) with director Brian Gibson (who had previously invited him to work on *The Tourist*). However, Giger was less than happy with the visual transformations of his ideas. 'I got mixed up with the wrong project,' he reveals. 'The producers gave me the impression that I would be able to create something really new for this film and that the script could be adjusted if need be. Unfortunately things went differently.'

In 1987 he was commissioned by Japanese director Akio Jitsusoji to create the monster Goho Dohji for *Tokyo The Last Megalopolis,* and more recently he designed Sil, the shape-changing alien hybrid for *Species* (1995).

'Giger's efforts on this movie were just enormous,' explains Frank Mancuso Jr, producer of *Species.* 'Way above and beyond any issue of money – I expect, in fact, that he may have lost money on this project, given the time and care he lavished on it; we talked for hours on

F

'In mapping the tribal lands of our psyches, Giger gives us fresh access to them. He frees us, in essence, to wander there, encouraged by the fact that others have gone before. He makes us brave, and I can think of few higher ambitions for any art.'

Clive Barker

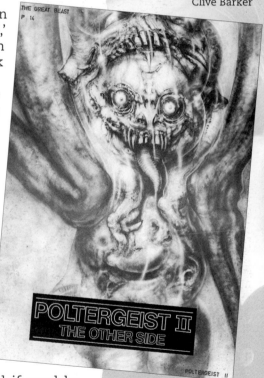

THE GREAT BEAST
P 14

POLTERGEIST II
THE OTHER SIDE

POLTERGEIST II

'Giger's work disturbs us, spooks us, because of its enormous evolutionary time-span. It shows us, all too clearly, where we come from and where we are going.'

Timothy Leary

F

Opposite: *Landscape XVIII*
by H.R. Giger (1973).

the phone about the most minute details of the design. He approached this project as an artist; he really gave it his all.'

However, after seeing the finished film, the artist's reaction was somewhat muted: 'Sometimes I ask myself why they used me on this film instead of someone else, because there are so many excellent film designers. I become so excited about a project that I lose my ability to make good business decisions and give far more than I am paid for.

'What is important is the final quality of my work and how it is presented. Nobody ever asks, after the years have passed, how much I got paid or whether I actually paid half of the costs for a particular sequence.'

Hans Rudi Giger was born in Switzerland in 1940. When he was five years old, Giger's mother was given a copy of *Life* magazine by an American soldier staying at their holiday home. Inside the magazine, Giger found a photo-spread from Jean Cocteau's magical film *La Belle et la Bête* (1946). 'I liked Cocteau,' he explains, 'because he was a man who did a lot of different things, just as I like to do.'

At the age of eighteen, Giger was employed as a draftsman by an architectural firm, where he developed his skills in composition and symmetry. From 1962–66 he attended the School of Applied Arts in Zürich, where he studied architectural and industrial design. The year that he graduated, he met actress Li Tobler, and the couple carried on an often turbulent love affair until her suicide in 1975.

'Li and I lived as lovers right up to her death,' he recalls. 'As an actress she adored anything unusual and loathed every form of mediocrity. It bored her to tears. When she finally left the theatre she opened her own art gallery in 1974. Her life was short but intense in every way, and her uniqueness stayed imprinted in the mind of everyone who ever met her.' Tobler's influence on the artist is apparent in a series of paintings he named after her.

In 1973, as Giger's international reputation began to grow, he was commissioned to design a record sleeve for the rock group Emerson, Lake and Palmer. Since then he has designed a prize, the Prix Tell, for the Swiss TV channel DRS; in Japan, Sony launched its first laser disc in 1986 with cover motifs by Giger; books by Aleister Crowley, H.P. Lovecraft and Timothy Leary were published in slipcases with Giger motifs in 1988 and, the same year, a Giger Bar was built in Tokyo, with another following in his hometown of Chur, Switzerland, in 1992. Numerous art books and prints of

his work are available worldwide.

Many of Giger's early drawings were done in india ink on tracing paper. In the late 1960s he experimented briefly with oils but found the medium too time-consuming and turned to the airbrush technique in 1971. 'Ridley Scott said that what he liked about my work was not the fantasy of it, it was the reality,' explains the artist. 'The airbrush was very new for me then, and only a few people in Switzerland were using it. With the airbrush you create a kind of reality because it comes very close to the photographic eye.'

However, these days he once again prefers to work in ink: 'After twenty years I have done enough airbrush. I changed because of the fax machine. Now I do a sketch in pencil and then ink because it comes out better on the fax, and in the movie business time is the most important thing. After you have a meeting they need a painting they can work with, and if you have first to create a painting with an airbrush, then take it to a photographer and then send a transparency over, it takes several days. If you can do it right away on paper and fax it through, they have it immediately.'

Giger's world is unlike any other. On entering, you are first repelled and then drawn in by its strange beauty.

'Giger's work leaves in its emotional wake the sensory equivalent of biting down on tinfoil. Most strongly put, he is our latter-day Hieronymus Bosch, the Dutch fabulist come again, demonic and erotic, exalting the more Baudelairean elements of the dark human psyche and affirming our now almost totally committed embrace with rust, stainless steel, the malevolent servo-mechanism, and the inescapability of clockwork destiny.'

Harlan Ellison

Above and top: The interior of Giger's home.

Much of the artist's work has been described as nightmarish, and the artist admits that some of his earlier paintings were done as a way of banishing disturbing dreams: 'I had a diary – a dream book. I had been having the same dreams again and again, and they were nightmares. They were horrifying. But I found that when I made artwork about them, the dreams went away. I felt much better. It was sort of self-psychiatry. In my dreams I think I always know where I am, but although these places must exist somewhere, I don't know where.

'I never think that I really paint horror. When I was a child I loved the ghost trains and things like that. But I also like castles and old buildings.'

He refers to his paintings as 'landscapes' or 'environments', and many of them are produced on large sheets of waterproof paper which have been mounted on chipboard or plywood panels. 'If I have an idea then I just make a sketch so that I don't forget it,' he says. 'The colours I use are pink and white, so they give the colour of something which has been lying a long time in a basement. Not very healthy colours.

'Sometimes people come and see my paintings and they see only the horrible, terrible things. In my paintings there are a lot of archetypes. People look at them and feel uncomfortable, and perhaps they think it's me, but it's them. I always have two elements in my paintings – the horrible things and the nice things. I mean, I like elegance, I like Art Nouveau; a stretched line or a curve. These things are very much in the foreground of my work.

'My stuff is not completely fresh. I have been influenced by Gaudi, Kubin, Dali and, first and foremost, by Hieronymus Bosch. When I do my work, everything influences me, it comes directly into my work.'

Many of these influences are reflected in his dystopian depictions of a world sinking beneath ecological horror, overpopulation and modern warfare. 'Other representations of our infected planet strike me as sentimental,' he says. 'More often than not, they give us only an imprecise idea of the shape we and our environs are in.

'Sex and death are all around us. It's so important, all the problems we have are to do with these things. I like to warn people about overpopulation in my work. Every problem comes from that, and it's ridiculous. It's really crazy that this world is so full of people that it's going to explode.'

The new landscape of horror is the body – its diseases, decay and secretions. It's a world that Giger explores with the insight of the other great artists of the horrific, such as Goya and Bacon. Like them, he creates strange places in which, eventually, we find a home.

It is a clear theme that runs through much of Giger's work, along with claustrophobia and a fascination with babies and reproduction. These are perhaps best defined in his 1973 painting *Landscape XVIII*, produced in acrylic on paper and wood. 'Landscapes formed from babies' heads have always given me a particular thrill,' admits the artist. 'Babies are so beautifully innocent and yet when I see them *en masse* (a canvas, thank God, has its limits) they become threatening and seem to me to represent the beginning of all evil. When a baby is born it already has a brain and that brain is not completely empty. It is aware of the heart beating. That's a reason why I have these strange, claustrophobic dreams: I remember when I was a little seed, I was swimming like crazy and I could see others.

'I asked my mother about my birth and she said it

F

Above: The alien, Sil, in *Species*.

F

Above: *Alien.*

was very difficult. It took a long time. I remember that I saw these passages and at the end I saw something round and like steel. It was probably an instrument the doctor used.

'Through the paintings I found out many things about myself. My work is a kind of therapy for me. I probably make other people sick, but for me it's healthy.'

Despite his worldwide fame, Giger remains content to live in Zürich. 'I'm an artist on the fringe,' he maintains. 'In Zürich I think I'm alone. Switzerland is not a very fantastic land. I like to stay here. It's very safe.'

'I visited him at his studio,' recalls *Species* director Roger Donaldson, '– quite an amazing place. Two little row houses, where he's punched a hole from one into the next one. Walls completely covered with his paintings and drawings, paintings on the ceilings, strange artifacts everywhere, bones and machinery. I remember sitting by a table and thinking, my God, that looks like a shrunken head – and indeed it was, a genuine shrunken head sitting there on the table.'

Giger's home is also filled with many bizarre presents that people have given him over the years. 'It's just like a warehouse,' he admits. 'I could fill a huge hall and I'd still never have enough space for my stuff. You can't find a two metre square, every space is taken.

'I like things like skulls for instance. When I was five years old I got this skull from a pharmacy. That was something special, having a real skull. I could do what I wanted with this skull. It was my skull. People sometimes send me very strange things, like an English "shrunken head" or some magical stuff. Sometimes it is uncomfortable to live with these objects, so I have to give them away.

'I'm not superstitious about the thirteenth or something like that,' maintains the artist. 'But I *am* sometimes superstitious. I have certain feelings that are like a warning that something could happen. The world of magic has always held a fascination for me, and this in turn has left its mark on my painting. Perhaps it has also helped me overcome my fear of such forces, a fear so bound up with my fascination. Because what you don't know, you're afraid of.'

G For Grim Tales

G

Right: Laurence Harvey and Karl Boehm create *The Wonderful World of the Brothers Grimm*.

There are two versions of childhood. The advertisers' childhood of cute remarks and freckles and wide eyes full of wonder. And then there's another, more vicious scenario: the perverse childhood of sudden violence and scary toys and eyes full of blankness.

Fairy tales abound in images of horror and dark fantasy – Snow White choking to death on an apple, a cannibal witch keeping Hansel and Gretel like animals in a cage to fatten them up for the oven, and Tom Thumb being eaten alive...

Once upon a time, long, long ago, there lived a rich man who had two children.

His little boy was given him by his first wife, who died when the boy was born. So the man married again, and had a little girl, borne him by his second wife, and when she looked at her own daughter, and then looked at the little boy, it pierced her heart to think that he would always stand in the way of her own child.

This evil thought took possession of her more and more, and made her behave very unkindly to the boy. She would drive him from place to place with her duffings and buffetings, so that the poor child went about in fear.

'I think if you went into a shopping mall and asked a

hundred people what their perception of a fairy tale was,' says Tim Burton, director of *Edward Scissorhands* (1990), 'it would be like a children's story. Then if you showed them some of Grimm's fairy tales, they might be a little horrified to see that it's probably worse than most of the *Friday the 13th* movies. Things aren't always as simple or what they seem, and I think that's what I like about the fairy tale form: that it's not cut and dried, it's open to interpretation.'

And so it came to pass one day, when the boy came back from school, the wife said to him: 'My child, will you have an apple?'

But she gave him a wicked look, because the evil thought had come into her head that she would kill him.

'Come with me,' she said, and she lifted the lid of the great

> 'He'd always been a solitary child, as much through choice as circumstance, happiest when he could unshackle his imagination, and let it wander…into a world more pungent and more remote than the one he knew. A world whose scents were carried to his nostrils by winds mysteriously warm in a chill December; whose creatures paid him homage on certain nights at the foot of his bed, and whose peoples he conspired with in sleep.'
>
> FROM WEAVEWORLD BY CLIVE BARKER

Above: The Brothers Grimm.

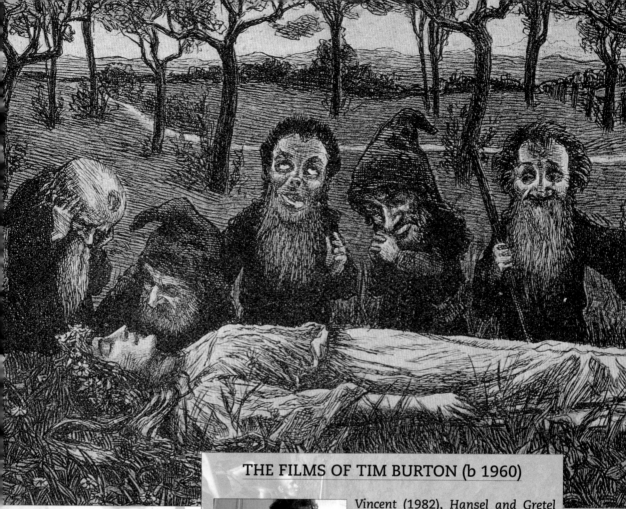

Above: Alfred Zimmerman's illustration of 'Snow White and the Seven Dwarfs' in *Jugend*, circa 1903.
Opposite: *The Nightmare Before Christmas*.

'These macabre exercises are pure escapism, and to claim they harm children is the veriest nonsense. For them they are simply fairy tales, no grimmer than the Grimm their grandmothers used to read to them at bedtime.'

Vincent Price

THE FILMS OF TIM BURTON (b 1960)

Vincent (1982), *Hansel and Gretel* (TV, 1983), *Frankenweenie* (1984), *Pee-Wee's Big Adventure* (1985), *Fairie Tale Theatre: Aladdin and His Wonderful Lamp* (TV, 1985), *Beetle Juice* (1988), *Batman* (1989), *Edward Scissorhands* (1990), *Batman Returns* (1992), *The Nightmare Before Christmas* (producer, 1993), *Cabin Boy* (producer, 1993) *Ed Wood* (1994), *Batman Forever* (producer, 1995), *James and the Giant Peach* (producer, 1996), *Mars Attacks!* (1996).

big chest where she kept the apples. 'Take one for yourself,' she said, and she smiled at the boy.

So the boy bent over the chest, and as he did so, the evil spirit urged her and crash!, down went the lid, and off went the little boy's head.

'"The Juniper Tree" is an extraordinarily violent story,' says Hanna Castien, Reader in Modern Languages at London University. 'It is therefore somewhat surprising that it formed the nucleus of a story book for children, a famous collection of fairy tales which the Brothers Grimm collected in the early nineteenth century. The brothers shared with their fellow romantics a predilection for violence, I suppose, and a deep interest in the dark side of the mind, which finds such strong expression in these tales.'

Many of the folk legends that the Grimm Brothers went on to collect erupt into similar images of intense horror. 'Clearly, when the Grimm Brothers collected their tales,' continues Hanna Castien, 'what they found were stories that were at times pretty crude.

'They were pretty prudish about the sexual aspects of this, and about body functions, and they almost eliminated them entirely. However, they were less prudish about the violent aspects. They felt that children could take these. Children were not easily frightened. They would not be damaged by this violence at all.'

The woman was overwhelmed with fear at the thought of what she had done. 'No one must know I have killed him,' she thought. 'So I will make him into puddings.'

So she took the little boy and cut him up, and made him into puddings, and put him in the pot. But his little sister stood looking on, and wept and wept, and her tears fell into the pot, so that there was no need of salt.

When the husband came home, the wife gave him a large dish of black pudding, and told him that his son had gone away into the country. The father was very sad that his son had gone away and not said good-bye, but he went on with his dinner. He asked his wife for more pudding, and threw the bones under the table.

'When I was six years old I read "The Princess and the Goblin", and images from that fairy story have never left

'The fascination of the "horror" film is perhaps because it is make-believe. Most people like to pretend that there is something just beyond the door. It transports the audience to another world. A world of fantasy and of imagination. A world inhabited by the characters of Hans Andersen and the Brothers Grimm. The "horror" film is concocted more or less from the folk tales of every country. When I am asked if these films are harmful to children, my answer is always the same: Do Grimm's fairy tales do any harm to children? I have never heard of fairy tale books being used in evidence in a juvenile delinquency case!'

Boris Karloff

83

G me since,' recalls award-winning horror novelist Ramsey Campbell. 'One in particular has a palace guard seeing a figure whose head is as round as a ball and with a face that one might have carved on a pumpkin, but a head twice the size it ought to have been for the body.

'Now these things stayed with me, particularly in the dark, and peopled my bedroom for nights after I'd read them. It just set my imagination off, and probably that's where I've come from as a writer ever since.'

But for Ramsey Campbell, it was not just his childhood reading that influenced him as a writer, but also the peculiarities of his early family life.

'Very shortly after I was born, or when I was no more than a year old, I suppose, my parents became estranged. And before I was more than three or four years old, my parents lived almost totally apart but in the same small house – three bedrooms, two rooms downstairs. Because I had to side with one parent or the other, I stayed with my mother. My father became a totally unseen presence in the same house.

'I suppose that there was a sense in which all that was going on in the house became magnified. I mean, not merely the footsteps coming upstairs in the dark, but also my bedroom became a kind of place of, if

> 'The shadows moved things. The mesh of the fireguard fluttered enlarged on the wall; sometimes, at the edge of sleep, it became a swaying web, and its spinner came sidling down from a corner of the ceiling... The room grew in the dark: sounds outside, footsteps and laughter, dogs encouraging each other to bark, only emphasized the size of my trap of darkness, how distant everything else was.'
>
> FROM 'THE CHIMNEY'
> BY RAMSEY CAMPBELL

'But for want of a typewriter, Ramsey Campbell might well have emerged at birth with an essay on the darker side of life in the womb. For Ramsey possesses a vision of the world, and all it contains, unlike any other; he finds shadows with unerring skill, and picks out from scenes and situations that most of us would find quite unremarkable, pieces of darkness embedded there like glass shards in a car wreck victim.'

Clive Barker

BOOKS BY RAMSEY CAMPBELL (b 1946)

NOVELS: *The Doll Who Ate His Mother* (1976), *The Face that Must Die* (1979), *The Parasite* (aka *To Wake the Dead*, 1980), *The Nameless* (1981), *The Claw* (aka *Night of the Claw*, 1983), *Incarnate* (1983), *Obsession* (1985), *The Hungry Moon* (1986), *The Influence* (1988), *Ancient Images* (1989), *Midnight Sun* (1990), *Needing Ghosts* (1990), *The Count of Eleven* (1991), *The Long Lost* (1993), *The One Safe Place* (1995), *The House on Nazareth Hill* (1996), *The Last Voice They Hear* (1997).

COLLECTIONS: *The Inhabitant of the Lake and Less Welcome Tenants* (1964), *Demons by Daylight* (1973), *The Height of the Scream* (1976), *Dark Companions* (1982), *Cold Print* (1985), *Night Visions 3* (with Clive Barker and Lisa Tuttle, 1986), *Black Wine* (with Charles L. Grant, 1986), *Scared Stiff: Tales of Sex and Death* (1987), *Dark Feasts: The World of Ramsey Campbell* (1987), *Waking Nightmares* (1991), *Strange Things and Stranger Places* (1993), *Alone with the Horrors* (1993), *Far Away and Never* (1997).

not exactly terror, then certainly of fears in the corners.

'When I read my story 'The Chimney' to an audience, then I realized that clearly what I was writing about was the terror of my father coming into my room. Indeed, the story actually contains the line that this terrible thing which invades this young chap's childhood was in some sense his father – it's a kind of projection of his fears about his father which makes this figure monstrous.'

Although the little boy was cooked and eaten, he didn't die. His sister buried his bones under the Juniper Tree, and he came back to life as a little bird. But he was determined to have his revenge upon his wicked step-mother.

He picked up a huge mill-stone in his beak, and flew with it to the cottage, singing:

'My mother killed me,
My father ate me,
Keewit, keewit, what a fine bird am I.'

Horror stories and fairy tales are united by a dark core. They construct fearful menacing worlds which we are drawn into as a way of exploring our own private terrors.

'When I read a fairy tale nowadays, I don't really understand it,' admits Tim Burton, 'but you do understand it on an emotional, visceral level. I think that was the whole purpose of those things: to help children to understand the horrors and complexities of life.'

Upon hearing this song, the woman fell to the floor in fear and trouble, and then she sprang up, her hair standing out from her head like flames of fire, and ran out of the cottage.

As she crossed the threshold, crash! the bird threw the mill-stone down on her head, and she was crushed to death. There was a huge flame, and a great ball of smoke, and there, on exactly the same spot, appeared the little boy.

When we look at a number of fairy tales, we can observe certain patterns of plot, as Hanna Castien explains: 'One of the simplest patterns is that a hostile

---

THE WONDERFUL WORLD OF THE BROTHERS GRIMM

USA/Germany, 1962. Dir: Henry Levin. With: Laurence Harvey, Karl Boehm, Claire Bloom, Walter Slezak, Barbara Eden, Oscar Homolka. George Pal/Metro-Goldwyn-Mayer. Colour.

Co-scripted by Charles Beaumont and based on *Die Brüder Grimm* by Dr Herman Gerstner, this features three fairy stories within the framework of the rise to fame of Wilhelm and Jacob Grimm (Harvey and Boehm, respectively). Russ Tamblyn stars in 'The Dancing Princess', the tale of a princess who dances all night with the gypsies; Harvey plays a cobbler whose wooden elves come to life (courtesy of producer Pal's Puppetoons) on Christmas Eve in 'The Cobbler and the Elves', and Terry-Thomas and Buddy Hackett are forced to battle a superb stop-motion dragon (animated by Jim Danforth) in 'The Singing Bone'. In the end, the sick Wilhelm is visited by all the characters he will write about: fairies, elves, Snow White and Tom Thumb (Tamblyn, recreating his role from the 1958 film). With Yvette Mimieux, Jim Backus, Ian Wolfe and Beulah Bondi. Filmed in CinemaScope. SJ.

'We have all been brought up with these mini-horror stories from nursery rhymes and the Brothers Grimm – so what I am doing is nothing different, I am not doing anything new...it's just more graphic these days.'

James Herbert

> 'He did not even like opening the door to flick on the light because he always had the idea – this was so exquisitely stupid he didn't dare tell anyone – that while he was feeling for the light switch, some horrible clawed paw would settle lightly over his wrist ...and jerk him down into the darkness that smelled of dirt and wet and dim rotted vegetables.'
>
> FROM *IT*
> BY STEPHEN KING

'I don't ever remember a time that I wasn't genuinely interested in horror in some form or another. It was always the grisly bits of fairy tales that I was interested in. I've always liked fantastical literature of some kind, and I've always liked the darker aspects of that.'

Clive Barker

Above right: Warwick Goble's illustration of 'The Juniper Tree' in *The Fairy Book*.

force intrudes into an established simple order of things. For example, the family unit intruded upon by the step-mother: that basic pattern is included in modern horror fiction. An example would be Stephen King's *It*, where a small community is invaded by a very powerful and dangerous force which threatens the whole town.

'A group of weaker individuals manage to conquer and overpower this force. They do it by using the virtues of the child in the fairy tale – a bit of cunning, a lot of courage, and an innate goodness which is victorious at the end. "The Juniper Tree" is such an empowering story.

'The boy does come back to avenge himself. He finds strength to defeat the intruder mother, and he actually kills her. So that at the end of the story it's not only he who's empowered, but the rest of the family. We have restored harmony and we have a stronger child at the end of it.'

H for Harlequinade

'I'm very interested in fools. Fools obsess me and always have, clowns too...Punch has always fascinated me because he's so cruel and so funny at the same time.'

Clive Barker

'I want my make-up simply to add to the picture, to show at a glance the sort of character I am portraying. But I want my roles to go deeper than that. I want to dig down into the mind and the heart of the role. But as a man's face reveals much that is in his mind and heart, I attempt to show this by the make-up I use; and the make-up is merely the prologue.'

Lon Chaney Sr

THE GREAT SILENT HORROR actor Lon Chaney Sr once said, 'A clown is funny in the circus ring, but what would be the normal reaction to opening a door at midnight and finding the same clown standing there in the moonlight?' Adults seem to think that clowns are great entertainment and good for you, too. Kids, being younger and somewhat wiser, aren't so sure...

Robert Bloch, the author of *Psycho,* agreed with Chaney: 'That, to me, is the essence of true horror – the clown, at midnight. Horror is something peculiar to the individual – a small child's (and quite frequently an adult's!) fear of the dark...and most particularly the phantoms of the imagination that populate the dark. The fear of a human being who doesn't act, think or look like a human being.'

According to Jason Covatch, a clown with the anarchic circus Archaos, 'The natural response to terror is initially to laugh, which is why if a child fears that he or she is threatened they will laugh, because they're not actually aware of the possible violence and damage and pain.

'I think an audience comes on a journey with you, and with us it is always a bumpy ride. There's the sense of a ghost train, of a funfair ride, of a roller coaster where you can guarantee that you'll get to the end, but you're not sure in between...'

The fine line between horror and humour is something that ex-punk rock singer turned writer/director Simon Sprackling explored in his low-budget British horror movie *Funny Man* (1994), which featured a harlequin from hell played by Tim James.

'I think the idea of the smile is an interesting one,'

CLOWNS IN THE MOVIES

L'Homme Qui Rit (1909), *The Man Who Laughs* (aka *Das Grinsende Gesicht;* with Franz Hobling, 1921), *He Who Gets Slapped* (with Lon Chaney Sr, 1924), *The Man Who Laughs* (with Conrad Veidt, 1928), *Laugh Clown Laugh* (with Lon Chaney Sr, 1928), *The Hunchback of Notre Dame* (1939), *Night of the Demon* (aka *Curse of the Demon,* 1957), *The Clowns* (aka *I Clowns;* with Rhum and Bario, 1965), *The Man Who Laughs* (aka *L'Uomo Che Ride;* with Edmond Purdom, 1965), *Harlequin* (aka *Dark Forces;* with Robert Powell, 1980), *Blood Harvest* (with Tiny Tim, 1987), *Killer Klowns from Outer Space* (1987), *Clownhouse* (1989), *It* (with Tim Curry, TV 1990), *Funny Man* (with Tim James, 1994).

says Sprackling. 'The clown has this painted smile, and the painted smile can read two ways. Kids will pick this up in their own way – because either they will have a trust of the adult world dressed up or they won't.

'What I really like about clowns and jesters is that they have this very long history which takes us back through the pack of cards, where you have the Joker, to the Tarot, where you have the Fool. The great thing about jesters for me, as the maker of a horror movie, is that I've got a character who links me to the past, and I think that can be very effective. Particularly if you're using old houses and that sort of Hammer Films feel, you need a sort of archaic character.'

'Throughout the film there are strong elements of dark humour in the horror,' says *Funny Man* co-star

Right and below: Archaos clowns.

Left: Tim James as the *Funny Man*.
Below: Federico Fellini's original design for *The Clowns*.

FUNNY MAN

UK, 1994. Dir: Simon Sprackling. With: Tim James, Christopher Lee, Benny Young, Ingrid Lacey, Pauline Black, Matthew Devitt. PolyGram. Colour.

Low-budget horror comedy in which the mysterious Callum (veteran Lee in a brief cameo) purposely loses his ancestral home in a poker game to Max (Young). When the winner, his family, friends and assorted travellers arrive at the creepy old mansion, they are brutally killed off one by one by a demonic court jester, the Funny Man (James in make-up by Neill Gorton), who has an evil sense of humour. S.J.

Christopher Lee, 'and powerful horrific elements to the black comedy. I think those two strands combine and work well together. The Funny Man's witty one-liners always work in the context of what he's done, what he's going to do. He's brutal, but funny…by which I mean he's genuinely eerie.'

'We didn't hold back on the violence,' agrees Neill Gorton, who was responsible for the special make-up effects in the film, 'and the comedy was our way around that. Instead of making a straight gory horror film, with *Funny Man* you're laughing one moment, then going "*Jesus Christ!*" the next.

'Basically, the character of the Funny Man in the script was that of the Joker from a pack of cards,' continues Gorton. 'He was Mr Punch, the Harlequin.'

Part Two opens in darkness. We've moved from the breathless dawn of Part One into a darker world, a haunted world. Distantly, the sound of whale-song. But closer, horses gallop, distant incoherent shouts, the clash of arms.

A light comes up on the Old Clown, who is sitting astride a knackered old Pantomime Horse, preferably piebald. He is dressed ridiculously, as a general. His hat bristles with tatty feathers. A wooden sword hangs forlornly at his side. He stares out at us, unblinking.

Enter Crazyface, not seeing the horse and rider. He is breathless, having run a long way.

He realizes that he has left the Pig Breeder's house a long way behind. He's safe. And he still has his coat.

The horse neighs. Crazyface turns around.

CRAZYF: You. Are you everywhere?

(The Clown blows out a long, slow column of water, his eternal greeting)

CRAZYF: What are you doing here? You'll get yourself killed. We'll all get killed.

(The Clown shrugs)

CRAZYF: What am I going to do? He took my box. And he tried to kill me. Ah, what do you care? I was going to go to Rome, but there isn't much use now is there? I'd go home...except that I keep seeing Lenny.

(The Old Clown looks at him sharply)

CRAZYF: Oh, so you know Lenny do you?

(The Old Clown shrugs)

CRAZYF: You do, don't you? He's my brother. Somebody once told me all the clowns in the world were related, however distantly. All parts of one great big family. Do you think that's possible?

(The Clown shrugs)

CRAZYF: Nah. Neither do I.

FROM *CRAZYFACE: A COMEDY (WITH LIONS)*,
A PLAY BY CLIVE BARKER

'I am distrustful of a man who laughs too readily.'

Lon Chaney Sr

'The thing about clowning breaking the rules is fundamental for us,' says Jason Covatch of Archaos. 'We use our clown-like abilities to make people feel that they aren't safe, to make them feel that they might lose things – that they might lose their limbs, that they might lose their security, that they might lose their clothes, that they might become wet, or that they might lose their wallet, their children. So it's essentially a crossing over, breaking down that spectator/performer boundary.'

In 1970 in Des Plaines, Illinois, prosperous and popular building contractor John Wayne Gacy began working as a children's entertainer, Pogo the Clown. Eight years later, on 10 May, Robert Piest, aged fifteen, of Des Plaines, disappeared. Police investigators were led to the

home of Gacy, where they discovered human remains covered by lime in the crawl space beneath the house.

After an insanity hearing lasting just over five weeks, Gacy was convicted of luring thirty-three young men and boys between the ages of fourteen and eighteen to his home in a modest suburban neighbourhood near O'Hare International airport, where, from 1972–1978, he strangled them and buried them beneath the floorboards.

'Two of the Keystone Cops they had following me were eating a meal at a restaurant,' said Gacy, 'and they were asking me why I did clowning with all the other things I was doing, that I wouldn't have time. I told them because it was fun and it was relaxing from my business. Going to the hospitals, visiting kids and old folks, was rewarding as well; and the parades were the most fun, as you could run off into the crowd, kiss the women, squeeze their breasts with husbands and boyfriends watching, and run off with them laughing, thinking it was funny. When you're in make-up, clowns can get away with murder and nobody gets mad. Trouble is, the only part quoted is, "Gacy says: clowns can get away with murder."'

Above: A cornucopia of clowns in *He Who Gets Slapped*.
Opposite: Conrad Veidt in *The Man Who Laughs* (1928).

'He looked up and saw Pennywise the Clown standing at the top of the lefthand staircase, looking down at him. His face was white with grease-paint. His mouth bled lipstick in a killer's grin. There were empty sockets where his eyes should have been. He held a bunch of balloons in one hand and a book in the other.'

FROM IT BY STEPHEN KING

'I used to love being a clown, it meant you could get away with murder.'

John Wayne Gacy

Right: John Wayne Gacy as Pogo the Clown.

'My art talent is a gift from God, and what I do with it is my gift back to God. I have done nearly 1600 paintings now, and mostly clowns and some Disney characters upon request.'

John Wayne Gacy

At one minute past midnight on 11 May 1994, 52-year-old John Wayne Gacy was finally executed on Death Row for his crimes. His death took more than twice as long as scheduled due to a partial failure of the lethal injection device at the Stateville maximum security prison in Joliet, Illinois.

Hundreds of demonstrators gathered outside the prison as the deadline approached, many carrying placards displaying such slogans as 'Justice, Justice, Not Too Late, John Wayne Gacy, Meet Your Fate' and 'Say Goodbye, It's Time for You to Fry'.

'What's interesting about the relationship between clowns and children is that we, as adults, assume that children find them funny,' says Simon Sprackling. 'But that's our presumption. I think that when kids are looking they're seeing an adult behaving in this rather peculiar fashion, which they can either find funny or they think, "There's something wrong with this".'

I For Innocents

I

'From all around the children were coming. Some of them were laughing gaily. They held knives, hatchets, pipes, rocks, hammers. One girl, maybe eight, with beautiful long blonde hair, held a jackhandle.'
FROM 'CHILDREN OF THE CORN'
BY STEPHEN KING

'There are few children who have not pulled the wings off a few flies at some point in their development, or squatted patiently on the sidewalk to see how a bug dies.'
Stephen King

SINCE THE GARDEN OF Eden, kids have been getting worse. At least that is what some adults, forgetting that they were ever kids themselves, will tell you. Did you really bring up your little angels to behave like little devils? And if it was not you, then what exactly is driving them...?

Ever since Ray Bradbury opened up the dark side of childhood in 1947 with his short story of a murderous baby, 'The Small Assassin', horror has claimed our kids. These days everything in the nursery looks both enchanting and cruel...

'There is a view of the child,' says Hanna Castien, Reader in Modern Languages at London University, 'that we perhaps have inherited from the nineteenth century, which sees the child as a wild animal. As such, it poses a threat to society and to its order, which the parents subscribe to. How do the parents go about taming this wild animal? Well, in the nineteenth century, there were examples that parents could look for.

'One of them was Heinrich Hoffman's book *Der Struwwelpeter*. Here a number of children actually pay with their lives for their disobedience.'

For centuries we have been unsettled by our children. Out of the adult fictions of wicked children and brutal punishment, comes one of the most dishonest ideas in modern horror, that of the Evil Child.

'I've always been very dubious of this notion of children as evil,' says horror author Ramsey Campbell. 'Sometimes this use of them in the horror genre is actually a way of reading what we don't want to admit about ourselves into a convenient scapegoat.

'I think the notion of childhood innocence involves a morality, but I also think that the prevailing idealization of children makes people feel betrayed if children act the way we used to act as kids. I'm inclined to feel that what is really going on here is the forgetting of what it was actually like to be children.'

According to Paul Wells of the Department of Media Studies at De Montfort University, Leicester, 'By the mid-1950s Americans had seen the Korean War, they had seen McCarthyism, the rise of commercial television, and suddenly the American Dream didn't seem as solid as it used to be. The scapegoat for this was the youth culture. Suddenly, America turned its head towards the youth culture and children in particular.'

A society obsessed with moulding children into shape was fertile ground for the horror genre to plant the nightmarish idea of an uncontrollable child. In 1956, the

Above: The face of evil?
Eleven-year-old Patty
McCormack in *The Bad
Seed* (1956).

first film to make a child the focus of fear was released. *The Bad Seed* had started life as a bestselling book and a hit play, but it was to have its biggest impact as a movie. Horror no longer had the twisted face of a monster. For the first time it was to be found in the smile of a little girl.

    The Bad Seed tells the story of Rhoda Penmark, an eight-year-old child murderess (played by eleven-year-old Patty McCormack, who starred in the play and received an Academy Award nomination for her portrayal in the film). Rhoda beats and drowns a young classmate, and then proceeds to burn alive the caretaker who discovers her crime.

97

I

'What motivated Rhoda was a sense that her own morality was about taking care of herself,' explains McCormack. 'She didn't weigh up right and wrong the way other people did. She had no sense of not being good or not being bad, she just took care of business.'

'Children are naturally transgressive,' says Paul Wells. 'They go to places where they are not supposed to go. They behave in a way that they are not supposed to. Horror movies like *The Bad Seed* take that one step further. They say, "What if a child is allowed to break all those rules and regulations that their parents have given them? What will happen then, just how far will they go?"'

When the film was released, the activities of such an evil child were met with public dismay. The official response to such transgression was immediate. Concerned about copycat behaviour, the American authorities banned all children from the movie theatres where *The Bad Seed* was playing – something unheard of in the days before official film classification in the US.

'I know that from first-hand experience,' reveals McCormack, 'because when we went to a theatre, I can't remember where, they objected to my going in. It had to be explained I was in the film before they let me in.'

What made the film even more controversial were the debates about the story's ending. In the original stage adaptation, Rhoda's crimes went shockingly unpunished. The play's producers knew that the public

---

THE BAD SEED

USA, 1956. Dir: Mervyn LeRoy. With: Nancy Kelly, Patty McCormack, Henry Jones, Eileen Heckart, Evelyn Varden, William Hopper. Warner Bros. B&W.

Macabre but stagey version of Maxwell Anderson's play, based on the novel by William March, about a pigtailed murderess possessed by an inherited evil – the bad seed of the title. McCormack gives an Oscar-nominated performance as the precocious cold-blooded killer, and Jones plays LeRoy, the mentally handicapped caretaker who sees through her lies, until she burns him to death. After the girl's mother (Kelly) shoots herself and the little girl is struck by lightning while looking for a medal (not in the play), a tacked-on Curtain Call plays it for laughs as Kelly spanks McCormack. With Paul Fix and Jesse White. *S.J.*

Remake: *The Bad Seed* (1985).

THE BAD SEED

USA, 1985. Dir: Paul Wendkos. With: Blair Brown, Lynn Redgrave, David Carradine, Carrie Wells, Richard Kiley, David Ogden Stiers. Warner Bros. Colour.

Surprisingly impressive TV movie remake of the 1956 film, also based on the play by Maxwell Anderson and William March's novel. Wells is chilling as *Rachel* Penmark, a nine-year-old child who will kill to get what she wants. Thanks to George Eckstein's superior script, director Wendkos coaxes fine performances from Redgrave as a flamboyant neighbour, Ogden Stiers as a crime novelist and Carradine as LeRoy Jessup, the simple gardener who suspects the child's secret. *S.J.*

"Talk all you want about the man and the woman-- but please don't tell about the girl!"

"THE BAD SEED" IS THE BIG SHOCKER!

WARNER BROS. PRESENT THE TWO-YEAR-RUN STAGE SENSATION WITH ITS ORIGINAL CAST!

NANCY KELLY AND INTRODUCING PATTY McCORMACK WITH HENRY JONES · EVELYN VARDEN · A MERVYN LeROY PRODUCTION · Screen Play by JOHN LEE MAHIN

MAXWELL ANDERSON and the novel by WILLIAM MARCH · DIRECTED BY MERVYN LeROY · A WARNER BROS. PICTURE

Above: *The Bad Seed* (1956).

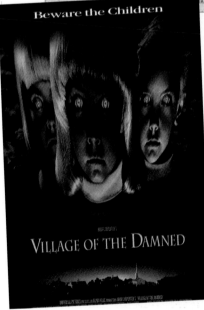

would not tolerate this lack of retribution. 'When Nancy Kelly took her curtain call,' recalls McCormack, 'she added bringing me out. I had already had my curtain call, and she told me to come here. Then she sat on the couch and flipped me over her lap and spanked me, which was very satisfying for the audience, who I suppose also wanted to do that.'

The film's producers were even more certain that such an evil child would have to be properly punished, and they took retribution one step further.

'It caused problems when it was made into a film,' explains Paul Wells, 'because the original ending of the play had the child murderess getting away with her

'I believe children can rid themselves of feelings of hatred and violence while watching us on the screen, instead of taking it out on their parents, friends and schoolteachers.'

Vincent Price

EVIL CHILDREN IN THE MOVIES

The Bad Seed (with Patty McCormack, 1956), *Village of the Damned* (with Martin Stephens, 1960), *The Innocents* (with Pamela Franklin and Martin Stephens, 1961), *Children of the Damned* (with Clive Powell, 1963), *Lord of the Flies* (with Tom Chapin, 1963), *Let's Kill Uncle* (with Pat Cardi and Mary Badham, 1966), *The House that Screamed* (aka *La Residencia*; with John Moulder Brown, 1970), *A Little Game* (with Mark Gruner, TV, 1971), *The Nightcomers* (with Verna Harvey and Christopher Ellis, 1971), *Unman, Wittering and Zigo* (with Colin Barrie, 1971), *The Other* (with Chris and Martin Udvarnoky, 1972), *Child's Play* (with Jamie Alexander, 1972), *Death Is Child's Play* (aka *Quien Puede Matar un Niño?/Island of the Damned*, 1975), *Kiss of the Tarantula* (with Suzanne Ling, 1975), *Carrie* (with Sissy Spacek, 1976), *Communion* (aka *Alice, Sweet Alice/Holy Terror*; with Mildred Clinton, 1976), *The Little Girl Who Lives Down the Lane* (with Jodie Foster, 1976), *The Omen* (with Harvey Stephens, 1976), *Cathy's Curse* (with Randi Allen, 1977), *The Child* (with Rosalie Cole, 1977), *Ruby* (with Janet Baldwin, 1977), *Shock* (aka *Shock Transfert-Suspence-Hypnos/Beyond the Door II*; with David Colin Jr, 1977), *The Spell* (with Susan Myers, TV, 1977), *Damien Omen II* (with Jonathan Scott-Taylor, 1978), *The Brood* (1979), *The Children* (1980), *Bloody Birthday* (with Elizabeth Hoy, Billy Jacoby and Andy Freeman, 1980), *Children of the Corn* (with John Franklin, 1984), *The Bad Seed* (with Carrie Wells, 1985), *Lord of the Flies* (with Chris Furrh, 1990), *The Reflecting Skin* (with Jeremy Cooper, 1990), *The Addams Family* (with Christina Ricci and Jimmy Workman, 1991), *Omen IV: The Awakening* (with Asia Vieira, 1991), *Children of the Corn II: The Final Sacrifice* (with Ryan Bollman, 1992), *Addams Family Values* (with Christina Ricci and Jimmy Workman, 1993), *The Good Son* (with Macaulay Culkin, 1993), *Children of the Corn III: Urban Harvest* (with Daniel Cerny and Ron Melendez, 1994), *Village of the Damned* (with Lindsey Haun, 1995), *Children of the Corn IV* (with Naomi Watts, 1996).

THEY COME TO CONQUER THE WORLD . . . *so young, so innocent, so DEADLY!*

ALL-NEW SUSPENSE THRILLER

METRO-GOLDWYN-MAYER presents
A LAWRENCE P. BACHMANN PRODUCTION

IAN HENDRY

CHILDREN OF THE DAMNED

...even more eerie than "Village of the Damned"!

With
ALAN BADEL
BARBARA FERRIS
Screenplay by
JOHN BRILEY
Produced by
BEN ARBEID
Directed by
ANTON M. LEADER

'I was by no means alone in my fascination with the chilling stuff; most children show a healthy appetite for the monstrous. It's only later we're shamed and bullied into suppressing that appetite, so that for many readers horror fiction is still a guilty pleasure.'

Clive Barker

crimes with absolutely no remorse whatsoever. The ending in the film now shows the child being punished by a bolt of lightning – the ultimate Divine Intervention!'

With this extravagant climax, adult audiences had the satisfaction of seeing the rebellious child quelled for good. At least, in their imaginations...

J for Japan

'I can mutate the whole world into metal.'

From *Tetsuo – The Iron Man*
(1989)

'A bizarre wet dream, a horrifying sex death...and ghastly special effects... Unmissable!'

City Limits on *Tetsuo – The Iron Man*

Above: *Tetsuo II Body Hammer*.

HORROR PLAYS ON UNIVERSAL fears – sex, death, change – but it also has a charming habit of knowing what scares the wits out of a particular culture at a particular time. If horror is a laboratory, then the thrill starts when such experimental notions break out of the building. Every once in a while someone, somewhere, comes up with an all-new, rogue viewpoint that spreads and multiplies. And finally these new contagions invade horror itself and change all the rules...

Since the Second World War, Japan has put its faith in technology, but sometimes technology can seem to have a life of its own. Tokyo-based film-maker Shinya Tsukamoto makes movies about men turning into machines – the hero in his *Tetsuo – The Iron Man* is part warrior insect and part driller killer. He's just a guy mutating the best way he can.

Tsukamoto was born in Shimokita, Tokyo, in 1960. He began making Super-8 films at the age of fourteen and took up acting at the age of seventeen. While still only in his teens, he managed to persuade the Japanese TV show *Ginza Now* to run his short films over three consecutive evenings.

In 1979 he built mobile theatres and made a series of seven Super-8 films to screen in them around Tokyo. He studied painting in the Fine Arts Department of Nihon University and graduated in 1982. After joining an advertising agency, he made commercials for a couple of years, before leaving in 1985 to concentrate on his work in theatre and film.

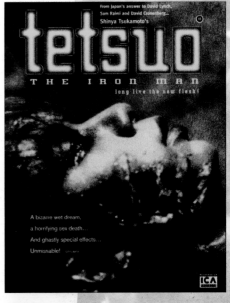

He founded, and still leads, the Kaijyu Theatre group. In the mid-1980s the Kaijyu Theatre staged his play *The Adventures of Denchu-kozo*, a live-action video game in which the central character develops a bizarre affinity with electric cables. The production became so popular with the theatre group's young audience that Tsukamoto adapted it for the screen in 1987 as a Super-8 film. It won the top prize at Tokyo's Pia Film Festival in 1988. The success of his next film, *Tetsuo – The Iron Man* (1989), in Japan and overseas, resulted in an offer to direct his first professional 35mm feature, *Hiruko the Goblin* (1991), before he returned to the bio-mechanical nightmares of *Tetsuo II Body Hammer* (1991).

'If the city becomes too big it will overwhelm human beings,' says Tsukamoto. 'The people will fight back, turning against the city so that it will not crush them. Weak and fragile humans will turn into strong monsters.

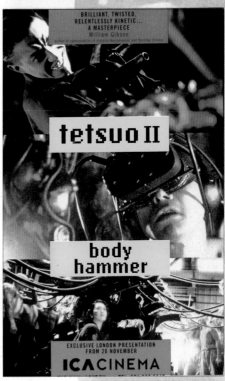

'The frightening aspect of city life for me is that reality and real sensations are fading. I believe that people have a need to live their lives in a physical way. With the earthquake, you become aware of how easily the city can be destroyed. The city is no match for nature. I think that it's a good idea to develop technology, but people have forgotten that the world was created by natural forces, and I'm frightened that we rely too much on technology.

'If people never communicate directly with each other physically, through touch – if it's just through electronic means like the telephone or television – it's like a beehive, a "brain world". It's a very sophisticated way of living, but there's never any real, physical act of communication. Nothing physical ever happens. And if we lose the way of feeling things physically, we lose our sense of reality, which I think is dangerous.

'I wanted to make a film about the juxtaposition of the natural world against the "brain world" of technology.

My film portrays the idea in a simple way: the people who live in the city bring about its destruction. *Tetsuo* is a simple story about a man who turns into metal. I've taken an extreme point of view by asking: "What would happen if humans turned into metal?"

'I was pretty much impressed by Cronenberg's *Videodrome*,' he continues. 'Then the cyberpunk movement came along. I saw many articles on the movement, which was about the assimilation of the flesh and the material, particularly the iron. I was haunted by this idea. That's the reason I wanted to make *Tetsuo*.'

There is a character called 'Tetsuo' in Katsuhiro Otomo's comic strip and movie *Akira*. It is a common Japanese name and many different Chinese characters (*kanji*) can be used to write it. The title of Tsuka-moto's film is written with two characters: 'Tetsu', meaning 'iron', and 'o', meaning 'male'. Hence the film's English title, *Tetsuo – The Iron Man*.

Although there is no character in the film actually named 'Tetsuo', the title clearly refers to the film's young metal fetishist (portrayed by the director himself).

TETSUO – THE IRON MAN
(Orig: Tetsuo)

Japan, 1989. Dir: Shinya Tsukamoto. With: Tomoroh Taguchi, Kei Fujiwara, Nobu Kanaoka, Shinya Tsukamoto, Naomasa Musaka, Renji Ishibashi. Kaijyu Theatre/ Japan Home Video/K2 Spirit/S.E.N. B&W.

Bizarre low-budget horror movie, shot on 16mm by producer/director Tsukamoto, who also stars as a punk metal fetishist (the opening scenes of him pushing a metal bar into an open wound on his thigh are truly disturbing). Injured in a hit-and-run accident, he possesses the driver of the car (rock musician Taguchi in his first film role) and gradually transforms the young 'salary man's' body into a bio-mechanical monstrosity. The violence is often brutal and explicit, but there is also enough unintentional humour to take some of the edge off the often dark, surreal imagery. S.J.

Sequel: *Tetsuo II Body Hammer* (1992).

'*Tetsuo* goes beyond almost anything else currently being made in the mainstream, harking back to the Kurosawa of *Do'des-ka Den* (1970), the Cronenberg of *Videodrome* (1982) or the Lynch of *Eraserhead* (1976). In its stylized, shrieking kabuki horror, *Tetsuo* establishes Shinya, a fringe theatre director and rock promoter, as a potential dingbat genius.'

The Aurum Film Encyclopedia: Science Fiction

SELECTED FILMS OF SHINYA TSUKAMOTO
(b 1960)

Genshi-san (Super-8 short, 1974), *Tsu-basa* (Super-8 short, 1980), *Futsu-size No Kaijin* (aka *The Phantom of Regular Size*; Super-8 short, 1986), *Denchu-kozo No Boken* (aka *The Adventures of Denchu-Kozo*; Super-8 short, 1987), *Tetsuo* (aka *Tetsuo – The Iron Man*; 16mm, 1989), *Hiruko Yokai Hunter* (aka *Hiruko the Goblin*; 1991), *Tetsuo II Body Hammer* (1992), *Tokyo Fist* (1995).

'The film is about a world where humans become metal and at the same time become inseparable from technology,' says Tsukamoto. 'I was asking: "What would happen in a world where metal brains thought for themselves?" As the city expands, we are entering a world of virtual reality where all communication takes place electronically. It's like a beehive with brains in all the holes. The purpose of *Tetsuo* is to destroy such a world.

'In *Tetsuo* I was concentrating on creating a sensual image,' explains the director, 'on showing the relationship between the metal – the material – and the flesh – the body. In *Tetsuo II*, I wanted to broaden the perspective. I came up with the idea that it's the relationship between the big city – urban society – and the human body, while the relationship between metal and flesh remains. Those two themes are synchronized, so the motive of the film becomes the end of the world.'

When Tokyo critics described the *Tetsuo* films, they invoked comparisons with the work of David Cronenberg, David Lynch and Sam Raimi, but Tsukamoto's remarkable vision of sadomasochistic mutation not only has its roots in Katsuhiro Otomo's legendary comic, but also in all the other fantasy and science-fiction entertainment that the children of Tsukamoto's generation grew up with: Toho's Godzilla movies, TV science fiction, *manga* comic strips and 'hardcore' rock music.

'Our land has been destroyed many times,' explains Japanese film critic Ken Okubo, 'because of the H-bomb, because of the earthquakes and big fires. We have a tendency to like to watch this destruction because we don't believe in our prosperity.

'Godzilla destroyed the big cities and we enjoy watching that. The first movie came out after the Second World War, after the experiment of the H-bomb in the South Pacific by the United States, and Godzilla reflects those memories.'

'I didn't experience the Bomb myself,' says Tsukamoto, 'but Godzilla has a big, black body which, for me, symbolizes death. It makes me feel that death is attacking me, and I wanted to use a black monster – the

TETSUO II BODY HAMMER

Japan, 1991. Dir: Shinya Tsukamoto. With: Tomoroh Taguchi, Nobu Kanaoka, Shinya Tsukamoto, Keinosuke Tomioka, Sujin Kim, Min Tanaka. Kaijyu Theatre/Toshiba EMI. Colour.

When his son is captured by two murderous skinheads, rage causes the body of a Tokyo businessman to mutate into a ferocious cyber-gun. Fascinated by this potentially lethal weapon, the leader of the skinheads forces the businessman to undergo a series of bizarre medical experiments. Following the full biomechanical mutation of the two protagonists, a pair of metal titans confront each other. *S.J.*

Above: Godzilla *King of the Monsters.*

GODZILLA (aka GOJIRA) IN THE MOVIES

Godzilla King of the Monsters (1954), *Gigantis the Fire Monster* (1955), *King Kong vs. Godzilla* (1963), *Godzilla vs. the Thing* (aka *Godzilla vs. Mothra*; 1964), *Ghidrah the Three-Headed Monster* (1964), *Monster Zero* (aka *Invasion of the Astro-Monsters/Invasion of Planet X*; 1965), *Ebirah Horror of the Deep* (aka *Godzilla vs. the Sea Monster*; 1966), *Son of Godzilla* (1967), *Destroy All Monsters* (1968), *Godzilla's Revenge* (1969), *Bambi Meets Godzilla* (short, 1969), *Godzilla vs. the Smog Monster* (1971), *Godzilla vs. Gigan* (aka *War of the Monsters/Godzilla on Monster Island*; 1972), *Godzilla vs. Megalon* (1973), *Godzilla vs. the Bionic Monster* (aka *Godzilla vs. the Cosmic Monster*; 1974), *Monsters from an Unknown Planet* (aka *The Terror of Godzilla/Terror of Mechagodzilla*; 1975), *Hollywood Boulevard* (1976), *Godzilla 1985* (1984), *Pee-Wee's Big Adventure* (1985), *Godzilla vs. Biollante* (1989), *Godzilla vs. King Ghidorah* (1991), *Waxwork II: Lost in Time* (1991), *Godzilla vs. Mothra* (1992), *Godzilla vs. Mechagodzilla* (1993), *Godzilla vs. Space Godzilla* (1994), *Godzilla vs. Destroyer* (1995), *Godzilla* (1998).

image of death – in my film.

'I've been having fun with the character of Tetsuo and I don't know if that's a good thing. It might be bad. There's no easy answer. If brain and body really did turn into metal we'd really be on an unstoppable course. These are horrific ideas but, even so, I'm enjoying them.'

K for Killing Joke

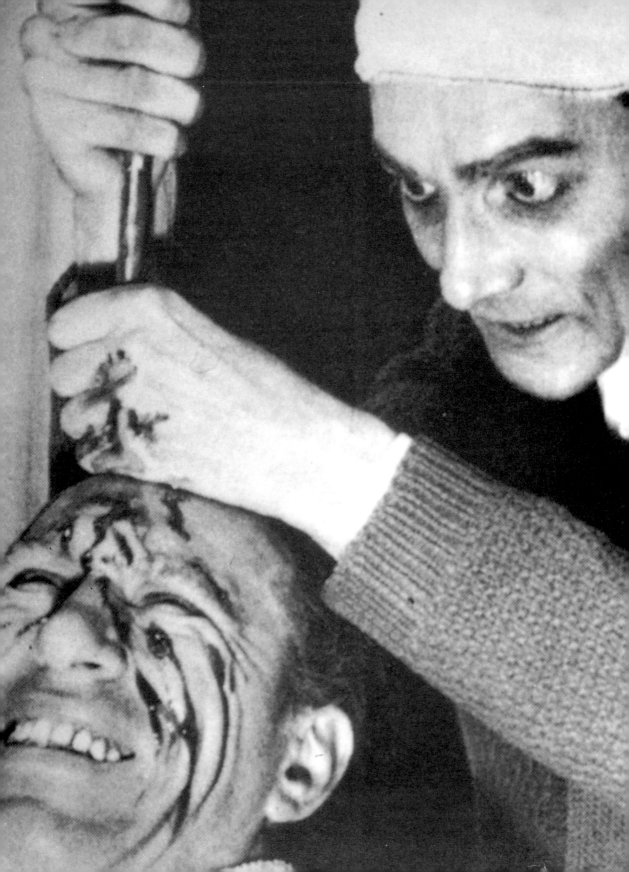

A T ITS BEST, THEATRICAL horror can be overwhelmingly intense – think of classic Greek Tragedy and Shakespeare. But for sheer *spectacle* you can't beat the French Théâtre du Grand Guignol. 'Grand Guignol' is a term that has entered our language to describe the most gruesome events. But was there anything quite so harrowing as the events enacted on a small stage in Paris almost one hundred years ago...?

'The Grand Guignol was opened on 13 April 1897, by Oscar Méténier,' says historian Agnes Pierron. 'He was a very strange character. He was secretary to a police commissioner. One of his duties was to accompany a condemned man to his death. He was not a literary man or a poet. He was a man of the flesh. Suffering flesh. Flesh that was going to die.'

For sixty-five years, various troupes of actors titillated Parisian audiences with one-act performances of murder, mayhem and revenge. Every night on stage they performed stabbings, mutilations, beheadings, gougings, tortures and dismemberments in gloriously graphic detail.

'The Grand Guignol is more sophisticated than it first appears,' says Pierron. 'Its speciality was horror, terror and blood. What is original is that there were no monsters, nothing as obvious as that. What it explored was not ancient fears, but those of today. Characters such as the madman, the condemned man – ordinary people you meet on the street. The seemingly normal person who goes off the rails.'

The Théâtre du Grand Guignol was situated at 20 bis rue Chaptal in Pigalle, a somewhat sleazy part of Montmartre. The building had once been a convent, which was destroyed during the French Revolution, and only the chapel remained. The wooden Gothic auditorium, consisting of a ground floor and balcony, could accommodate almost three hundred people when full.

'When you arrived in the rue Chaptal it was dark,' recalls audience member Peche who, as a young girl in the late 1950s and early 1960s, would accompany her family to the Grand Guignol. 'It felt as if Paris life had been left far behind. I was a bit scared and checked to see if anyone was following me.'

'Suddenly, you were in this cobblestoned alleyway,' explains actor and director Robert Hossein, who worked at the Grand Guignol during the 1950s. 'A mysterious

Grand Guignol (grahn genyol) *n.* dramatic entertainment in which short sensational or horrific pieces are played successively [name of theatre in Paris].

The Concise Oxford Dictionary

K

alleyway. If you didn't know the area and the street, you'd miss it. At the end of the street was this theatre, an old wooden chapel.'

'Inside, there was a certain atmosphere and smell,' continues Peche. 'Being an old chapel, maybe the smell was incense or maybe wax – I don't know. It felt like plunging into a tomb. But the point was, it created a spooky atmosphere.'

'I was a young actor in this theatre,' says Hossein. 'I was bewitched by the atmosphere. It was as if the religious fervour brought devil-worshippers to the Grand Guignol. The stage manager always shouted for more blood! The rain sometimes leaked through the roof. The audience thought it was raining blood!'

Among the many famous authors and playwrights whose work was adapted for the stage of the Grand Guignol were James Hadley Chase, Henri-Georges Clouzet, Charles Dickens, Théophile Gautier, Rudyard Kipling, Gaston Leroux, Guy de Maupassant, Edgar Allan Poe, Mary Robert Rinehart, Robert Louis Stevenson, Mark Twain and Emile Zola, to name only a few.

One of the more memorable plays performed there was titled *On the Telephone* or *Au Téléphone*, by Charles Foley and André de Lorde.

'Some of the plays were masterpieces,' enthuses Hossein. 'Extraordinary theatre. Like the one about the man on the telephone. He's talking to his wife. She tells him that burglars have broken in and are going to kill her. She's telling him over the phone, but there's nothing he can do. So the phone becomes an instrument for horror.'

'The Grand Guignol was based on the ideas of Naturalism,' explains Agnes Pierron, referring to the theatrical movement of the late 1880s, inspired by the French novelist Emile Zola. 'If meat was needed in a scene, *real* meat was used on stage. So real objects, everyday objects – without being transformed from normal everyday use – were transposed to the stage. And it was *this* that was so scandalous at the time.'

'I often had my eyes poked out,' says actor André Chanu. 'I was regularly strangled. That was how I spent my time at the Grand Guignol – much to my pleasure and everyone else's pain!'

After Méténier mysteriously disappeared in 1889, the theatre continued to thrive under various owners and managers, and the Grand Guignol progressed from pantomimes and morality plays to much more gruesome fare. By

1910 it was the best-known tourist attraction in Paris.

'I worked at the Grand Guignol from 1933,' remembers actress Mado Maurin, 'and it was a fairy tale come true. It was the happiest time of my life because that is where I started. I was only seventeen. The Grand Guignol at that time was a real classic. People came from all over. They'd go to the Opéra, Comédie Française, but *also* to the Grand Guignol. It was a must.

'There was this scene, it was horrible. A man was gasping for air, not being able to speak. He was held down and had his eyes gouged out. Blood pouring. Horrible!'

'Of course, blood was the most important of all special effects,' agrees Agnes Pierron. 'Grand Guignol was about horror, but also about the eroticism which underpinned horror. Don't forget that this theatre was in a deconsecrated church. Therefore, what pleasure to indulge in the forbidden and live out the impossible.'

'At the back of the theatre were discreet boxes fronted by wire mesh,' recalls Maurin, 'where certain members of the audience would go as an alternative to a hotel room!

'With almost half a century of unbroken history behind it, the world-famous institution has given the French language the phrase: *C'est du Grand Guignol*, to denote any theatrical piece, performed anywhere, that is emotionally terrifying.'

Boris Karloff

K

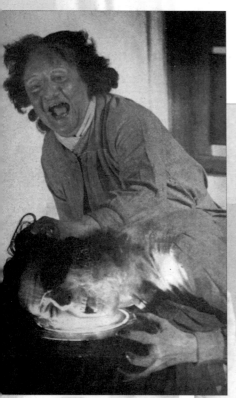

It is no surprise to me that some got a certain physical pleasure out of watching horror and would perhaps like to share it.'

'The cleaning ladies would find traces of sexual pleasure from the audience,' Agnes Pierron continues. 'Ejaculating, yes. Vomiting, no. You can't do it all at once!'

'You could see these boxes from the stage,' laughs actor Bernard Charlan, 'and once I shouted: "You enjoy yourselves in there!"'

One of the undisputed stars of the Théâtre du Grand Guignol was an actress named Maxa, who the newspapers of the day dubbed as 'The High Priestess of the Temple of Horror'. During her career, she is said to have been murdered more than ten thousand times in over sixty different ways, raped more than three thousand times,

GRAND GUIGNOL IN THE MOVIES

On the Telephone (Dir: D.W. Griffith, 1909), *Fumeur d'Opium* (Dir: Emile Chautard, 1911), *Une Nuit d'Épouvante* (Dir: Emile Chautard, 1911), *Le Justice du Mort* (Dir: Victorin Jasset, 1911), *Le Cabinet d'Affaires* (Dir: Victorin Jasset, 1911), *Le Cercueil de Verre* (Dir: Emile Chautard, 1912), *Le Système du Docteur Goudron et du Professeur Plume* (Dir: Maurice Tourneur, 1912), *Figures de Cire* (Dir: Maurice Tourneur, 1912), *Le Sculpteur Aveugle* (Dir: Emile Chautard, 1913), *La Malédiction* (Dir: Emile Chautard, 1913), *Bagnes d'Enfants* (Dir: Emile Chautard, 1914), *Le Fauseur de Fous* (Dir: Emile Chautard, 1914), *Le Château de la Mort Lente* (Dir: Donatien), *Unheimliche Geschichten* (aka *Tales of the Uncanny*; Dir: Richard Oswald, 1919), *Grand Guignol* (series; Dir: Fred Paul and Jack Raymond, 1920), *Gosses de Misère* (Dir: Georges Gauthier, 1933), *Fünf Unheimliche Geschichten* (aka *Tales of the Uncanny*; Dir: Richard Oswald, 1932), *Mad Love* (aka *The Hands of Orlac*; Dir: Karl Freund, 1935), *L'Armoire Volante* (Dir: Carlo Rim, 1948), *Les Yeux sans Visage* (aka *Eyes without a Face/The Horror Chamber of Dr Faustus*; Dir: Georges Franju, 1959), *The Blood Beast Terror* (aka *The Vampire-Beast Craves Blood*; Dir: Vernon Sewell, 1967), *Le Viol di Vampire* (aka *La Reine des Vampires/The Vampire's Rape*; Dir: Jean Rollin, 1967), *The Thirteen Chairs* (aka *12 + 1*, 1970), *La Mansión de la Locura* (aka *Dr Tarr's Torture Dungeon*; Dir: Juan Lopez Moctezuma, 1972), *Grand Guignol* (Dir: Jean Marboeuf, 1986), *Interview with the Vampire: The Vampire Chronicles* (Dir: Neil Jordan, 1994).

and cried 'Help!' nearly a thousand times. Perhaps her worst fate was when she was cut up into ninety-three pieces and then glued back together again!

The Théâtre du Grand Guignol reached its peak of popularity during the 1920s. But by the end of the following decade its reputation started to wane as the real-life horrors of Adolf Hitler began to engulf the world. Although Field Marshal Hermann Goering of the Luftwaffe was a regular patron during the early 1940s, the occupying Nazi forces condemned the Grand Guignol as 'Entartete Kunst' (degenerate art).

According to historian Agnes Pierron: 'The fact that the Grand Guignol was frequented by the Nazis contributed to its downfall. No doubt about it. It was part of the tourist trail at the end of the 1930s. The Nazis couldn't avoid coming across it. The Grand Guignol never recovered after the Second World War. It was supposed to show the worst kind of horror, but the war itself *was* that kind of horror.'

'There were a lot of Germans in the audience,' agrees actor André Chanu. 'They had nothing like it back home, neither did the Americans who followed. They had nothing which resembled the Grand Guignol, which is why they were so keen on it. On several occasions, the German officers came backstage to offer their compliments after the show without realizing I was in the Resistance.'

However, the Grand Guignol could not hope to compete with the horrors of the modern world, and the theatre limped on as a tourist attraction, becoming increasingly a parody of its own finest achievements. It finally closed its doors for the last time in 1962. The building still stands, now operating as a theatre school.

'This specialized form of theatre no longer exists,' laments Agnes Pierron.

During its existence, the Grand Guignol inspired imitators in Rome (1908–1928), London (1920–1922, starring Sybil and Russell Thorndike) and New York (1923), and it has arguably influenced everything from the Expressionist movement of the silent German cinema to the gore films of Herschell Gordon Lewis and others. Over the years there have been several efforts to revive the Grand Guignol in America, most notably with the productions of the Aboutface Theatre Company in New York City. Horror writers involved with more recent attempts included Robert Bloch and David J. Schow.

Even today, its legacy is still with us.

L For Lynch Mob

L

IN AMERICA, THE LATEST thing in popular music has been called 'Horrorcore'. Horrorcore is a strain of rap music that puts the shroud and the sepulchre into urban New York, and proves that horror is as old as time itself and as new as a freshly spun hook.

Such performers as Ozzy Ozborne and Alice Cooper have used horror movie imagery extensively in their music, but now a new breed of rap acts are reworking those concepts. They include groups with such names as Gravediggaz, Flatliners and Half Pit, Half Dead.

The brainchild of legendary New York rap producer Prince Paul, the Gravediggaz, whose 1995 album 6 *Feet Deep* includes such tracks as '1-800 Suicide', 'Diary of a Madman' and 'Graveyard Chamber', consist of the Grym Reaper, the Undertaker, the Gatekeeper and the RZArector.

'Because we'd all been buried as far as the music industry is concerned, we chose the name Gravediggaz,' explains the Undertaker (aka Prince Paul). 'We had to resurrect ourselves. There was a darkness, and within that context (the music) fed off that negative vibe, and so anger is the underlying element.'

'The industry was sceptical about all of us,' says the Grym Reaper (aka Poetic). 'They felt we'd had our chance and we were over. But we have the creative stamina to overcome any obstacles that the industry put before us. We discovered our music trapped the mind in the fourth dimension by going into areas that haven't been explored in hip hop before, both in subject matter and production. You got to dig deeper than the songs to get the message.'

TALES FROM THE CRYPT PRESENTS DEMON KNIGHT

USA, 1995. Dir: Ernest Dickerson. With: Billy Zane, William Sadler, Jada Pinkett, Brenda Bakke, CCH Pounder, Dick Miller. Universal. Colour.

Loosely inspired by the HBO TV series, which in turn is based on the EC horror comics of the 1950s. Brayker (Sadler), the enigmatic guardian of an ancient key that keeps the forces of darkness from overwhelming mankind, is forced to protect the residents of a remote boarding house from an army of flesh-eating demons unleashed by the Collector (Zane), who wants to regain the supernatural talisman that contains the blood of Jesus Christ. Special make-up effects designed by Todd Masters. Introduced by the irritating Crypt Keeper (voiced by John Kassir). S.J.

'In our video we don't intend to promote any violence or any form of satanism,' says the RZArector (aka RZA, aka Prince Rakeem). 'No sir. Nor are we trying to disrespect anybody's religious belief. We're just trying to manifest the horrors of modern day life so that we can all recognize them, man. Because positive education has to be constant elevation. That means peace.'

'I guess the horror I'm interested in is the horror that is about something else than just scaring people,' says Ernest Dickerson, who was the cameraman on Spike Lee's early pictures and directed *Tales from the Crypt*

'No need to cry, 'cause we all die.'
From '1-800 Suicide'
by Gravediggaz

Presents Demon Knight (1994), which included a Gravediggaz track on the soundtrack. 'To me, the best horror has always been a metaphor for the human condition. The life we live is like a horror movie. Some of the stuff that we go through is like a horror movie. We are just feeding off of everyday situations and showing you the horror of everyday life.'

According to the Gatekeeper (aka Fruitkwan), the Gravediggaz' music 'comes from the thoughts of a man who has been suppressed or a people who have been suppressed'.

'The story of Africans in America is a horror story,' continues Dickerson. 'One of the things that rap does is bring this up. Rap talks about it, rap hits it out there, rap talks about a lot of things that a lot of people would rather just ignore, just deny that they even exist.'

'When I sit out here and look at these people in the ghetto,' says the Grym Reaper, 'all these mentally dead people, I'm not happy. Know what I'm saying? The theme is like, the nastiness, the real dark side of life.'

'So many people are slaves of mental death,' explains RZArector, 'they don't know what's going on. Our idea is

'A rap-horror concept was starting to gel. A roughneck, jokey sound that spoke with the voice of street rap, but which, underneath the Hammer Films bullshit, had something positive to say.'

New Musical Express,
17 September 1994

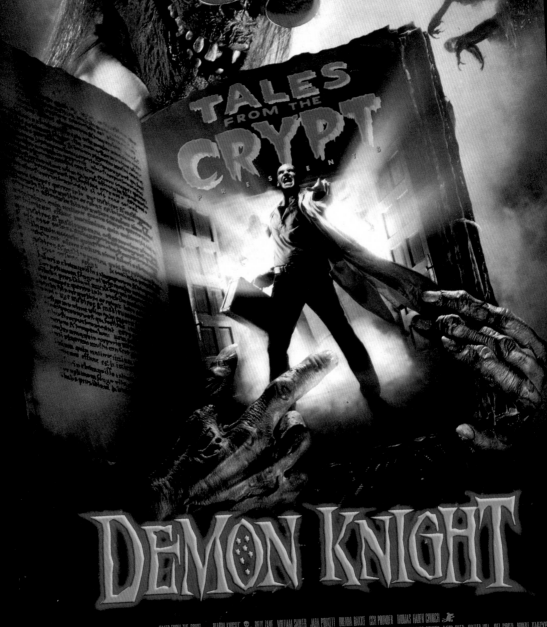

to dig up their mental grave, and shed on them a little light about what time it is. Poetic is the Grym Reaper, he brings them in. Then Prince Paul, the Undertaker, prepares them. Fruitkwan's the Gatekeeper. He sees who's gonna go through the gate, and decides whether to let them burn, or whether to give them to me, the RZArector... I bring them back to life, I'm the antidote to make them see what's going on.'

'There seems to be a problem with Western society in thinking that everything we see here is the world,' says Dickerson. 'That you should only believe in what you see. I don't believe that, and I think that's part of our culture that has really manifested itself, you know, having a lot of fall-out from our homeland, Africa. I think we take the supernatural for granted in our daily life.'

Black horror is not a new phenomenon. In the 1930s and 1940s there were such all-black horror movies as *Drums o' Voodoo* (1934) and *Son of Ingagi* (1939), while during the early 1970s, a new type of exploitation film briefly appeared for a few years in inner-city theatres. Such horror titles as *Blacula* (1972), *Blackenstein* (1972) and *Dr Black and Mr Hyde* (1975) were at the forefront of this fleeting movement, which was quickly dubbed 'blaxploitation'.

More recently, with the help of executive producer Spike Lee, director Rusty Cundieff and producer Darin Scott made *Tales from the Hood* (1995), a $6 million urban horror anthology.

'I really liked the idea of doing a black anthology film,' says Scott, 'because there's never been one. And usually when there's a black horror film, which is rare, it's a spoof. So what we're trying to do here is truly scare people and tell good stories.

'The social issues really had to be laid into the story and be intrinsic. We deal with everything from police brutality and child abuse to racist politicians and black-on-black violence. And when you do stories about those things, whatever the message is or whatever the social consciousness is has to come out in the story. It's subtle

" TALES FROM THE HOOD

One Of The Year's Best Entertainments

USA, 1995. Dir: Rusty Cundieff. With: Clarence Williams III, Corbin Bernsen, Wings Hauser, Rosalind Cash, David Alan Grier, Anthony Griffith. 40 Acres/Mule Filmworks/Savoy Pictures. Colour.

Urban horror anthology in which three black gang members (Joe Torry, De'Aundre Bonds and Samuel Monroe Jr) are taken on a tour of a creepy funeral parlour by mysterious mortician Mr Simms (Williams III). He explains how each person ended up in their respective casket: a trio of racist cops kill a community activist (Tom Wright), who returns from the grave for revenge; a battered boy (Brandon Hammond) confronts the monster living in his house; a corrupt supremacist politician (Bernsen) encounters the restless spirits of plantation slaves, and a crazy murderer (Lamont Bentley) is put in the care of a ruthless doctor (Cash). In the end – surprise, surprise! – Mr Simms turns out to be the Prince of Darkness himself. With director Cundieff in a cameo role as a teacher. Special effects created by Screaming Mad George, KNB EFX and the Chiodo Brothers. Executive produced by Spike Lee. S.J.

'So you want to die, commit suicide dial 1-800 cyanide line. As far as life, yo ain't worth it. Put a rope around your neck and jerk it.'

From '1-800 Suicide' by Gravediggaz

119

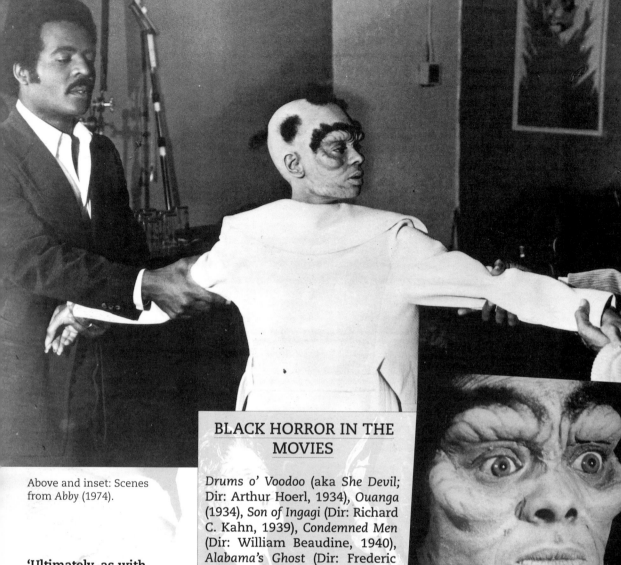

Above and inset: Scenes from *Abby* (1974).

'Ultimately, as with all music, you can read anything you like into the Gravediggaz lyrics. Maybe their scary tales will find them in court defending themselves from ludicrous claims of backmasking, a 'Diary of a Madman' scenario made real.'

New Musical Express,
17 September 1994

BLACK HORROR IN THE MOVIES

Drums o' Voodoo (aka *She Devil;* Dir: Arthur Hoerl, 1934), *Ouanga* (1934), *Son of Ingagi* (Dir: Richard C. Kahn, 1939), *Condemned Men* (Dir: William Beaudine, 1940), *Alabama's Ghost* (Dir: Frederic Hobbs, 1972), *Blackenstein* (aka *Black Frankenstein;* Dir: William A. Levy, 1972), *Blacula* (Dir: William Crain, 1972), *Scream Blacula Scream* (Dir: Bob Kelljan, 1973), *Ganja & Hess* (aka *Blood Couple/Double Possession/Black Evil/Black Out: The Moment of Terror/Black Vampire;* Dir: Bill Gunn, 1973), *Abby* (Dir: William Girdler, 1974), *House on Skull Mountain* (Dir: Ron Honthaner, 1974), *Sugar Hill* (aka *Voodoo Girl;* Dir: Paul Maslansky, 1974), *Lord Shango* (Dir: Raymond Marsh, 1975), *Dr. Black and Mr. Hyde* (aka *The Watts Monster;* Dir: William Crain, 1975), *J.D.'s Revenge* (Dir: Arthur Marks, 1976), *Crossroads* (Dir: Walter Hill, 1986), *Def By Temptation* (Dir: James Bond III, 1990), *Tales from the Crypt Presents Demon Knight* (Dir: Ernest Dickerson, 1994), *Tales from the Hood* (Dir: Rusty Cundieff, 1995), *Vampire in Brooklyn* (Dir: Wes Craven, 1995).

enough that it's going to speak to certain people that it's directed at, but for everyone else it's just another horror story. Maybe when they're discussing it afterwards, the other stuff will come out.'

According to writer and critic Nelson George: 'Discrimination, racism, the kind of barriers both physical and almost kind of spiritual that are in America, come through and end up appearing in the artist's work.

'So much of it is ripe with the imagery of possession, demonology. I mean, the greatest Delta blues musician ever, Robert Johnson, reputedly sold his soul to the Devil at a crossroads. Everyone talks about the blues as a great American resource, but there's some pretty evil stuff in it, which may be why it's so American.'

'Es-cape, I have al-ready mu-talated your brain like Dr Arcane...even if you escape you'll be going insane.'
From 'Diary of a Madman' by Gravediggaz

'What we're doing,' says Gravediggaz's RZArector, 'is flashing them different things that happen every day, things that we see, or have seen, or you have seen.

'Everyone goes around talkin' 'bout what they do to people,' explains the Undertaker, 'but a lot of our tracks deal with what people do to themselves.'

'We talk about the social conscience as well as the political aspects of the dark side,' agrees the Grym

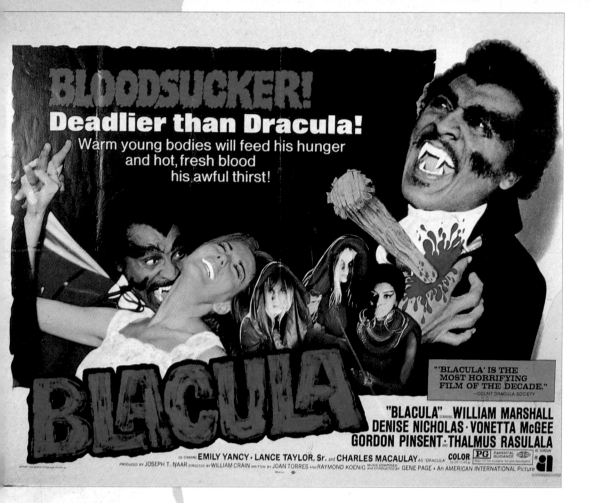

BLOODSUCKER!

Deadlier than Dracula!

Warm young bodies will feed his hunger
and hot, fresh blood
his awful thirst!

"'BLACULA' IS THE
MOST HORRIFYING
FILM OF THE DECADE."
—COUNT DRACULA SOCIETY

BLACULA

"BLACULA" STARRING WILLIAM MARSHALL
DENISE NICHOLAS · VONETTA McGEE
GORDON PINSENT AND THALMUS RASULALA

CO-STARRING EMILY YANCY · LANCE TAYLOR, Sr. AND CHARLES MACAULAY AS 'DRACULA' COLOR PG PARENTAL GUIDANCE
PRODUCED BY JOSEPH T. NAAR DIRECTED BY WILLIAM CRAIN WRITTEN BY JOAN TORRES AND RAYMOND KOENIG MUSIC COMPOSED AND CONDUCTED BY GENE PAGE · An AMERICAN INTERNATIONAL Picture

'Bare witness, as I exercise my exorcism. The evil that lurks within, the sin, the terrorism. Possessed by evil spirits, voices from the dead, I come forth with "Gravediggaz" and a head fulla dread. I've been examined ever since I was semen. They took a sonogram and seen the image of a demon.'

From 'Diary of a Madman'
by Gravediggaz

Reaper. 'People say we're morbid, but if you wanna be morbid, turn on the damn news!'

'We have our rhythms,' says Ernest Dickerson. 'These are rhythms that only come from the African-American community, only from our music. These are things that nobody else does. It's our own specific way of talking about things, our own specific way of addressing things.

'I think that, especially in black music, these issues are dealt with – the supernatural or aspects of horror.'

Nelson George believes that, 'If you can make a link between hip hop or some of the other stuff and horror at all, it's because of the imaginative element of it.

'So just like the great horror directors, Brian De Palma and Alfred Hitchcock and John Carpenter, the Gravediggaz use imagery of violence to entertain. And one of the things we have to acknowledge in America is that violence is entertaining. People are entertained by action, excitement, danger, threat. And these are the things that good rap music provides, these are the things that good horror provides.'

M For Mistress of the Night

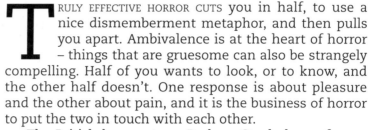

M

'The face of Steele explains why her mere presence suffices to trigger the perverse but fundamental and pleasurable fantasies that form the raw material of the horror genre itself and why her image, more than any other, is the emblem and fetish of the genre.'

The Aurum Film Encyclopedia: Horror, edited by Phil Hardy

TRULY EFFECTIVE HORROR CUTS you in half, to use a nice dismemberment metaphor, and then pulls you apart. Ambivalence is at the heart of horror – things that are gruesome can also be strangely compelling. Half of you wants to look, or to know, and the other half doesn't. One response is about pleasure and the other about pain, and it is the business of horror to put the two in touch with each other.

The British-born actress Barbara Steele has a face, a look, unlike anyone else in movies. Most of her Italian-made horror movies, in fact all of her movies, are modern-day cults. She does what few actresses are capable of doing – she lets you see both destruction and delight in the same pair of eyes.

'Once you see Barbara Steele you know you will never forget her,' says director Tim Burton. 'She is probably one of the only real horror goddesses. There is a timelessness that she has.'

Roger Corman, who directed the actress in *The Pit and the Pendulum* (1961) agrees: 'There was a depth to her. On the surface she was a beautiful brunette woman. Beneath that – and you could almost get poetic here – looking into her eyes, you could see layer upon layer. I could probably best, inadequately, describe it as a kind of exotic mystery.'

According to J. Arthur Rank publicity sources, Barbara Steele was born at Birkenhead, near Liverpool, on 29 December 1937. However, most sources list her birth date as 1938, and the actress herself has said, 'I was born in Ireland on the same day as Fellini but not the same year. I am, therefore, a Capricorn.'

Her professional stage debut came in a comedy opposite Robert Morley in the mid-1950s, and she appeared in a number of repertory parts before she was spotted in John Van Druten's *Bell, Book and Candle* and put under long-term contract by the Rank organization.

Her first Rank film was the light comedy *Bachelor of Hearts* (1958), quickly followed by roles in the colour remake of *The 39 Steps* (1959), *Upstairs and Downstairs* (1959), *Sapphire* (aka *Operation Scotland Yard*, 1959) and *Your Money or Your Wife* (1960).

When Rank sold her contract to Twentieth Century Fox, the actress moved to Hollywood. It was an unhappy period for Steele. The studio said she was too big and that she should change her hair colour, and she spent most of her time sitting on the beach waiting for the phone to ring. 'That's how I came to the States,' she recalls. 'But I don't know why the studio got it into its

head to make me a blonde, but this is something that they did. I felt like a total lie as a blonde, because it didn't suit my nature, which is pretty dark. And I said to myself, I'm out of here.'

The bleached-blonde actress spent three days working on Don Siegel's Elvis Presley movie *Flaming Star* (1960) before she fled to Europe and was replaced in the picture by Barbara Eden. 'I found myself in Rome and I was wildly grateful to be in Italy,' she says. 'It felt right. I felt centred. I felt embraced and adored. I find it very interesting that, in this great period of phenomenal optimism in Italy, these horror movies came out, because the dark side is always going to express itself somewhere. And the kick-off was *Black Sunday*.'

Directed by the great Italian stylist Mario Bava, *Black Sunday* (1960) starred Steele in the dual roles of Asa, a resurrected vampire witch, and her innocent descendant Princess Katia.

'She played this sexy witch,' remembers Joe Dante,

Top and opposite: Barbara Steele, *circa* 1960s.

125

Opposite: *The Ghost*.

BLACK SUNDAY
(Orig: LA MASCHERA DEL DEMONIO. UK: REVENGE OF THE VAMPIRE/THE MASK OF SATAN)

Italy, 1960. Dir: Mario Bava. With: Barbara Steel (Steele), John Richardson, Andrea Checchi, Ivo Garrani, Arturo Dominici, Enrico Olivieri. Galatea/ Jolly/American International. B&W.

Based on Nikolai Gogol's story 'The Vij'. British actress Barbara Steele became a cult star in the dual roles of heroine Princess Katia and Asa, a seventeenth century witch accidentally released from her tomb by a drop of blood. With the aid of her vampire helper (Dominici), she plans to replace Katia, who is her exact double. Atmospherically photographed by co-writer/director Bava, this begins with a memorable scene in which a spiked mask is hammered on to Asa's face. The American version replaced Roberto Nicolosi's moody score with an inferior one by Les Baxter. It was banned in Britain until 1968, when it was finally released in a cut version. S.J.

Remake: *La Maschera Del Demonio* (1990).

'Ah! Barbara Steele... extraordinary! In *The Ghost*, her eyes are metaphysical, unreal, impossible, like the eyes of a Chirico painting. There are times, in certain conditions of light and colour, when her face assumes a cast that doesn't appear to be quite human, which would be impossible for any other actress.'

Riccardo Freda

who directed the actress in *Piranha* (1978). 'She did a lot of smouldering, basically, which was just the thing for kids who were beginning to get interested in sex but were still more interested in monsters; and Barbara was a sexy monster, so it was sort of okay.'

'There was always a high level of sexuality in every horror film,' says Steele, 'because you are dealing with death and very primal things and you've always got to have this juxtaposition of a subtext, of a very powerful, sexual subtext, whatever is going on. I mean, you try and invest it with a kind of force.'

After appearing opposite Vincent Price in the American production *The Pit and the Pendulum* (1961), the actress went on to make a string of horror films in Italy.

'She already had a bit of a cult following when she came to us,' recalls Roger Corman. 'I think she went back to Italy afterwards. Those were days of tremendous activity in Rome and she was a major star for that kind of filming.'

Directors such as Riccardo Freda and Antonio Margheriti were quick to capitalize upon her distinctive features and they cast her in a number of similar parts.

'I usually played these roles where I represented the dark side,' explains Steele. 'I was always a predatory bitch goddess in all of these movies, with all kinds of unspeakable elements of necrophilia and rising from the dead and perpetuating curses.

'The women that I played were usually very powerful women and they suffered for it. You saw these powerful women – usually adulteresses, full of lust and greed, playing out all this repressed stuff – and then in the end I always seemed to get it. And there was always this sort of morality play, this sort of final pay-off, and that was very consoling to everybody. Because the dark goddess can't just go on wreaking hubris and havoc ad infinitum. She gets her come-uppance, too.'

'What I think these films do is they basically fill you with a psychic dread and they address the soul,' says Tim

BARBARA STEELE
PETER BALDW
LE SPECTRE !
TECHNICOLO
HET SPOOK !

Burton. 'When I was younger my parents boarded up my room. I had two big windows and they boarded them up like a small kind of slit window. After seeing movies like *Pit and the Pendulum*, when you see her eyes glaring out of the iron maiden, I could certainly relate that to looking out of my window and feeling kind of trapped.

'I always found those Italian horror films actually made me feel psychologically comfortable. There's something about her and those films that taps into the unconscious and makes you actually feel better about the abstractions of life.'

According to Joe Dante: 'A number of the pictures that Barbara made in the 1960s, like *The Ghost*, *Castle of Blood* and *The Long Hair of Death*, although they played double bills at drive-ins and movie houses, they were a little more sexually daring than certainly the domestic pictures. Even though most of them had been re-edited before they got to America, it was very difficult to take out all of the undertones of necrophilia and lesbianism.'

'*Castle of Blood* was quite a scandal when it opened in Rome because of its lesbian love scene,' recalls director Antonio Margheriti, 'but she did it without making any fuss.'

'I liked doing all of those scenes that had these forbidden aspects to them,' she admits. 'Necrophilia, incest, all these violent kinds of repressed emotions. I liked that a lot. I think that's a really great arena to work in.'

Despite her appearance in such films as Federico Fellini's critically acclaimed *8½* (aka *Otto e Mezzo*, 1962) and Volker Schlöndorff's *Young Törless* (1966), the quality of some of the horror movies Steele appeared in gradually began to deteriorate. Even her co-starring role opposite those maestros of menace Boris Karloff, Christopher Lee and Michael Gough couldn't save the British-made *Curse of the Crimson Altar* (1968).

'It's the producers,' Steele told a magazine at the

THE HORRIBLE DR HICHCOCK
(Orig: L'ORRIBLE SEGRETO DEL DOTTORE HICHCOCK. UK: THE TERROR OF DR HICHCOCK/RAPTUS: THE SECRET OF DR HICHCOCK)

Italy, 1962. Dir: Robert Hampton (Riccardo Freda). With: Barbara Steele, Robert Flemyng, Montgomery Glenn (Silvano Tranquili), Teresa Fitzgerald (Maria Teresa Vianello), Harriet White, Spencer Williams. Panda Film. Colour.

A minor classic, shot in only eight days. English actor Flemying plays the eponymous turn-of-the-century scientist who is only sexually aroused by necrophilia. After he accidentally kills his first wife (Fitzgerald) with an overdose of drugs during sex, his new wife Cynthia (Steele) is menaced by her ghostly predecessor, who has returned from the grave seeking blood. Director Freda uses the colour photography to create some wonderful images, and Steele has never looked better as the much-put-upon heroine. Some prints include scenes of Flemying fondling the bodies of dead women, which were cut from the film's original release in both Britain and America. *S.J.*

Sequel: *The Ghost* (1963).

SELECTED FILMS OF BARBARA STEELE
(b 1938)

Black Sunday (aka *La Maschera del Demonio/ Revenge of the Vampire/The Mask of Satan*; Dir: Mario Bava, 1960), *The Pit and the Pendulum* (Dir: Roger Corman, 1961), *The Horrible Dr. Hichcock* (aka *L'Orribile Segreto del Dottore Hichcock/The Terror of Dr Hichcock/Raptus: The Secret of Dr Hichcock*; Dir: Riccardo Freda, 1962), *The Ghost* (aka *Lo Spettro*; Dir: Riccardo Freda, 1963), *Castle of Blood* (aka *La Danza Macabre/ Castle of Terror*; Dir: Antonio Margheriti, 1964), *The Long Hair of Death* (aka *I Lunghi Capeki della Morte*; Dir: Antonio Margheriti, 1964), *The Faceless Monster* (aka *Amanti d'Olretomba/Nightmare Castle*; Dir: Mario Caiano, 1965), *Terror Creatures from the Grave* (aka *Cinque Tombe per un Medium/Cemetery of the Living Dead*; Dir: Massimo Pupillo, 1965), *Revenge of the Blood Beast* (aka *La Sorella di Satana/Il Lago si Satana/The She Beast*; Dir: Michael Reeves, 1965), *An Angel for Satan* (aka *Un Angelo per Satana*; Dir: Camillo Mastrocinque, 1966), *Curse of the Crimson Altar* (aka *The Crimson Cult*; Dir: Vernon Sewell, 1968), *Shivers* (aka *The Parasite Murders/They Came from Within*; Dir: David Cronenberg, 1974), *Piranha* (Dir: Joe Dante, 1978), *The Silent Scream* (Dir: Denny Harris, 1980), *Dark Shadows* (Dir: Dan Curtis, TV, 1990) *The Island of Dr. Moreau* (role deleted, 1996).

> 'Barbara is very good in horror films; she has a very magical presence and a very charismatic face.'
>
> Antonio Margheriti

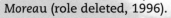

Top: *An Angel for Satan*.
Above: *Black Sunday*
Left: *Curse of the Crimson Altar*.

'She has a great, otherworldly quality – her bone structure, her face, the way of movement. I was struck by it and used it as much as I possibly could.'

Roger Corman

'The horrors are the only films one hears about, which is a drag. I always used to think they'd end up only in Sicily. It's not so. They end up at the Marble Arch Odeon in London, while the things you did for love and nothing end up in late-night showings at the Tokyo Film Festival.'

Barbara Steele

time. 'They have a completely false image of me, I think. Once and for all, they've cast me as a sorceress. People are intellectually very lazy. They prefer not to change the image they have of me. What is one to do?'

In 1974, after a four-year absence from the screen, she made her comeback as the sadistic warden in *Caged Heat!*, a slice of women-in-prison exploitation that marked the directorial debut of screenwriter Jonathan Demme. She went on to appear in David Cronenberg's feature debut, *Shivers* (1974), Joe Dante's *Piranha* (1978) and Louis Malle's *Pretty Baby* (1978).

According to Dante, 'In the 1970s, I think Barbara found herself being cast by people like David Cronenberg, Jonathan Demme and me because we had all seen her when we were growing up, and she had made an indelible impression on us that a lot of her contemporaries didn't.'

'Everybody wanted to chat to me about my sixties' horror films,' says Steele, 'and I just wouldn't talk about it. I was in total denial about them. I pushed them all aside because I felt that they had tripped me up in terms of working and I didn't want to deal with them. I didn't want anyone to love me for the horror movies.'

These days Barbara Steele is more comfortable about that period of her career. She teamed up with Dan Curtis and served as a producer on the popular ABC-TV mini-series *The Winds of War* (1983) and *War and Remembrance* (1988), and she returned to the horror genre in the early 1990s as Dr Julia Hoffman in Curtis's briefly revived vampire TV series *Dark Shadows*. However, she is still surprised by the fan following her horror films command.

'I've met a lot of my fans and a lot of them are completely charming. But I don't know what it is I represent to them. It's a mystery to me.

'I can only imagine that they sense something in me, and maybe what it is that they sense is some kind of psychic pain. Some kind of childhood grief. Some kind of isolation and some unresolved pain.'

'It's funny that people see it as kind of scary and dark and psychotic,' says Tim Burton, 'when in fact everybody has that duality. The healthiest people are the ones who explore it. She's had the opportunity to do that on film, which is a really healthy way of doing it. She's got an incredible strength and yet a mystery which is something you don't learn in acting school. It's just something you have or you don't have. And she has it.'

N for Nightmare

N

WE ALL HAVE NIGHTMARES. Some of us, like Wes Craven, make films about them... 'The cinema lends itself to dreaming,' says Craven. 'It is, in a sense, a dream itself. People go into a dark room very much like a bedroom. They see phantasmic images that aren't really there on a screen. It's part and parcel of dreams.'

Wes Craven was born in Cleveland, Ohio, to a working-class family. He showed an early interest in drawing, 8mm films and music, and began writing for his schools' newspapers, including a regular comedy column. He continued his writing at Wheaton College, Illinois, and earned a BA in English. Offered a full scholarship, he continued his education at the Johns Hopkins Graduate Writing Seminars, studying under the Baltimore poet/scholar Eliot Coleman, where he earned a Masters in Writing and Philosophy.

The same year Craven married, started a family and began teaching Humanities, first at Westminster College in New Wilmington, Pennsylvania, then at Clarkson College in Potsdam, New York.

'When I was about five years old we moved down to Brooklyn Heights,' recalls his son, producer Jonathan Craven, with a wicked grin. 'I was kept in a closet for the majority of my childhood. That's the type of man my father is: he fed us scraps that were weeks old and threw them into the closet. We never had any light and were only allowed to look at out-takes from his films...'

While at Clarkson, Wes Craven bought a 16mm camera and began making amateur films. Within a year he quit his teaching post and headed for New York, determined to break into the movies.

'He started out as a runner for a trailer-editing company,' says Jonathan Craven. 'He began by cutting trailers, and then he raised the $70,000 to make a feature called *Last House on the Left* (1972). It disgusted and repulsed many people who saw it because it was so close to reality and so graphic in its storytelling. It came out a couple of years before *The Texas Chainsaw Massacre* (1974), and those were the two films that established a new sub-genre in horror films. You actually had the human side of horror, as opposed to a monster in a bogeyman outfit. You finally saw what human beings are capable of.'

Jonathan Craven was seven when his father started making films, as he remembers: 'At first I thought it was really cool that my dad made movies, but most of the people that I grew up with had no idea. He was not a big director. When I was a kid, my friends were not into horror films like *Last House on the Left* and, later, *The Hills*

N

Have Eyes (1976). Those were for a real cult horror following who were a little bit older.

'It was an interesting concept to me that my father had become a film-maker, I liked the idea. It wasn't until I was in college, my sophomore year, that *A Nightmare on Elm Street* came out and made him a commercial name.'

Made on a budget of just $1.5 million by a small Hollywood company called New Line Cinema, *A Nightmare on Elm Street* opened in 1984 with very little advance hype and was originally perceived by the critics and public alike as just another low-budget stalk 'n' slash thriller.

'Whatever You Do, Don't Fall Asleep...' warned the ads and, within a few days, word-of-mouth recommendation had sent the film's box office takings through the roof.

'One of the most interesting things that I ran across was a newspaper article about young men who were dying in their sleep after having severe nightmares,' says Wes Craven. 'Not just any nightmares, but nightmares where they would tell their family, "I've never had one like this before, it's totally different from anything before."

'The most extraordinary example was that of a young man who had such a nightmare, told his family, and decided to stay awake for as long as he could because he was convinced he was going to die if he slept again. Finally he collapsed into sleep. His family carried him up to his room and everybody else went to bed.

'In the middle of the night, everybody is dreaming away when suddenly there are these horrible screams. They run back to his room, and he is thrashing in his bed. They get to him and try to wake him up. But he falls still – dead.

'I thought that was so dramatic that I devised it into a movie situation where somebody is attacked in his sleep. That became the basis of *A Nightmare on Elm Street,* which generated six direct sequels and a billion dollar industry just off of one or two gripping newspaper articles.'

'My father actually ended up moving out to Los Angeles while I grew up in New York,' explains Jonathan

A NIGHTMARE ON ELM STREET

USA, 1984. Dir: Wes Craven. With: John Saxon, Ronee Blakley, Heather Langenkamp, Amanda Wyss, Johnny Depp, Robert Englund. New Line Cinema/Media Home Entertainment/Smart Egg Pictures. Colour.

Writer/director Craven's much-imitated chiller about a psychopathic killer, burned to death years ago, who returns for revenge by murdering his killers' teenage offspring through their dreams. Englund's horrific killer, Freddy Krueger, is a marvellous creation, but too many plot holes and the telegraphed shock moments reduce an imaginative idea to low-budget popcorn entertainment. S.J.

Sequels: *A Nightmare on Elm Street Part 2 Freddy's Revenge* (Dir: Jack Sholder, 1985); *A Nightmare on Elm Street Part 3 Dream Warriors* (Dir: Chuck Russell, 1987); *A Nightmare on Elm Street 4 The Dream Master* (Dir: Renny Harlin, 1988); *Freddy's Nightmares* (TV, 1988–1990); *Nightmare on Elm Street The Dream Child* (Dir: Stephen Hopkins, 1989); *Freddy's Dead The Final Nightmare* (Dir: Rachel Talalay, 1991); *Jason Goes to Hell: The Final Friday* (1993); *Wes Craven's New Nightmare* (Dir: Wes Craven, 1994).

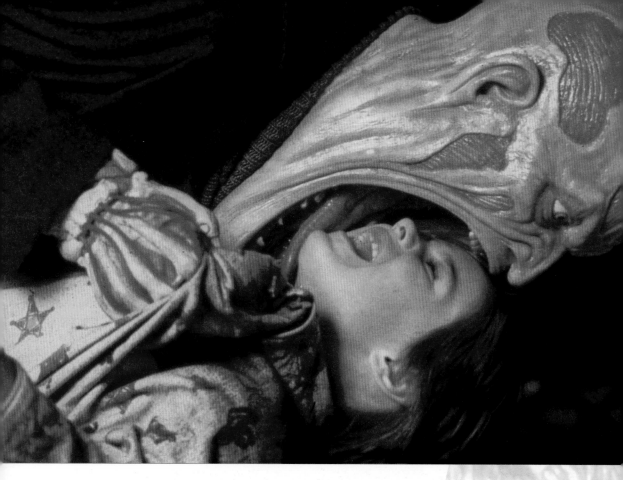

Craven. 'At the beginning he wanted just to have more flexibility as a director, but found himself writing scripts that people found very disturbing, that came from somewhere within him.

'I think that, if there is a family trait, it's that we're emotional, intuitive people who are also introspective. When you meet my father, he comes off as a very polite person, reserved – more the college professor, the academic, than the typical Hollywood type. He's an extremely intelligent man.'

Combining all the elements of the traditional horror movie with impressive special effects, *A Nightmare on Elm Street* tells the story of a group of suburban teenagers who discover that they all share a common nightmare. One by one, as they sleep, they are dispatched by a disfigured killer with wicked steel claws, who waits for them in their darkest nightmares.

With her friends ending up in a welter of blood, gutsy Nancy Thompson (Heather Langenkamp) decides to fight back before it's too late. Yet, despite drinking gallons of coffee and popping countless pills down her throat, Nancy can't resist a quick snooze during class, and she

'The first *Nightmare* was my film and I controlled it all the way through except for the last few minutes. I ended it in the script this way. The heroine turns her back on Freddy. He leaps for her and he goes screaming off into nothingness. The kids drive off into the fog and you never know if the whole thing is a dream or not. It's like a full circle. You start in a dream, you end in a dream.'

Wes Craven

135

Right: *The Hills Have Eyes.*
Below: *Deadly Friend.*

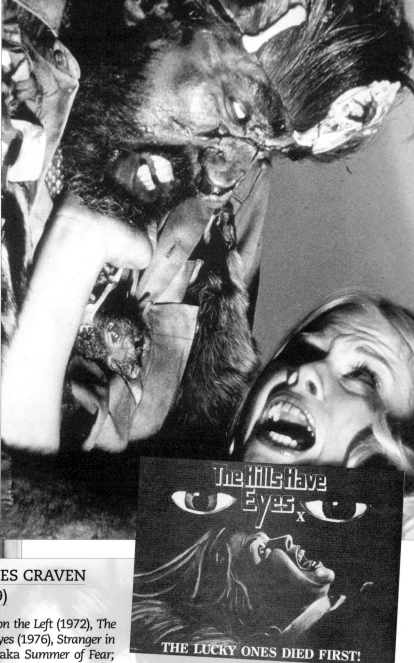

THE FILMS OF WES CRAVEN
(b 1949)

Last House on the Left (1972), *The Hills Have Eyes* (1976), *Stranger in Our House* (aka *Summer of Fear;* TV, 1978), *Deadly Blessing* (1980), *Swamp Thing* (1981), *Invitation to Hell* (TV, 1982), *Chiller* (TV, 1983), *The Hills Have Eyes Part II* (1984), *A Nightmare on Elm Street* (1984), *Casebusters* (TV, 1985), *Deadly Friend* (1986), *A Nightmare on Elm Street Part 3 Dream Warriors* (co-writer/co-executive producer, 1987), *The Serpent and the Rainbow* (1987), *Shocker* (1989), *Night Visions* (TV, 1990), *The People Under the Stairs* (1991), *Laurel Canyon* (co-creator/executive producer, TV, 1993), *Wes Craven's New Nightmare* (1994), *The Fear* (actor only, 1994), *Mind Ripper* (executive producer, 1995), *Vampire in Brooklyn* (1995), *Scream* (1996), *Scream 2* (1997).

The Hills Have Eyes
X

THE LUCKY ONES DIED FIRST!

ends up in a hellish world of flames and hissing steam.

After barely escaping with her life, Nancy learns from her gin-soaked mother (Ronee Blakley) and stalwart cop father (John Saxon) that the pizza-faced bogeyman plaguing her dreams is Fred Krueger, a real-life child killer who was finally hunted down and burned to death by a mob of vigilante parents (including Nancy's). Now Freddy has returned through the teenagers' dreams to avenge himself on those parents who originally destroyed him.

Finally realizing that she must rely on her own wits to survive, Nancy enters Krueger's boiler room of hell one last time to drag him into the waking world, where he can be destroyed...

The film had been beset with problems during production: lack of money, a short shooting schedule and last-minute script changes all added to the writer/director's problems. But what made A *Nightmare On Elm Street* stand out from other horror movies was dream killer Freddy Krueger ('the bastard son of a hundred maniacs'), memorably portrayed by actor Robert Englund.

Audiences remembered the nightmarish figure of Freddy – his greasy red and black striped sweater, battered felt hat pulled down over his horribly burned features, and a right-hand glove fitted with razor-sharp blades. Freddy Krueger quickly became the moviegoer's quintessential bogeyman.

'Freddy is an entity that has been around for a very long time,' explains Wes Craven. 'He stands for something ancient and probably goes back to the very roots of mankind. In each age storytellers try to grab on to those elements that are mysterious and hidden and ineffable and give them shape and give them names. In my case, I called it Freddy.'

'Originally they wanted a very big man to play Freddy,' reveals actor Robert Englund, 'and I don't think he was going to talk at all. I had a hiatus between TV shows and this was the only project that would fill the time for me. I also wanted to work with Wes Craven.

'I was breaking up with my wife when I went to meet Wes, and I was in a sort of punk stage then: I had gel on my hair and pencilled circles under my eyes, and I just sat there staring at him. I guess I rang a bell or something, because he went with me.'

Critics called the film 'a high-octane shocker', 'a state-of-the-art horror film', and announced that it was 'destined for horror history'. They were right, and A *Nightmare on Elm Street* went on to gross an impressive $30 million.

'You have to remember that we make them for little

'It astonishes and depresses me because there's nothing in a Freddy movie that hasn't been created a thousand times better in an oil painting.'

Clive Barker

'The *Elm Street* films use the dream theme to have some fun with surreal images of the sort sometimes found on comic book covers – the clawed hand coming out of the bath, the telephone receiver with a tongue, the monster leaning out of a wall in A *Nightmare on Elm Street,* or the old-dark-house-of-the-psyche finale of *Dream Warriors,* which seems to take place inside Freddy's head.'

Kim Newman

Opposite: *A Nightmare on Elm Street Part 2.*

or no money,' Englund points out. 'We worked a hard six weeks on that first one. I had a day-and-a-half off a week, which gave my skin a chance to breathe and heal from the make-up.'

Not surprisingly, New Line quickly decided to put a sequel into production, and *A Nightmare on Elm Street Part 2 Freddy's Revenge* (1985) reached the screen just over a year later. Wes Craven was missing from the sequel, as were the original cast members, except for Englund.

'Artistically, I think the first film was an intact, whole film, and it makes the statement I started out to make,' says Craven. 'I never intended to make a sequel.'

'A lot of Freddy's humour was encouraged by Wes in *Nightmare 1*,' according to Englund, 'but most of it hit the cutting-room floor. They were a little wary of giving this creature a personality. However, Jack Sholder – who did some editing on *Nightmare* 1 and directed *Nightmare* 2 – had seen some of this material and put a lot of the humour back into the sequel.

'*Nightmare 2* is a very creepy, very kinky film,' continues the actor. 'It reverses the first one – instead of having a teenage girl in jeopardy, we have a bisexual male, and this factor is exploited by Freddy. There's a lot of stuff implied with the S&M bar, stringing up the coach in the shower room in a bondage situation, and going to his boy friend's house for protection – the two of them take their clothes off as much as possible. All that adolescent mad teenage hormone stuff is explored, which of course Freddy is privy to.'

Freddy Krueger quickly became an unlikely cult figure. During the late 1980s, he was *the* screen monster, outstripping such rivals as *Psycho*'s Norman Bates, *The Texas Chainsaw Massacre*'s Leatherface, *Halloween*'s Michael Myers and *Friday the 13th*'s hockey-masked Jason.

Teenagers dressed up in Freddy drag for midnight screenings; an American heavy metal rock group released a song entitled 'The Ballad of Freddy Krueger'; young people in India saw him as the contemporary manifestation of a traditional evil spirit, and teenagers in the former Yugoslavia told Freddy jokes ('They don't translate well,' laughs Englund). Books and toys appeared, and he even had his own anthology TV show – *Freddy's Nightmares*.

'I just felt that Freddy was the paradigm of the threatening adult,' explains Craven. 'Freddy stood for the savage side of male adulthood. He was the ultimate bad father. It's a sickness where youth is hated. Childhood and innocence are hated. From the very beginning that's how I saw him.'

'I don't play Freddy as evil incarnate,' says Englund,

Above: *Nightmare on Elm Street The Dream Child.*

'One of the reasons I liked *Nightmare on Elm Street Part 3* was because we understood that Freddy was the bastard child of a hundred maniacs; we got to meet his mother, a nun, and all that kind of thing. I like that texture. It's something that audiences have fun with, too, because you can fit bits of the plot together. Having said that, there have always got to be bits of the mystery that remain unfinished.'

Clive Barker

'although I believe that is what he is on a symbolic level. The evil has come home – Freddy is the sins of the parents revisited on the children. Freddy is a child murderer and that means he is killing innocence, killing the future. I don't play Freddy as a symbol, I play Freddy as a man – a man who hates the future of youth.

'I use those things as an actor, and occasionally some of Freddy's predicament shows through. I don't want people to be sympathetic towards him, but I like the idea that he is out there thrashing around in a middle-class stronghold: Elm Street represents everything that is safe about suburban America and Freddy enjoys taking revenge there because I don't think he was ever allowed to be a part of it.'

Wes Craven made a welcome return to the series as co-writer and co-executive producer of *A Nightmare on Elm Street Part 3 Dream Warriors* (1987), and he wrote, directed and played himself in the film-within-a-film, *Wes Craven's New Nightmare* (1994).

'Now, in a sense, he's embraced by younger kids,' explains Craven, 'and they can make fun of him. In a way he's dangerous and in a way he's a joke. It's probably safer to deal with him that way. In his first incarnation, he was just terrifying.'

'Our films are not "slashers",' insists Englund, who has become firmly identified with the role of the deadly dream demon. 'They are much more surrealistic, much more stylized. They take place in a dream, not reality, and if you took the gore out of them you'd still have an interesting gimmick. Horror has always been a part of our society, a fascination with abomination that we all have. The *Nightmare* films are several rungs up the evolutionary ladder in terms of the horror genre.'

'I think horror films serve the same function as nightmares serve in the human condition,' continues Craven. 'They are a vent for disturbing but very powerful and important thoughts. I think films process very powerful primal fears and trepidations. It's life and death, blood and guts. But people come out of it at the end. There's a sense of exhilaration. They survive.'

For the time being, at least, Freddy Krueger also looks set to survive and to continue stalking the dreams of unwary teenagers. With his claw-like hand tipped with glittering razors, he will turn dream into reality and reality into horrifying nightmare.

'Freddy enjoys his work...' laughs Robert Englund in that distinctive death-rattle chuckle that has made him famous, '...his revenge is sweet.'

O for Open Vein

'Only be sure that thou eat not the blood: for the blood is the life; and thou mayest not eat the life with the flesh.'

Deuteronomy 12:23

'Before we do anything, let me tell you this; it is out of the lore and experience of the ancients and of all those who have studied the powers of the Un-Dead. When they become such there comes with the change the curse of immortality; they cannot die, but must go on age after age adding new victims and multiplying the evil of the world; for all that die from the preying of the Un-Dead become themselves Un-Dead, and prey on their kind. And so the circle goes on ever widening, like as the ripples from a stone thrown in the water.'

FROM *DRACULA* BY BRAM STOKER

HORROR DELIGHTS IN DREADFUL pleasures – the things that are gruesome yet strangely compelling. Of all the dreadful pleasures, none is quite so dreadful or so pleasurable as blood. Some people have a *thing* about blood: its texture, its danger. Actually, don't we all...?

Since ancient times, humans have associated blood with the powers of life and death. Over the centuries, throughout numerous cultures, blood has been ascribed diverse magical and sacred properties and used in a variety of ways during rituals and ceremonies.

Some races believed that by drinking the blood of their victims, they absorbed the qualities of those they conquered. Its redness endowed items of a similar colour with a special potency – such as red wine, drunk by the devotees of Dionysus as a symbolic gesture of consuming the Greek god's blood. In Christianity, the red wine of the Eucharist is still used to signify the blood of Christ.

'Blood is a very basic substance,' explains criminal psychiatrist Dr Roderick Anscombe, author of the novel *The Secret Life of Laszlo, Count Dracula* (1994). 'There aren't too many things in nature that are bright red, and that's why we use that colour as a signal of emergency or danger. So when people see blood spilled, there's a very deep-seated emotional response that tells you there's something dangerous happening to this person. They're losing their life force.'

'Blood is life,' says David J. Skal, author of the acclaimed non-fiction studies *Hollywood Gothic*, *The Monster Show* and *Dark Carnival*, 'but the sight of blood represents death, because blood is such a powerful and non-specific metaphor. I think this is why the vampire is such a persistent myth in human culture.'

The vampire is a concept that can be found in one form or another throughout most of the world's mythology. It can be a mythical creature, either animal or human, or a reanimated corpse (the 'Undead') that rises from the grave and retains its semblance of life by drinking the blood of others. In the Bible there are numerous references to blood

'"The blood is the life! The blood is the life!"'

From *Dracula* by Bram Stoker

Above: Countess Elizabeth Bathory

'After binding their hands, the servants would whip the girls until the skin of their bodies ripped and they became a mass of swollen wounds... The blood spurted like fountains and the white dress of the nocturnal lady would turn red. So red, that she would have to go up to her room to change. The walls and ceiling of the chamber would also turn red.'

From *The Bloody Countess* by Alejandra Pizarnik

sacrifices and warnings against people consuming blood. Therefore, by drinking blood, the vampire directly defies the teachings of God.

Unfortunately, there are also numerous real-life examples of people who have been inspired by the vampire myth to commit atrocities. Perhaps one of history's most notorious examples is the Countess Erzsebet (Elizabeth) Bathory (1560–1614), the infamous 'Blood Countess', who allegedly killed more than 650 young women for their blood.

The daughter of aristocrats George and Anna Bathory, she was born on the Hungary-Slovak Republic border and raised at the family estate in Ecsed, Transylvania. As a child she was subject to fits of rage and uncontrollable epileptic seizures. In 1575 she married Count Ferenc Nadasdy and took on the duties of managing his family estate. It was there she began her reign of terror by sadistically torturing her servants, often to death.

The Count died in 1604 and Elizabeth began to spend more time at Castle Cachtice, once part of north-western Hungary and now located in Slovakia. In conjunction with two other women, Anna Darvulia (who died in 1609) and Erzsi Majorova, she continued to torture and murder. As rumours of her activities spread, an inquiry into her crimes was begun, and she was arrested on 29 December 1610. Her trial was conducted by Count Thurzo, an agent of King Matthias II, whose main purpose was to confiscate her large property holdings and so escape having to repay a substantial loan her husband had made to the crown. As evidence, a journal listing the names of 650 victims, all noted in her own handwriting, was introduced. While her accomplices were tortured and burned to death, she was sentenced to life imprisonment in solitary confinement. For the next three years she was walled up in a room in her castle at Cachtice, where she died on 21 August 1614.

'Today we tend to think of Elizabeth Bathory as a kind of female Dracula who lived in the 1500s,' says David Skal. 'She was quite blood-thirsty and her crimes fed a whole oral tradition. Then, later, the idea that she bathed in the blood of virgins became popular – that she thought she could rejuvenate herself, actually become younger.'

One hundred years after the trial records were sealed, a Jesuit priest, Laszlo Turoczy, located the original documents and collected stories of the Countess eating the flesh of her victims, draining their blood and bathing in it to retain her youth and beauty. Later stories would

ELIZABETH BATHORY IN THE MOVIES

Countess Dracula (1970), *Necropolis* (1970), *The Werewolf vs. the Vampire Woman* (aka *La Noche de Walpurgis/Nacht der Vampire/Blood Moon/Shadow of the Werewolf*; 1970), *Vampyros Lesbos die Erbin des Dracula* (aka *El Signo del Vampiro/Las Vampiras*; 1970), *Daughters of Darkness* (aka *La Rouge aux Levres/Blut auf den Lippen/Children of the Night*; 1971), *The Legend of Blood Castle* (aka *Ceremonia Sangrienta/The Female Butcher/Blood Ceremony*; 1972), *The Vampire's Night Orgy* (aka *La Orgia Nocturna de los Vampiros/La Noche de los Vampiros/Orgy of the Vampires*; 1972), *Curse of the Devil* (aka *El Retorno de Walpurgis*, 1973), *Immoral Tales* (aka *Contes Immoraux*; 1974), *Mamma Dracula* (1979), *Thirst* (1979), *The Craving* (aka *El Retorno del Hombre Lobo*; 1980), *Krvava Pani* (1981), *The Mysterious Death of Nina Chereau* (1988).

embellish her crimes with tales of vampirism and werewolfism. Bram Stoker, the creator of *Dracula* (1897), read about Elizabeth Bathory in *The Book of Werewolves* (1865) by the Protestant minister Sabine Baring-Gould, and it has been suggested that her legend played a major role in the creation of his famous fictional vampire.

'The metaphor was very powerful,' continues Skal, 'and many writers of Gothic fiction probably came across these accounts. The image of the vampire as a bloodthirsty aristocrat, who could prolong his or her youth, probably owed much to the Bathory legend.'

Poppy Z. Brite was born in 1967 in New Orleans. She has worked as a gourmet candy-maker, mouse caretaker, artist's model and exotic dancer. She began her first novel, *Lost Souls* (1992), when she was nineteen, but it was not published until she was twenty-five. She describes it as 'a homoerotic, southern Gothic, rock 'n' roll vampire tale set partly in New Orleans and partly in my fictitious town of Missing Mile, North Carolina'. She has followed it with a collection, *Swamp Foetus* (1993), the erotic

> 'These cuts he had made over the years were more in the nature of experimentation: to test his domain over his own malleable flesh, to know the strange human jelly below the surface, part layer upon cell-delicate layer of skin, part quickening blood, part pale subcutaneous fat that parted like butter at the touch of a new blade.'
>
> FROM *DRAWING BLOOD* BY POPPY Z. BRITE

> 'I'm a gay man in a woman's body.'
>
> Poppy Z. Brite

> 'Big talent gives off thermonuclear vibes. I can feel them. The last time I said it, I was talking about Dan Simmons. Now I'm saying it about Poppy Z. Brite.'
>
> Harlan Ellison

vampire anthology *Love in Vein* (1994), and two further novels, *Drawing Blood* (1993) and *Exquisite Corpse* (1996).

'My teenage years were a difficult period of my life,' she recalls. 'I was never happy in school, I was never particularly happy with people my own age. They thought that I was strange for wanting to be a writer and for dressing the way that I did.

'I started cutting my wrists when I was about eighteen or nineteen. I did it with single-edged razor blades mostly. Sometimes exacto knives that I'd swiped out of the school biology lab. As for why I did it, it was a release of pain.

'It made me able to, not so much like myself, as feel sympathy for myself that I didn't have otherwise, because it was a time of great self-hatred and self-disgust for me. Seeing my own blood, using my own blood, made it easier for me to get through this pain and to turn some of this pain into creativity.

'When I started writing *Lost Souls* around this time, I already had such an intimacy with my own blood that it was easier to turn blood into a very sexual motif in the story, which of course is about vampires.'

'I wanted to write a novel about Count Dracula, the vampire,' says Roderick Anscombe, 'because although it is a traditional and well-trodden path, the reality is so compelling. I've interviewed perhaps a hundred murderers, often very soon after they've committed their actions. So I was interested in a man who commits murder after murder, and I wanted to bring my experience as a doctor and as a psychiatrist to this myth and to infuse it with reality, because as a psychiatrist I have a professional interest in reality.'

So-called 'real' vampires – people who drink blood for nourishment or sexual pleasure – are suffering from a condition that psychologists call 'hematomania'. According to author and critic Colin Wilson, 'The whole vampire legend has joined the great sort of confluence of horror and sex crime which flows on into the twentieth century. And of course, nowadays, with serial killers and so on, we once again are seeing a strange merging of the vampire legend with the legendary aspect of serial killers.'

Although the Marquis de Sade, Gilles de Rais and even Ed Gein are often cited as vampiric criminals, one of the earliest reported cases was a German man called Sorgel who, during the early nineteenth century killed a man in

> 'Sometimes he would hold his arm over a page of his sketchbook, let the blood fall on clean white paper or mingle with fresh black ink; sometimes he would trace it into patterns with his finger or the nib of a pen.'
> FROM *DRAWING BLOOD* BY POPPY Z. BRITE

> 'Dazed, I watched her heart continue to pump blood through the wound for several more seconds, and it was not until the flow finally petered out that I began to realize what I had done... Gently, I pressed my lips against the soft, surrendering edges of the wound and tasted the still unclotted blood which welled there.'
> FROM *THE SECRET LIFE OF LASZLO, COUNT DRACULA* BY RODERICK ANSCOMBE

Above: Poppy Z. Brite. Opposite: Vlad Tepes, the original Dracula, from a German pamphlet published in Strasbourg, *circa* 1500.

COUNT DRACULA IN THE MOVIES

Drakula (1921), Nosferatu (1922), Dracula (1930), Dracula (Spanish version, 1930), Hollywood on Parade (1933), Mickey's Gala Premiere (1933), Dracula's Daughter (1936), G-Man Jitters (1939), Son of Dracula (1943), Gandy Goose in Ghost Town (1944), House of Frankenstein (1944), House of Dracula (1945), Mighty Mouse Meets Bad Bill Bunion (1945), The Jailbreak (1946), Meet Frankenstein (aka Abbott and Costello Meet the Ghosts; 1948),

Abbott and Costello Meet Dr Jekyll and Mr Hyde (1953), Drakula Istanbulda (1953), The Return of Dracula (aka Curse of Dracula/The Fantastic Disappearing Man; 1957), Dracula (aka Horror of Dracula; 1958), House on Bare Mountain (1962), Escala en Hi-Fi (1963), Sexy Proibitissimo (1963), Batman Dracula (1964), Dracula (1964), Kiss Me Quick! (1964), Mga Manugang ni Drakula (1964), Billy the Kid versus Dracula (1965), Chappaqua (1966), Dracula Prince of Darkness (1965), Dr Terror's Gallery of Horrors (aka The Blood Suckers/Return from the Past/Alien Massacre/Gallery of Horror; 1966), El Imperio de Dracula (1966), Mad Monster Party? (1966), Mondo Keyhole (aka The Worst Crime of All!; 1966), La Sombra del Murcielago (1966), Batman Fights Dracula (1967), Blood of Dracula's Castle (1967), Dracula's Wedding Day (1967), The Naked World of Harrison Marks (1967), A Taste of Blood (aka The Secret of Dr Alucard; 1967), Dracula Has Risen from the Grave (1968), Santo y Blue Demon vs los Monstruos (aka Contra los Monstruos/Santon y Blue Demon contra los Monstruos/Santo contra los Monstruos de Frankenstein; 1968), Santo y el Tesoro de Dracula (aka El Vampiro y el Sexo; 1968), Does Dracula Really Suck? (1969), Dracula (The Dirty Old Man) (1969), Dracula vs. Frankenstein (aka El Hombre Que Vino del Ummo/Dracula jagt Frankenstein/Los Monstruos del Terror/Assignment Terror; 1969), Men of Action Meet Dracula (1969), Taste the Blood of Dracula (1969), Bram Stoker's Count Dracula (aka El Conde Dracula/Nachts wenn Dracula Erwacht/Il Conte Dracula/Count Dracula; 1970), Dracula vs. Frankenstein (aka Blood of Frankenstein/They're Coming to Get You/ Revenge of Dracula; 1970), Guess What Happened to Count Dracula (aka The Master of the Dungeon; 1970), Jonathan (aka Jonathan, Vampire Sterben Nicht; 1970), One More Time (1970), Scars of Dracula (1970), A Trip with Dracula (1970), Gidget Gets Married (TV,

Above: Dracula (1930).
Right: Dracula (Spanish version, 1930).
Opposite top: Dracula (1979).
Opposite bottom: Dracula's Great Love.

1971), *Lake of Dracula* (aka *Chi O Suu Me*; 1971), *The Mad Love Life of a Hot Vampire* (1971), *Blacula* (1972), *Dracula A.D. 1972* (1972), *Dracula Prisoner of Frankenstein* (aka *Dracula contra Frankenstein/Dracula contra el Doctor Frankenstein/Dracula le Prisonnier de Frankenstein/The Screaming Dead*; 1972), *The Dracula Saga* (aka *La Saga de los Dracula/Saga of the Draculas/Dracula – The Bloodline Continues*; 1972), *Dracula's Great Love* (aka *El Gran Amor del Conde Dracula/Dracula's Virgin Lovers/Cemetery Girls/Vampire Playgirls*; 1972), *La Fille de Dracula* (aka *La Hija de Dracula*; 1972), *Go for a Take* (1972), *La Invasion de Los Muertos* (aka *Blue Demon y Zovek el la Invasion de los Muertos*; 1972), *Santo y Blue Demon contra Dracula y el Hombre Lobo* (1972), *Blood for Dracula* (aka *Dracula cerca Sangue di Vergine e... Mori di Sete/Andy Warhol's Dracula*; 1973), *Dracula* (TV, 1973), *The Satanic Rites of Dracula* (aka *Count Dracula and His Vampire Bride*; 1973), *Son of Dracula* (aka *Young Dracula*; 1973), *The Legend of the 7 Golden Vampires* (aka *The Seven Brothers Meet Dracula*; 1974), *Vampira* (aka *Old Dracula*; 1974), *Deafula* (1975), *The Evil of Dracula* (aka *Chi O Suu Bara*; 1975), *Train Ride to Hollywood* (1975), *The Bride's Initiation* (1976), *Dracula and Son* (1976), *El Pobrecito Draculin* (1976), *Tiempos Duros para Dracula* (1976), *Count Dracula* (TV, 1977), *Doctor Dracula* (1977), *Dracula's Dog* (aka *Zoltan... Hound of Dracula*; 1977), *Lady Dracula* (1977), *McCloud: McCloud Meets Dracula* (TV, 1977), *La Dinastia Dracula* (1978), *Vlad Tepes* (aka *The True Life of Dracula*; 1978), *Dracula* (1979), *Dracula Blows His Cool* (aka *Graf Dracula in Oberbayern*; 1979), *Dracula Sucks*

(aka *Lust at First Bite/Dracula's Bride*; 1979), *Kyuketsuki Dorakyura Kobe Ni Arawaru: Akuma Wa Onna Wo Utsukushiku Suru* (1979), *Love at First Bite* (1979), *Nocturna, Granddaughter of Dracula* (1979), *Nosferatu the Vampire* (aka *Nosferatu Phantom der Nacht*;1979), *Star Virgin* (1979), *Blood Lust* (1980), *La Charlots conre Dracula* (1980), *Dracula* (1980), *Last Rites* (aka *Dracula's Last Rites*; 1980), *Dracula Exotica* (aka *Love at First Gulp*; 1981), *Buenas Noches, Señor Monstruo* (1982), *Dracula Rises from the Coffin* (1982), *Hysterical* (1982), *Dracula Tan Exarchia* (1983), *An Evening with Kitten* (1983), *Gayracula* (1983), *Hello Dracula* (1985), *¡Vampiros en la Habaña!* (1985), *Who Is Afraid of Dracula* (aka *Fracchia contro Dracula/Fracchia vs. Dracula*; 1985), *The Monster Squad* (1987), *Scooby-Doo and the Reluctant Werewolf* (1988), *Sundown The Vampire in Retreat* (1988), *To Die For* (1988), *Vampire in Venice* (aka *Nosferatu a Venezia/Vampires in Venice*; 1988), *Waxwork* (1988), *The Lost Platoon* (1989), *Bite!* (1991), *Son of Darkness: To Die For II* (1991), *Waxwork II: Lost in Time* (aka *Lost in Time*; 1991), *Bram Stoker's Dracula* (1992), *Dracula* (1992), *Dracula's Hair* (1992), *Dracula Rising* (1993), *Leena Meets Frankenstein* (1993), *Dracula* (1994), *Dragula* (1994), *Nadja* (1995), *Dracula, Dead and Loving It* (1995).

a forest and drank his blood in an attempt to cure himself of epilepsy. A more famous case involved Sergeant Victor Bertrand (1824–1849), who was convicted of opening graves in Paris and eating the flesh of the corpses. In Germany, Fritz Haarman (1879–1924), also known as 'the Vampire of Düsseldorf', killed and cannibalized more than twenty people, while Peter Kürten (1883–1931) mutilated a series of young children and women and then drank their blood. John George Haigh (1910–1949) killed nine victims in London, drank their blood and disposed of their bodies in a vat of sulphuric acid. In 1978, serial killer Richard Chase (1950–1980) of Sacramento, California drank the blood of his victims in the assumption that it would improve his physical health. As recently as 1992, Andrei Chikatilo of Rostov, Russia, was sentenced to death for murdering fifty-five people.

'The serial killer is a vampire for the new millennium,' says Poppy Z. Brite, 'the predator who feeds on humans. The vampire is usually seen as a different creature, a creature of a separate race or a reanimated corpse. Whereas the serial killer is – whether we like to

Opposite: Bela Lugosi as *Dracula* (1930).

'The horror film in general and the vampire film in particular confirms the feeling. Yes, it says; sex is scary; sex is dangerous. And I can prove it to you right here and now. Siddown, kid. Grab your popcorn. I want to tell you a story...'

Stephen King

DRACULA

6d.

BY BRAM STOKER

6d.

WESTMINSTER
Archibald Constable & Co Ltd
2 WHITEHALL GARDENS

Above: Behind-the-scenes, *Dracula* (1930).

"'I cannot afford to lose blood just at present: I have lost too much of late for my physical good.'"
From *Dracula* by Bram Stoker

'For the life of the flesh is in the blood...therefore I said unto the children of Israel, "No soul of you shall eat blood, neither shall any stranger that sojourneth among you eat blood."'
Leviticus 17:11-12

admit it or not – a member of the human race. One of the two serial killer characters in my novel *Exquisite Corpse* gets off on the texture of the blood, on the sight of it, being able to have his hands in it.'

'In the last one hundred years,' says David Skal, 'there's been a tremendous one-hundred-and-eighty degree change in the way we respond to the image of the vampire. A hundred years ago the vampire was something to be feared because it was going to take something from us. It was going to take power, it was going to take strength, it was going to take life, as represented by blood. Today we want that power for ourselves. We want to be the vampire.'

'The vampire is a subversive creature in every way,' agrees Brite, 'and I think this accounts for much of his appeal. In an age where moralists use the fact that sex is dangerous to "prove" that sex is bad, the vampire points out that sex has always been dangerous.

'The vampire is everything we love about sex and the night and the dark dream-side of ourselves: adventure on the edge of pain, the thrill to be had from breaking taboos. The vampire is not only perennially popular, he is the only supernatural creature who has become a role model.'

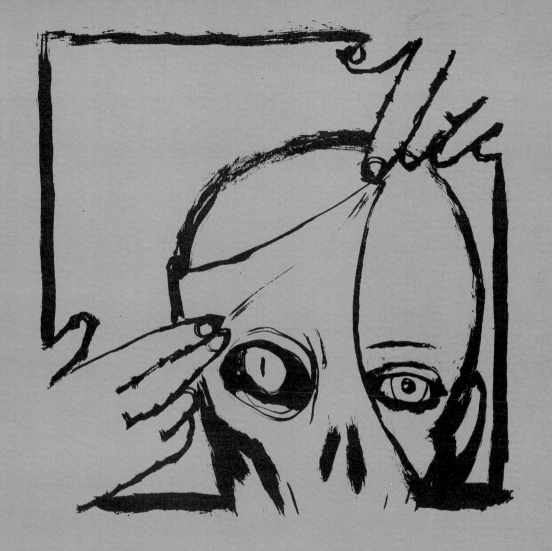

P for Pain

P

EOPLE HATE CHANGE, WHICH is probably why horror likes to give it a home. Transformation is perhaps the single scariest idea in horror – whether it is Dr Jekyll, werewolves or David Cronenberg's *The Fly*. All this shape-shifting scares us because it reminds us that we are not in control – of our own mind, our own body. What is here today could be gone tomorrow; *we* could be gone tomorrow. In a single breath we could be sick, be alien, or be crazy…

Among special effects artists, Tom Savini holds a unique place. He is affectionately known as 'The Wizard of Gore', the man who put splatter on the map. In films like *Dawn of the Dead* (1978) and *Friday the 13th* (1980) he makes us

believe that the carnage is for real. And he should know – he's *seen* carnage for real.

'Horror deals a lot with painful death because that's one of our fears,' says Savini. 'We hate pain, we are afraid of pain. Everyone knows pain, but no one knows death. They see other people in death, but they don't know it. Death is something that is quite difficult for people to relate to, but pain is actually quite easy to relate to. They know pain because they have experienced it, and that's what makes them afraid.'

Born and raised in Pittsburgh, Pennsylvania, Savini cites his first influence as the legendary silent actor and make-up artist, Lon Chaney Sr. At the age of thirteen he saw James Cagney's portrayal of Chaney in *Man of a Thousand Faces* (1957). 'Until that point I believed that Frankenstein, the Creature from the Black Lagoon, they were all real. For the first time in my life I was shown that somebody had to create those monsters, and I wanted it to be me.

'What was great about Lon Chaney was that he treated his face as a three-dimensional canvas. When he pulled his nose up to make his nostrils flare, he actually painted them larger. He didn't just depend on his own nostrils.

Above: *Friday the 13th.*
Opposite: *Night of the Living Dead* (1990).

'The impact of special make-up effects upon audience and industry is unquestionable.'

John Carpenter

Below: The great Lon Chaney Sr.
Right: Chaney Sr as the vampire in *London After Midnight* (1927).

That's an illusion, which is what make-up effects really are.'

When other children were out playing baseball, Savini was in his bedroom making up his face or those of the neighbourhood kids. At the age of fourteen he landed his first professional employment as part of a travelling act that performed horror and magic shows in movie theatres. The following year he found a non-paying job creating the make-up for horror host 'Chilly Billy' Cardille and various monsters on Pittsburgh television's *Chiller Theatre*.

Savini first met George Romero during his junior year in high school. Although the project they discussed never got made, Romero remembered him three years later when he was preparing *Night of the Living Dead* (1968). Romero asked to see samples of his make-up skills, but before that could happen Savini was called into the army and sent to Vietnam as a combat photographer.

'I've been called the "King of Splatter", the "King of Gore",' says Savini, 'and that's because the severed heads or the body parts have to be *real* to me. I have to get the same feeling that I had when I saw the real gore in Vietnam as a photographer. My job was to go in after a battle and photograph the damage to machines and people. I saw a lot of gore, the way the stuff really looks. I saw a lot of anatomically correct corpses.

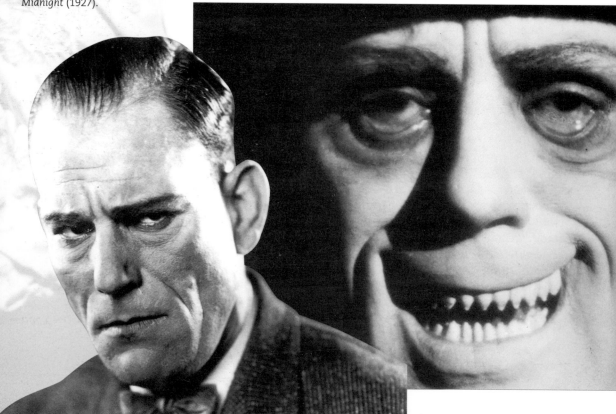

SELECTED FILMS OF TOM SAVINI (b 1947)

Deathdream (aka *Dead of Night;* 1972), *Deranged* (1974), *Martin* (1976), *Dawn of the Dead* (aka *Zombies,* 1979), *Effects* (actor only, 1980), *Friday the 13th* (1980), *Eyes of a Stranger* (1980), *Maniac* (1980), *The Burning* (1980), *Nightmare* (1981), *The Prowler* (aka *Rosemary's Killer;* 1981), *Knightriders* (actor only, 1981), *Creepshow* (1982), *Alone in the Dark* (1982), *Friday the 13th The Final Chapter* (1984), *Invasion USA* (1985), *The Ripper* (actor only, 1985), *Day of the Dead* (1985), *The Texas Chainsaw Massacre 2* (1986), *Creepshow 2* (1987), *Two Evil Eyes* (aka *Due Occhi Diabolici;* 1989), *Night of the Living Dead* (director only, 1990), *Heartstopper* (actor only, 1990), *Innocent Blood* (actor only, 1992), *Trauma* (1992), *Necronomicon* (1994), *From Dusk Till Dawn* (actor only, 1995).

'I hate it when I see a movie and someone dies and they shut their mouth and they assume this peaceful look on their face. Well, you're not pretty when you die. I try to show that more realistically. It's not just the physical damage – it's the *expression* of the body. It's a feeling that you have about that body. If I don't get the same feeling from the fake props as I did when I saw the real stuff, then it's not real enough for me.'

Following his discharge, Savini found work as an actor and make-up artist at a local theatre in North Carolina. He made some extra cash painting signs, and it was while he was delivering a consignment to a bar that he met art director Forrest Carpenter, who looked at his portfolio and hired him as Alan Ormsby's make-up assistant on Bob Clark's *Deathdream* (aka *Dead of Night,* 1972) and *Deranged* (1974), the latter based on the life of Wisconsin serial killer Ed Gein.

'A lot of violence you see in movies today is pornography,' says Savini. 'Some directors go in for a close-up of the cut throat or the gouged eye, and to me that is just like pornography. Personally, I'm not a gore hound. I think the less you show the better, because you can make it far more hideous than the scriptwriter wrote or something the effects guys created. What I imagine is a lot more horrible. I know that sounds strange coming from me.

'In *The Texas Chainsaw Massacre* (1974), there was hardly anything that you physically saw. It all happened

Surrounded by evil...

New Line Cinema presents A Robert Shaye Production

ALONE IN THE DARK

Starring JACK PALANCE   DONALD PLEASENCE
MARTIN LANDAU   DWIGHT SCHULTZ   ERLAND VAN LIDTH
Produced by ROBERT SHAYE Written and Directed by JACK SHOLDER in ☐☐ DOLBY STEREO

'When you're doing effects, you're just trying to get them to be okay and not look like effects... Less is more with these things, because the more you leave to people's imaginations, the better the stuff looks.'

Joe Dante

Above: Tom Savini and puppet head, behind-the-scenes.

'When it gets right down to it, it was Jack Pierce who really created the Frankenstein Monster. I was merely the animation in the costume.'

Boris Karloff

under the frame, above the frame, behind the door. But there are people who swear that they saw chainsaws ripping people apart because they *did* see it – they completed it in their own mind.'

Returning to Pittsburgh, he was quickly hired to do the make-up for George Romero's vampire film *Martin* (1976). Following the completion of that project, Savini moved back to North Carolina for a summer vacation. Then one day a telegram arrived from Romero. It read: 'Start thinking of ways to kill people.'

The film was *Dawn of the Dead* (aka *Zombies*, 1978), the second chapter in Romero's *Dead* series.

'A third of that movie was improvised,' explains Savini. 'We would sit around and think, let's tear his head off, or let's take a saw to his face and cut the top of his head off. We would go to the shopping mall at seven at night and leave at seven in the morning, and it was just the best fun you can imagine. The joy and happiness came from thinking of a way to kill people and then actually doing it. Sometimes when you're under pressure you come up with your best ideas.'

On some nights, Savini would have to turn three hundred extras into zombies. 'There was me and an assistant to do the straight make-up. For a few days we brought four or five friends in and made a little zombie assembly line. They would paint the zombies grey and I would do the gore make-up. If we knew that a zombie was going to die a glorious death hanging on to a car, then I would double them and do the stunt.

'We would ask some of the zombies if they would just leave the make-up on and come back tomorrow. They would go home and sleep in it and we'd touch it up a bit when they came back. Every day was Halloween – it was wonderful!'

After his work on Sean Cunningham's successful slasher movie *Friday the 13th* (1980), Savini went on to work on a string of similar splatter projects, including *Maniac* (1980), *The Burning* (1980) and *The Prowler* (aka *Rosemary's Killer*, 1981).

P

'Jack Pierce did really feel that he *made* these people, like he was a *God* who created human beings. In the morning he'd be dressed in white, as if he were in a hospital to perform an operation.'

Elsa Lanchester

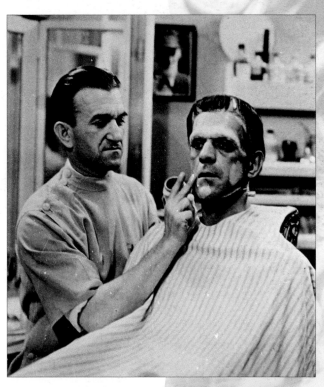

Above: Jack P. Pierce transforms Boris Karloff into the Monster in *Frankenstein* (1931).

'There was a plethora of splatter movies coming out,' he recalls, 'and I was going from one to another, using the same cut-throat appliance. The only thing that was changing was the murder weapon.

'It's been my job to show everything, and I've been called a sick puppy, but I always remind them that I don't write this stuff. My job is to take the script and create as realistically as possible what the writer has written.

'In my mind, what makes an effect successful is the fact that it's really an illusion. It's a magic trick. I have to misdirect you, I have to make you look over here while I am pulling the flowers out of my back pocket. In movies we misdirect you constantly with dialogue, with music, with sound effects. The best way to scare you is to get you off guard.

'Most of our effects are mechanical devices that pump and squirt, so to make the effect work we have to think of it as a magic trick. I imagine it on the screen, and that tells me what I have to see to make me believe that it is real. By imagining what I need to see, then I know what to show you.

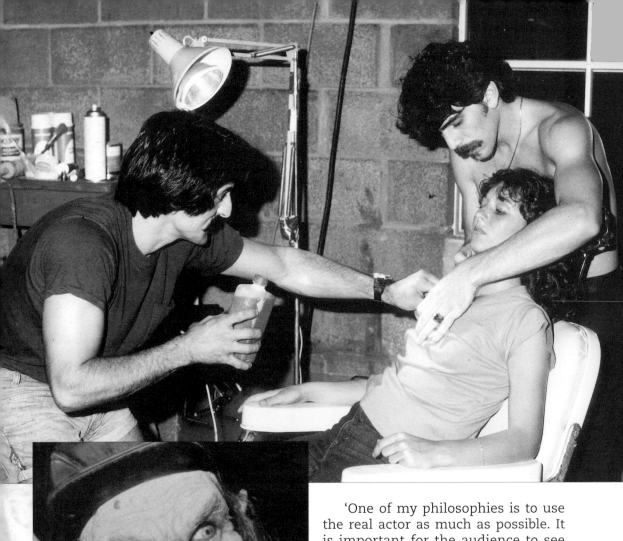

Top: Tom Savini (left)
behind-the-scenes, *Friday
the 13th.*
Above: Savini as The
Creep in *Creepshow 2.*

'One of my philosophies is to use
the real actor as much as possible. It
is important for the audience to see
the pain and the violence happen to a
real person. So if I have to cut a
throat, instead of taking a fake head
and using a real knife, I will take a
blade with a groove that looks like it is
in the throat when it's on. By using
the real actor you can have the changes
in facial expression, the scream and
even blood coming out of the knife.

'The blood is pumped in by a
hypodermic syringe that you don't know about. That's an
example of a mechanical device fooling you, just like a
magician would. What I try to do is to fool you by using a
real person as much as possible because you relate to the
real person. You can tell almost immediately if it's a fake
head, but when it's happening to a real face or a real
hand that is moving realistically, then you are just
sucked in.

'I think it is true when some critics say that our movie-makers are desensitizing people to violence,' he continues. 'When my daughter was five years old she would see us smacking people on the head with rubber hammers. One day she sneaked up on one of the effects guys and clobbered him with one of the real hammers. We had a long talk and now she knows the difference!'

Savini continued his association with Romero on such films as *Creepshow* (1982) and the third instalment in the *Dead* series, *Day of the Dead* (1985).

'In *Day of the Dead* there was a character called Rhodes, played by Joe Pilato. This guy's shooting people at random and blowing them away, so he had to die gloriously. So we said, let's just tear him in half. We could have done it with a fake body and torn him in half, but it would not have had the same impact or emotion.

'We used his real head and arms and gave him a fake foam rubber chest. His real body was under a platform, with a fake body placed under his armpits. It was stuffed with anything we could find from the food table and intestines that we had used throughout the film. Unfortunately, they were left in a refrigerator that was unplugged and the smell was incredible. We filled it with guts and chicken livers, shrimp dip and apple cores. Whatever we could find. We couldn't protect him with anything up his nose, but we sure protected ourselves with respirators. So he was getting that stench.

'We were actually pumping blood into this cavity as well, so it was pretty juicy as the zombies tore into the flesh and walked away with his lower body. His expression of sickness was very real because he was getting the stench from that stuff. It was even more real afterwards when the camera stopped rolling. Then he really looked like he was going to heave!'

When George Romero decided to remake his classic *Night of the Living Dead* for commercial and copyright reasons, he turned to his long-time make-up collaborator to direct.

'It is a film about people facing an external threat,'

Top: *Friday the 13th: The Final Chapter.*
Above: *The Prowler.*

161

NIGHT OF THE LIVING DEAD

USA, 1990. Dir: Tom Savini. With: Tony Todd, Patricia Tallman, Tom Towles, McKee Anderson, William Butler, Katie Finneran. 21st Century Productions/Columbia. Colour.

Savini's colour remake of executive producer George Romero's 1968 classic is surprisingly faithful and effective; cleverly shifting the emphasis away from Ben (Todd) and on to Barbara (a tough-looking Tallman) as the heroic protagonist. This time the flesh-eating zombies look genuinely dead and scary (thanks to John Vulich and Everett Burrell's make-up effects), and although Savini plays down the gore effects, there are some genuinely gruesome scenes. Unfortunately, this was not the box office success it should have been. S.J.

THERE IS A FATE WORSE THAN DEATH.

> 'It's as an audience member that I am most indebted to them, for those precious moments when the screen unveils a monster who will join the pantheon in my mind, and there remain to delight, appall and astonish me.'
>
> Clive Barker

says Savini. 'In a way, the threat doesn't matter. It's the people and their response that matters. If the people in this house can pull together, they can save themselves – if they can't, they'll die.

'I think zombies can still be scary. People have seen zombies and more zombies, so we knew if the zombies were going to be frightening, we had to do some things differently. We wanted the zombies to be people.

'It's more of a challenge today to frighten film audiences,' Savini believes. 'These days, you're not going to frighten audiences with more gore. Before effects became elaborate, a mere skeleton was scary. Effects guys like me spoiled people. The more we showed them, the more they wanted to see. We were in a position of trying to outdo ourselves.

In some ways, I became a captive of my own success.'

Q For Quiet Men

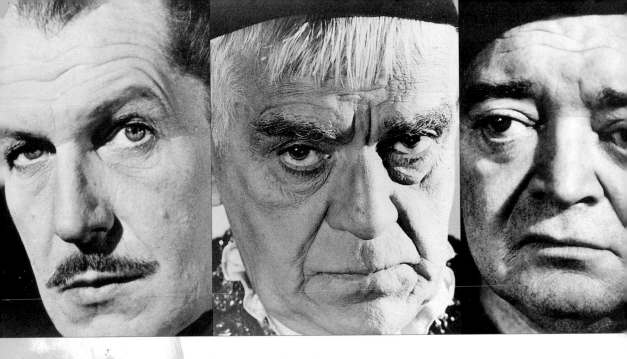

Above, left to right:
Vincent Price, Boris Karloff
and Peter Lorre.
Below: Roger Corman
lines up a shot.

S OME OF OUR BEST friends are monsters. However, it
has often been found that the actors who, on
screen, are the most hideous of creatures can, in
reality, be among the most pleasant of folk...

'I can remember two or three,' says director Roger
Corman, 'particularly Vincent Price, Boris Karloff and
Peter Lorre, three very fine actors who are not with us
any more and who have worked with me in horror films.'

Born in St Louis, Missouri, Vincent Price (1911–1993)
was one of the screen's more modern Masters of the
Macabre: by the time he appeared in his first genre film,
Lon Chaney Sr had been dead for nearly a decade, and
Boris Karloff, Bela Lugosi and Peter Lorre were already
established stars. Yet by the standards of today's audiences, Price is justly venerated as the cinema's Prince of
Peril. His suave, menacing looks and distinctive voice are instantly recognizable, and for more than five
decades he was regarded by
many as the epitome of the
horror film star.

'Vincent Price was the first I met,' recalls
Corman. 'He had started in Hollywood as a
young leading man, and when I met him he had
graduated to a more mature type of character
actor. Vincent's public persona was that of a
very elegant and established, rather formal,
Hollywood star, but he was also a very funny
man, and rather cultured in both his knowledge of art and of food.

SELECTED FILMS OF VINCENT PRICE
(1911–1993)

Tower of London (1939), The Invisible Man Returns (1940), House of Seven Gables (1940), Shock (1946), Dragonwyck (1946), Moss Rose (1947), Meet Frankenstein (aka Abbott and Costello Meet the Ghosts; 1948), House of Wax (1953), The Mad Magician (1954), Son of Sinbad (1955), The Ten Commandments (1956), The Story of Mankind (1957), The Fly (1958), House on Haunted Hill (1959), The Bat (1959), Return of the Fly (1959), The Tingler (1959), The Fall of the House of Usher (1960), Master of the World (1961), The Pit and the Pendulum (1961), Confessions of an Opium Eater (aka Evils of Chinatown; 1962), The Tower of London (1962), Tales of Terror (1962), The Raven (1963), Twice-Told Tales (1963), Diary of a Madman (1963), The Comedy of Terrors (1963), The Haunted Palace (1964), The Last Man on Earth (aka L'Ultimo Uomo della Terra; 1961/64), The Masque of the Red Death (1964), The Tomb of Ligeia (1964), City Under the Sea (aka War-Gods of the Deep; 1965), Dr Goldfoot and the Bikini Machine (aka Dr G and the Bikini Machine; 1965), Dr Goldfoot and the Girl Bombs (aka Le Spie Vengona dal Semifreddo/Dr G and the Love Bomb; 1966), House of 1000 Dolls (aka Das Haus der Tausend Freuden; 1967), Witchfinder General (aka The Conqueror Worm; 1968), The Oblong Box (1969), Annabel Lee (1969), Scream and Scream Again (1969), Cry of the Banshee (1970), The Abominable Dr Phibes (1971), Dr Phibes Rises Again (1972), The Aries Computer (TV, 1972), An Evening with Edgar Allan Poe (TV, 1972), Theatre of Blood (1972), Madhouse (1973), The Snoop Sisters: A Black Day for Bluebeard (TV, 1973), The Devil's Triangle (1974), Alice Cooper: The Nightmare (TV, 1975), The Butterfly Ball (1976), The Monster Club (1980), The Sorcerer's Apprentice (TV, 1980), I Go Pogo (aka Pogo, 1981), Vincent Price's Dracula (aka Dracula – The Great Undead, TV, 1982), Vincent (1982), House of the Long Shadows (1982), Thriller (1983), Bloodbath at the House of Death (1983), The Great Mouse Detective (aka Basil The Great Mouse Detective; 1986), Escapes (1986), From a Whisper to a Scream (aka The Offspring; 1986), The Little Troll Prince: A Christmas Parable (1987), Dead Heat (1988), Edward Scissorhands (1990), Arabian Knight (aka The Thief and the Cobbler; 1974/95).

'Vincent Price was extremely supportive. He's extremely intelligent and a very cultured man.'

Barbara Steele

'To me Boris Karloff was not only a great actor but a dear and long time friend. What I admired most about him was his enormous gratitude to the public and movie-makers who made it possible for him to have such a long and productive career. He often spoke of it with great feeling and always with humour. That humour was, of course, the secret of his charm; humour and genuine concern for his friends.'

Vincent Price

SELECTED FILMS OF BORIS KARLOFF
(1887–1969)

The Bells (1926), Tarzan and the Golden Lion (1927), Behind that Curtain (1929), King of the Congo (1929), The Unholy Night (1929), The Sea Bat (1930), King of the Wild (1930), The Mad Genius (1931), Frankenstein (1931), The Old Dark House (1932), The Mask of Fu Manchu (1932), The Mummy (1932), The Ghoul (1933), The Black Cat (aka The House of Doom; 1934), Gift of the Gab (1934), Bride of Frankenstein (1935), The Black Room (1935), The Raven (1935), The Invisible Ray (1936), The Walking Dead (1936), The Man Who Changed His Mind (aka The Man Who Lived Again; 1936), Juggernaut (1936), Charlie Chan at the Opera (1937), Night Key (1937), Mr Wong, Detective (1938), Devil's Island (1939), Son of Frankenstein (1939), The Mystery of Mr Wong (1939), Mr Wong in Chinatown (1939), The Man They Could Not Hang (1939), Tower of London (1939), The Fatal Hour (aka Mr Wong at Headquarters; 1940), Black Friday (1940), The Man with Nine Lives (aka Behind the Door; 1940), Doomed to Die (aka Mystery of the Wentworth Castle; 1940), Before I Hang (1940), The Ape (1940), You'll Find Out (1940), The Devil Commands (1941), The Boogie Man Will Get You (1942), The Climax (1944), House of Frankenstein (1944), The Body Snatcher (1945), Isle of the Dead (1945), Bedlam (1946), The Secret Life of Walter Mitty (1947), Lured (aka Personal Column; 1947), Dick Tracy Meets Gruesome (aka Dick Tracy's Amazing Adventure; 1947), Meet the Killer (aka Abbott and Costello Meet the Killer, Boris Karloff; 1949), The Strange Door (1951), The Emperor's Nightingale (1949/51), The Black Castle (1952), Abbott and Costello Meet Dr. Jekyll and Mr. Hyde (1953), Voodoo Island (aka Silent Death 1957), Frankenstein 1970 (1958), Grip of the Strangler (aka The Haunted Strangler; 1958), Corridors of Blood (1958), The Veil (TV, 1958), Jack the Ripper (TV, 1958), Destination Nightmare (TV, 1958), The Raven (1963), The Terror (1963), Black Sabbath (aka I Tre Volti della Paura; 1963), The Comedy of Terrors (1963), Monster of Terror (aka Die, Monster, Die!; 1965), Ghost in the Invisible Bikini (1966), The Daydreamer (1966), The Venetian Affair (1966), Dr. Seuss' How the Grinch Stole Christmas! (TV, 1966), Mad Monster Party? (1966), The Sorcerers (1967), Cauldron of Blood (aka El Coleccionista de Cadaveres/Blind Man's Bluff; 1967), Targets (1968), Curse of the Crimson Altar (aka The Crimson Cult; 1968), Cult of the Damned (aka La Muerte Viviente/La Isla de los Muertos/Isle of the Snake People/Snake People; 1968), Alien Terror (aka La Invasion Siniestra/The Incredible Invasion; 1968), The Torture Zone (aka La Camera Del Terror/Fear Chamber/The Torture Chamber; 1968), Dance of Death (aka Serenta Macabre/House of Evil/Macabre Serenade; 1968), Madhouse (1974), Transylvania Twist (1989).

'Although Vincent led what might be described as the good life, he was a very dedicated actor, and took his craft or his art very seriously. Vincent had been trained at London's Royal Academy of Dramatic Art as a classical actor – so he had the formal movements and techniques. But he and I were both looking for what we would call truth in performance.'

Vincent Price may have been the Prince, but Boris Karloff (1887–1969) was the undisputed King of Horror. Born William Henry Pratt in Camberwell, London, he used a £100 legacy from his mother to sail to Canada in 1909, where he found employment in a variety of jobs. When he applied to join a touring theatre company, he remembered a remote family name on his mother's side

'I have been more fortunate than some actors who have been in horror films, I know. It was a shame that Boris Karloff was confined to the playing of one type of role, because he was too good an actor.'

Christopher Lee

Q

THE MASTERS OF MENACE IN A BLAST OF ROBBERY, POISONING AND MURDER

THE COMEDY OF TERRORS

'SCOPE EASTMAN COLOUR

STARRING
VINCENT BORIS PETER
PRICE KARLOFF LORRE

WITH
JOYCE JAMESON · RHUBARB THE CAT

SPECIAL GUEST STAR · ALSO STARRING
JOEE BROWN · BASIL RATHBONE

Produced by JAMES H. NICHOLSON and SAMUEL Z. ARKOFF · Co-Producer ANTHONY CARRAS · Directed by JACQUES TOURNEUR · Written by RICHARD MATHESON · Music by LES BAXTER
An AMERICAN INTERNATIONAL Picture   From ANGLO AMALGAMATED for WARNER-PATHE release

168

SELECTED FILMS OF PETER LORRE (1904–1964)

M (1931), F.P.1 Antwortet Nicht (1932), Mad Love (aka The Hands of Orlac; 1935), Think Fast, Mr. Moto (1937), Thank You, Mr. Moto (1937), Mr. Moto's Gamble (1938), Mr. Moto Takes a Chance (1938), Mysterious Mr. Moto (1938), Mr. Moto's Last Warning (1939), Mr. Moto Takes a Vacation (1939), Strange Cargo (1940), Stranger on the Third Floor (1940), You'll Find Out (1940), The Face Behind the Mask (1941), Arsenic and Old Lace (1941), Invisible Agent (1942), The Boogie Man Will Get You (1942), The Beast with Five Fingers (1946), Der Verlorene (1951), 20,000 Leagues Under the Sea (1954), Around the World in Eighty Days (1956), The Story of Mankind (1957), Voyage to the Bottom of the Sea (1961), Tales of Terror (1962), Five Weeks in a Balloon (1962), The Raven (1963), The Comedy of Terrors (1963), Muscle Beach Party (1964).

and adopted 'Karloff' as a stage name. For a first name he pulled Boris 'out of the air'.

By the time he arrived in Los Angeles in 1917, he had established himself as a popular stage vil-lain. Beginning his movie career with appearances in crowd scenes and serials, he slowly began to establish himself, and a role in the 1931 gangster thriller The Criminal Code led directly to him being cast as the Monster in James Whale's classic Frankenstein (1931).

'Boris, when transforming himself into a mon-ster, was much more of a formalistic actor, using technique,' Corman remembers. 'I would tell him exactly what I wanted and he could play that. Peter Lorre, however, was an entirely different type of actor.'

If Karloff was King, and Price the Prince, then Peter Lorre (1904–1964) was the Jester among these three Merchants of Menace. Born Ladislav Loewenstein in Rózsahegy, Hungary, he decided to become an actor in the 1920s, joining a performing troupe in Vienna, where he was noticed by director Fritz Lang. In 1930, Lang cast the actor as the child-murderer in M, inspired by the exploits of serial killer Peter Kürten, the notorious 'Vampire of Düsseldorf'. Fleeing the rise of Nazism, Lorre escaped to France and then to England, where Alfred Hitchcock cast him in The Man Who Knew Too Much (1934).

Accepting a six-month contract with Columbia, Lorre travelled to America the day after completing his work for Hitchcock.

'He'd been trained in Germany in the 1920s in the German Expressionist technique,' explains Corman. 'So that when he came to Hollywood, he could work very well with American method actors and directors. On the set, I was more inclined to let him go, to encourage him to improvise, because he could stay with the truth of the scene and, at the same time, bring some very strange quirky humour to it.

'I did work with Peter, Boris and Vincent together on one film, *The Raven* (1963), and it was a wonderfully stimulating experience.

'We had to play *The Raven* for laughs,' continues Corman, 'because both Richard Matheson, our writer, and I were getting tired of the stock Poe pictures. In fact, it was his original idea that we should move into comedy. I was only too happy to agree. As it turned out, this film was the most fun we ever had on a Poe picture. It had the biggest look of

THE RAVEN

USA, 1963. Dir: Roger Corman. With: Vincent Price, Peter Lorre, Boris Karloff, Hazel Court, Olive Sturgess, Jack Nicholson. American-International Pictures. Colour.

After five years absence, Karloff was brought back to the screen by director Corman for this enjoyable romp. Matheson's script has less to do with Poe's atmospheric poem than the 1935 version did, but this tale of rival sorcerers Dr Erasmus Craven (Price) and the evil Dr Scarabus (Karloff) benefits from a star cast, including the ad-libbing Lorre as Dr Bedlo, magically transformed into the foul-tempered bird, a young Nicholson as the bumbling hero, and Court as the 'lost' Lenore. It also features a wonderful climactic duel of magic. It was given an 'X' certificate in Britain. *S.J.*

SELECTED FILMS OF ROGER CORMAN (b 1926)

The Day the World Ended (1955), *It Conquered the World* (1956), *Attack of the Crab Monsters* (1956), *Not of This Earth* (1956), *The Undead* (1957), *War of the Satellites* (1958), *The Saga of the Viking Women and Their Voyage to the Waters of the Great Sea Serpent* (aka *The Viking Women and the Sea Serpent*; 1957), *Teenage Caveman* (1958), *A Bucket of Blood* (1959), *The Wasp Woman* (1959), *The Little Shop of Horrors* (1960), *The Last Woman on Earth* (1960), *The Creature from the Haunted Sea* (1960), *The Fall of the House of Usher* (1960), *The Pit and the Pendulum* (1961), *The Premature Burial* (1962), *Tales of Terror* (1962), *The Tower of London* (1962), *The Raven* (1963), *The Terror* (1963), *X* (aka *The Man With X-Ray Eyes*; 1963), *The Haunted Palace* (1963), *The Masque of the Red Death* (1964), *The Tomb of Ligeia* (1964), *DeSade* (uncredited co-director, 1969), *Gas-s-s-s!* (1969), *Frankenstein Unbound* (1990).

Q

'One of my favourite movies was with Boris Karloff, Peter Lorre and Basil Rathbone, *The Comedy of Terrors*. What wonderful fun they all were and how I shall miss them all. All of them were highly intelligent, extremely kind and vastly amusing men. None of them felt other than privileged to have had a faithful public for so many years.'

Vincent Price

them all up until that time and certainly was the most colourful, with the sorcerers' duel at the end filled with lightning bolts and fireballs.

'But the best part of the movie was being on the set and watching everything between the actors. Peter kept everyone on their toes, myself included. He would just begin to improvise unexpectedly. Boris came in with all of his lines learned and he said, "Peter gives me replies that are not in the script. What can I do?" What I finally came up with, I said, "See if you can just modify your lines a little bit to fit what Peter is going to say, which none of us knows in advance, and I kind of think Peter doesn't know either." Vincent would really appreciate the new angles and actually play along with them, but it would drive poor Boris crazy. The two of them, and eventually the three of them, in their scenes work very well together.

'At one point, just to show you how this movie evolved, Vincent is talking with Peter, who is dressed in this oversized bird costume. Just the sight of Peter in that suit would be enough to make anyone crack up. But Vincent has to play it straight. Very sadly, he turns to Peter and says, "My wife's body is buried in a crypt beneath the house."

'Peter didn't bat an eye. "Where else?" he just shrugged. That sort of behaviour occurred throughout the shooting.'

Although they are no longer with us, Vincent Price, Boris Karloff and Peter Lorre have left behind them a lasting legacy of movies that are destined to chill and thrill generations to come.

According to Roger Corman, 'A horror actor's job – and I shouldn't use the words horror actor, I should really say an actor who is working in a horror film – just as any actor's job, is to deliver truth in a performance. If an actor can do that, I think he is a fine actor in any medium, and a particularly fine actor for a horror film.'

THE COMEDY OF TERRORS

USA, 1963. Dir: Jacques Tourneur. With: Vincent Price, Boris Karloff, Peter Lorre, Joyce Jameson, Joe E Brown, Basil Rathbone. American International Pictures. Colour.

Although not too successful in America and given a belated release in Britain, this fun horror/comedy teamed the three great horror stars under the direction of Val Lewton veteran Tourneur, who does the best he can with an uninspired Richard Matheson script. In a small New England town in the 1890s, the family funeral establishment of Hinchley and Trumbull is beset with financial difficulties. So the unscrupulous Waldo Trumbull (Price) and his assistant Felix Gillie (Lorre) set out to create their own clients. Unfortunately, their plans are thwarted by the senile Amos Hinchley (Karloff) and the wealthy Felix F. Black (Rathbone), who refuses to remain dead. Price is nicely nasty and Karloff has an amusing cameo, but the real stars are Rathbone, spouting Shakespeare at the most inopportune moments, and Lorre in his last horror role (a masked double is clearly visible in several scenes). Given the talent involved, this should have been much funnier, but it's still quite enjoyable. S.J.

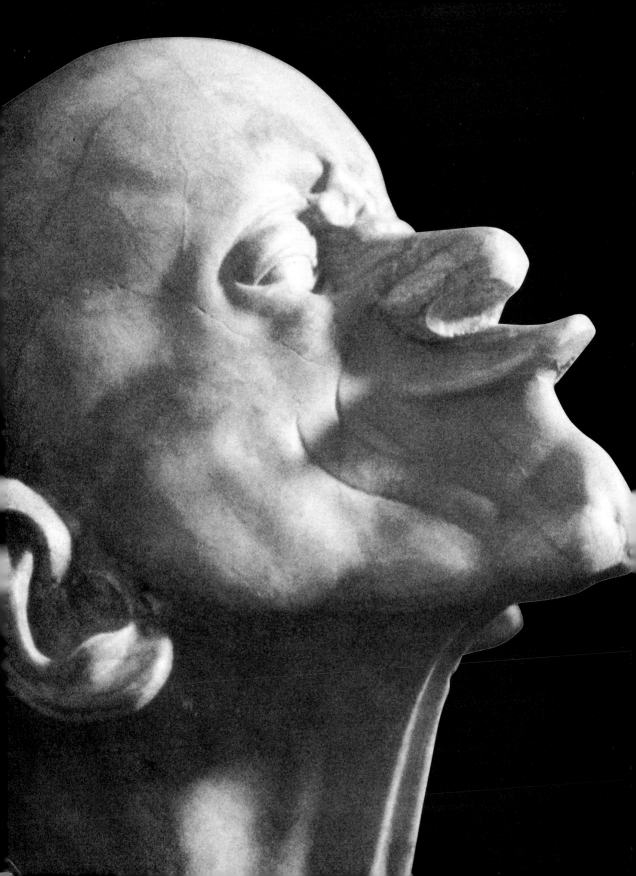

ONE OF THE MOST unendurable experiences we can have goes like this: we look into a human face and see madness there. Insanity is the most pure, the most undiluted horror of all. Look very closely at the faces on these pages. For me they are the most potent expressions of the horrors of madness, extraordinary works with an extraordinary story behind them.

At the end of the eighteenth century, the sculptor Franz Xavier Messerschmidt produced baroque figures for the Austrian court. Then, at the age of thirty-five, he was afflicted with what at the time was called a 'psychic illness'. He suffered from dementia, paranoia, hallucinations. Forced to withdraw from public life, he spent the rest of his days working on his series of 'Character-Heads'. These consisted of forty-eight busts representing the sculptor's own head in a variety of grimacing transformations, executed in marble, lead or plaster, which served as mementoes of his encounters with the spirits that tormented him.

His friend, Freidrick Nicolai, paid visits to his remote

'It is part of fantastic art's condition that, though time may blur its satiric purpose and confound its allegories, its appeal lies deeper than such superficial intentions. It calls us to the common ground of our subconscious, from which we may become estranged, but where we are never truly strangers. In other words, it calls us home.'

Clive Barker

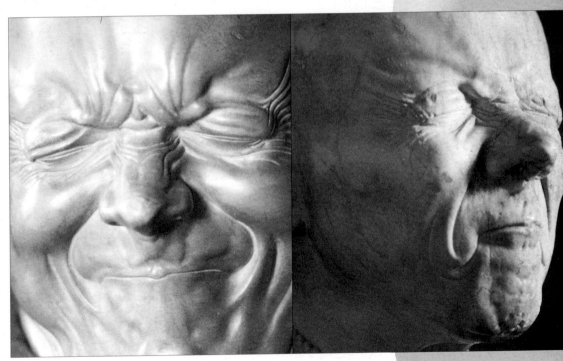

studio and recorded his impressions of this tortured man in his *Recollection of a Meeting with Messerschmidt in Pressburg in 1781*.

Messerschmidt was equally remarkable as an artist and as a man. In his art, an extraordinary genius. In common life, inclined a little to peculiarity. For a long

time he couldn't understand why.

In fact, Messerschmidt believed that evil demons came to him at night to persecute him: 'But eventually I realized that the spirit of proportion envies me for coming so near to perfection in my work,' explained the artist. 'So the spirit causes me physical pain.'

To ward off these demonic spirits, he devised a system of pinches carefully combined with certain facial contortions. He would pull faces in front of his mirror and deemed himself witness to the most amazing effects of his power over the spirits.

'I decided to fix these grimacing proportions permanently,' said Messerschmidt, 'an army of magical heads to protect me from the spirits.'

But in the corner of his room stood a rather different head; its form utterly curious and misproportioned; the face drawn almost into the shape of a beak.

'And the demon pinched me that time,' revealed the afflicted artist. 'I tell you, it nearly did for me. Luckily, it let off a sudden hellish fart and disappeared in the midst of a dreadful stench. Or it would surely have been the death of me…'

'I don't like to make a distinction between the writer and the painter, finally, because I do both things anyway. Everybody's dreaming and trying to put down their dreams in the way that their hand knows best. I feel as much a unity, as much comradeship, with painters as I do writers.'

Clive Barker

S For Sorceress

S

THE AMERICAN NOVELIST SHIRLEY Jackson (1919–1965) is perhaps best known for her novel, *The Haunting of Hill House* (1959), which was made into a very fine movie, *The Haunting* (1963). She is also known for a classic short story, 'The Lottery' (1948). Jackson is described now as a pioneer of what has been termed 'Modern Gothic', where houses, and neighbours, are never quite what they seem...

'I very much dislike writing about myself or my work,' she once said, 'and when pressed for autobiographical material can only give a bare chronological outline which contains, naturally, no pertinent facts.'

Born in San Francisco, she spent most of her early life in California. In 1940, after graduating with a BA from Syracuse University, she married the critic and numismatist Stanley Edgar Hyman. They settled in the quiet rural community of Bennington in Vermont. 'Our major exports are books and children,' she said, 'both of which we produce in abundance.' She described her book *Life Among the Savages* (1953) as 'a disrespectful memoir' of her children, Laurence, Joanne, Sarah and Barry, and she followed it in 1957 with an equally whimsical sequel, *Raising Demons*.

> 'I took my coffee into the dining room and settled down with the morning paper. A woman in New York had had twins in a taxi. A woman in Ohio had just had her seventeenth child. A twelve-year-old girl in Mexico had given birth to a thirteen-pound boy. The lead article on the woman's page was about how to adjust the older child to the new baby. I finally found an account of an axe murder on page seventeen, and held my coffee cup up to my face to see if the steam might revive me.'
>
> FROM *LIFE AMONG THE SAVAGES* BY SHIRLEY JACKSON

Shirley Jackson claimed to be the only practising amateur witch in New England. She owned a ouija board, tarot cards and more than five hundred books on the occult. In her obituary, her friend, the critic Brendan Gill, told how she believed she had caused an accident to an enemy by making a wax image of him with a broken leg.

'My mother was a great student of the supernatural,' says Laurence Hyman. 'On the back of a book it would say that she writes with a broomstick rather than a pen.'

'My mother did in fact say she was a witch,' agrees Joanne Holly, 'that she used her witchly powers. In the kitchen was a drawer. Shirley would open it up and she'd need something and it wouldn't be there, and she'd slam the drawer and say its name and open it up and it'd be on top. I've seen her do it. I can't do it myself, but I've tried.'

According to Sarah Stewart, 'My mother believed in the power of inanimate objects to "pack a wallop", as she used to say. When she gave me the typewriter, she said, "There are many more stories left in that typewriter."'

'My mother saw strong personalities in cats and cars. I certainly remember her driving and urging her car to do

certain tricks, and then almost always it would. She believed that houses also had personalities. She spoke often, and strongly, of the wills of inanimate objects and hoped to affect them with her will.'

'She and I used to drive around the countryside looking for buildings that she could use,' recalls Laurence. 'She didn't look at buildings so much from an architectural point of view, but from a personality point of view.

'The house was filled with music all the time,' he continues. 'My mother played the piano, my sisters and mother sang. My parents had a music box that actually had belonged to my great-great-grandmother and it was one of my mother's prized possessions. However, it was clear early on that the music box was haunted. It would turn itself on. In the middle of the night it would start playing itself over and over when no one had wound it. I think my mother really did believe in supernatural things – if something happened it was because magic was behind it.'

Despite being said to suffer from obesity, asthma, arthritis and acute anxiety, Jackson was also described as 'a neat cosy woman whose blue eyes looked at the world through light horn-rimmed spectacles'. She would only write after she had completed all her household chores.

Above: Shirley Jackson.

'Perhaps more than anything else, the horror story or horror movie says it's okay to join the mob, to become the total tribal being, to destroy the outsider. It has never been done better or more literally than in Shirley Jackson's short story "The Lottery", where the entire concept of the outsider is symbolic, created by nothing more than a black circle coloured on a slip of paper.'

Stephen King

177

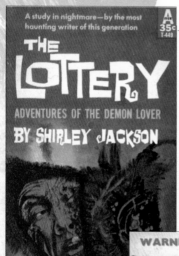

BOOKS BY SHIRLEY JACKSON (1919–1965)

The Road Through the Wall (aka *The Other Side of the Street*, 1948), *The Lottery, or, The Adventures of James Harris, the Daemon Lover* (1949), *Hangsaman* (1951), *Life Among the Savages* (1953), *The Bird's Nest* (aka *Lizzie*; 1954), *The Witchcraft of Salem Village* (1956), *Raising Demons* (1957), *The Sundial* (1958), *The Haunting of Hill House* (1959), *The Bad Children: A Play in One Act for Bad Children* (1959), *We Have Always Lived in the Castle* (1962), *Nine Magic Wishes* (1963), *The Magic of Shirley Jackson* (1966), *Come Along with Me: Part of a Novel, Sixteen Stories and Three Lectures* (1968), *The Masterpieces of Shirley Jackson* (1996), *Just an Ordinary Day: The Uncollected Stories of Shirley Jackson* (1997).

'Reading *The Haunting of Hill House* first in my teens, I found it genuinely don't-turn-out-the-lights frightening, and it went immediately into my pantheon of the "really scary" along with certain short stories by M.R. James, Walter de la Mare and L.P. Hartley. Like those other writers, Jackson invokes terror less by what she says than by what she doesn't say.'

Lisa Tuttle

According to Barry Hyman, 'One of the earliest memories I have of my mother was her in the kitchen, the warmth, the light, the feeling of family and security. But I realized there was more going on than that when I became aware of the typewriter going all the time. She tried to type ten pages a day, a first draft. She just kept working and I think that, in a sense, was her therapy.'

'She would always inevitably go up to her room,' says Laurence, 'shut the door and type, and we could just hear her up there. She'd type for half-an-hour, an hour, or two or three – whatever time she had, while at the same time running a household and keeping up with four very active children.'

Joanne recalls 'taking naps as a little child or going to sleep at night, my entire life – always the sound of the typewriter, pounding away, fast, very fast typing'.

'At those times we didn't even talk to her,' Sarah says. 'She wasn't our mother then, she was the typing person and she wouldn't be kind to us, or hear what we wanted. She was working.'

By the careful manipulation of atmosphere and lonely, often unreliable narrators, much of Shirley Jackson's fiction expertly balances psychological instability with an ambiguous supernatural horror.

'She was masterful at taking commonplace events,'

says Laurence, 'and turning them into spine-chilling horror stories by letting the reader become comfortable enough to let down their guard.'

Leonard Brown (to whom she later dedicated *The Haunting of Hill House*), her English professor at Syracuse University, told her that 'the aim of writing is to get down what you want to say, not to gesticulate and impress'. It was a lesson she never forgot.

'She'd write a story,' says Joanne, 'and trim it to the least possible number of words. Then she'd substitute the most vivid word possible for every adjective or noun, so that the reader could *see* it, so that reading itself wasn't a conscious act. It just jumped from her pen into your mind.'

Her first novel, *The Road Through the Wall*, was published in 1948, but it was the publication of 'The Lottery' in *The New Yorker* in August that same year that brought her fame and controversy as an author.

According to Sarah, 'She wrote in two hours

Below and bottom: Richard Boone and Eleanor Parker in *Lizzie*.

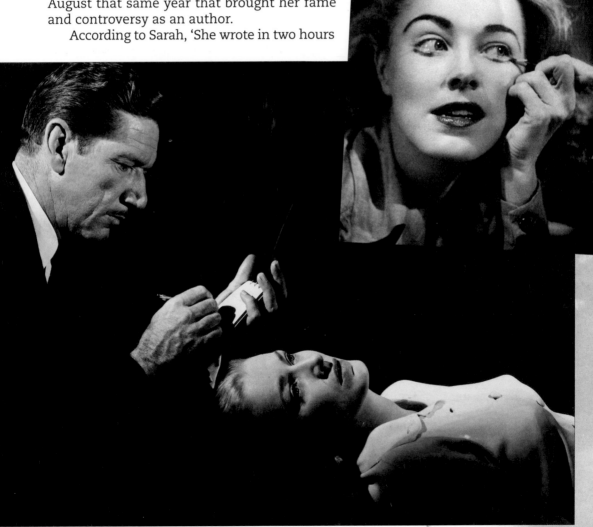

S

S

'Although the villagers had forgotten the ritual and lost the original black box, they still remembered to use stones. The pile of stones the boys had made earlier was ready; there were stones on the ground with the blowing scraps of paper that had come out of the box.'

FROM 'THE LOTTERY'
BY SHIRLEY JACKSON

'I think there are few if any descriptive passages in the English language that are any finer than this; it is the sort of quiet epiphany every writer hopes for: words that somehow transcend words, words which add up to a total greater than the sum of the parts.'
Stephen King on
The Haunting of Hill House

'No live organism can continue for long to exist sanely under conditions of absolute reality; even larks and katydids are supposed, by some, to dream. Hill House, not sane, stood by itself against its hills, holding darkness within; it had stood so for eighty years and might stand for eighty more. Within, walls continued upright, bricks met neatly, floors were firm, and doors were sensibly shut; silence lay steadily against the wood and stone of Hill House, and whatever walked there, walked alone.'

FROM *THE HAUNTING OF HILL HOUSE*
BY SHIRLEY JACKSON

this story that will probably never die, when she was pregnant with me. My mother read "The Lottery" to me at the kitchen table – I must have been around seven or eight. I remember hearing it, then feeling that I had to go and hug her. And also not wanting to.'

'The story was written two or three years after the end of the Second World War,' says Barry. 'I think the point of "The Lottery" is to make people realize that anyone and everyone can convert to mob behaviour – and that's where the horror sets in.

'"The Lottery", in a sense, is just a statement of how far people can go – normal people, everyday people. Only if you understand this, how humans can quickly cross the line into unacceptable behaviour, do you have a chance to put the brakes on it and step back. Don't join the crowd, don't throw one of the stones.'

'It created an enormous controversy and the mail just poured in,' recalls Laurence. 'More letters than any story had ever received.'

Many readers cancelled their subscriptions to the *New Yorker*. The tale was decried as 'violent', 'pointless' and 'un-American'. People wanted to know what it meant but, when asked, Jackson said, 'Well, really it's just a story.'

The story was reprinted in the collection *The Lottery, or, The Adventures of James Harris* in 1949, and she adapted it for television the following year. In 1951 she published *Hangsaman*, a description of college life with a fantastical edge, and followed it with *The Bird's Nest* in 1954. The story of a woman with multiple personalities, it was filmed as *Lizzie* in 1957, starring Eleanor Parker and Richard Boone. A decaying family awaiting the end of the world was the subject of *The Sundial* in 1958, and the following year she published perhaps her most enduring work, *The Haunting of Hill House*, which has justly been described as 'one of the greatest haunted house novels in literature'.

'When she decided to write *Hill House*,' says Joanne, 'what she did was take books out of the library on houses of New England where murders had occurred.'

She came across an account of a nineteenth century investigation of a haunted house and decided to go out and discover her own. 'I found it so exciting,' she said, 'that I wanted more than anything else to set up my own haunted house, and put my own people in it, and see what I could make happen.' Not only did she apparently discover one, but her research also revealed that it was built by her great-grandfather!

'Shirley could have created a house of enormous menace, horrifying implications,' continues Joanne, 'without ever having left her study. But she liked to work it out, get a good lather.'

'What she was trying to achieve was the feeling of a house substantial enough to be an entity on its own,' says Barry, 'with enough substance that you could seriously believe it might also have a will.'

In 1961 Shirley Jackson won the Mystery Writers of America Edgar Award for her story 'Louisa, Please', while her final novel, *We Have Always Lived in the Castle*, was published in 1963 and earned the National Book Award.

'I used to have to collect the mail,' recalls Sarah. They would send the mail to "The Lottery Lady, North Bennington, Vermont". She was the Lottery Lady. Sometimes letters came in that made my mother cry, about "The Lottery" and how it was some evil story.'

'I can remember growing up in the 1950s,' says Laurence, 'and there was certainly hostility from the townspeople because we were different. It is very hard to become accepted in a New England village in only one generation. This was no exception – these people were only several generations removed from the folks in Salem who burnt witches.'

THE HAUNTING

UK, 1963. Dir: Robert Wise. With: Julie Harris, Claire Bloom, Richard Johnson, Russ Tamblyn, Fay Compton, Rosalie Crutchley. Argyle/Metro-Goldwyn-Mayer. B&W.

Based on Shirley Jackson's classic novel. Director Wise brings to the film many of the subtle, atmospheric touches he learned while under the guidance of Val Lewton at RKO in the 1940s. Anthropologist Dr Richard Markway (Johnson) decides to open up the reputedly haunted Hill House after eighty years. With the help of Luke (Tamblyn), the sceptical heir, and two women who have already had contact with the supernatural, the lesbian psychic Theo (Bloom) and the repressed Eleanor (Harris), he uncovers the restless spirits that haunt the New England mansion. Nelson Gidding's literate screenplay and David Boulton's excellent Panavision cinematography imbue the house with a palpably evil force. Scenes like the ghostly presence outside Eleanor and Theo's room, the phenomena surrounding the locked nursery, and the sudden appearance of Mrs Markway's (Lois Maxwell) face are genuine high points of terror in one of the finest horror films ever made. *S.J.*

"'The concept of certain houses as unclean or forbidden – perhaps sacred – is as old as the mind of man. Certainly there are spots which inevitably attach to themselves an atmosphere of holiness and goodness; it might not then be too fanciful to say that some houses are born bad. Hill House, whatever the cause, has been unfit for human habitation for upwards of twenty years."'

FROM *THE HAUNTING OF HILL HOUSE* BY SHIRLEY JACKSON

'In a very real way, in spite of fine acting, fine direction, and the marvellous black and white photography of David Boulton, what we have in the Wise film is one of the world's few radio horror movies. Something is scratching at that ornate, panelled door, something horrible... but it is a door Wise elects never to open.'

Stephen King on
The Haunting

Top and above: *The Haunting.*

'There was a huge flurry of negative, very venomous letters,' remembers Joanne. 'You can't wade through that much venom without having a little bit of it stick to you. I think Shirley probably must have been unavoidably hurt by some of them.'

Suffering from bouts of depression and anxiety, Shirley Jackson left her final novel, the semi-autobiographical *Come Along with Me*, unfinished when she had a fatal heart attack in 1965 at the age of forty-five. The story of a middle-aged New England woman investigating the occult, it was included by her husband in a posthumous collection in 1968.

'I think Shirley Jackson's art was to tickle that nerve to remind you that at any moment the uncontrollable could start,' says Barry.

'After her death,' adds Sarah, 'her agent sent us a letter she had received a few days after Shirley died, in which she said: "I'm going to be doing something very different soon, and I'll be in touch."'

> 'My name is Mary Katherine Blackwood. I am eighteen years old, and I live with my sister Constance. I have often thought that with my luck at all I could have been born a werewolf, because the two middle fingers on both my hands are the same length, but I have had to be content with what I had. I dislike washing myself, and dogs, and noise. I like my sister Constance, and Richard Plantagenet, and Amanita phalloides, the death-cap mushroom. Everyone else in our family is dead.'
>
> FROM *WE HAVE ALWAYS LIVED IN THE CASTLE*
> BY SHIRLEY JACKSON

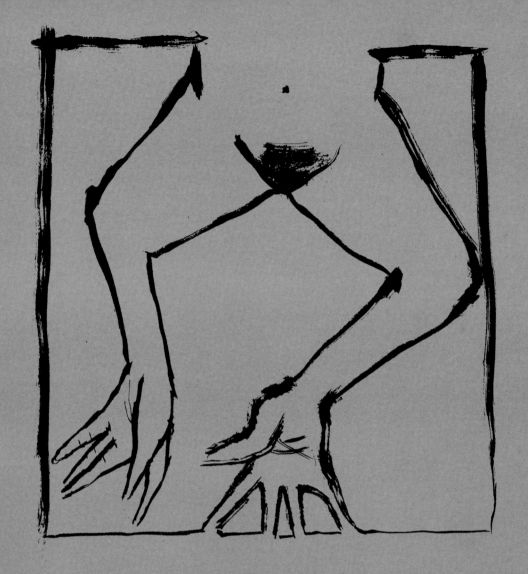

T For Torso

T

NOTHING REDUCES US TO the status of slaves quicker than sex. Which is, of course, part of the fun. Men do what they do and women do what they do – but women know their bodies are battle-grounds, and men know that they do very ugly things in the name of control...

The torso can be both a work of art and of horror. It denies personality, and without qualms focuses our thoughts on a limbless vulnerable sexuality. The torso in the picture frame, or on the pedestal, is a captive figure made subject to our will, to our fantasies.

Jennifer Chambers Lynch, the daughter of maverick film-maker David Lynch and the writer-director of the controversial *Boxing Helena* (1993), admits: 'I myself am obsessed with the torso – male and female – so I think that it is a phenomenal shape. It does so many things, it holds so many things, and it holds, interestingly enough, the parts of us that are most instinctual. The brain is excluded, the legs don't matter, the arms don't matter, but the genitals and heart are as vague as we are at times but have their purpose.

'I started this obsession with the Venus de Milo because my grandmother had a small statuette of it in her home, and I thought: "Well, what if this man in this story was obsessed with this statue and what if it was primarily due to the fact that it never hit him, it never struck out at him or moved away from him, it simply looked down at him lovingly and was easily embraced." So the Venus de Milo came into it and I thought, rather than tearing her apart, what if you simply moulded her into something that didn't make him afraid and didn't go away, as maybe his family had done. So of that was born *Boxing Helena*.

'I felt it had to be a love story,' continues Chambers Lynch. 'It can't be a horror film, and it can't be about condoning the act that takes place. It's more of an invitation to try something magical and different, rather than what it could have been: a very horrifying, degrading picture to women.

'I do think that when men are trying to

BOXING HELENA

USA, 1993. Dir: Jennifer Chambers Lynch. With: Julian Sands, Sherilyn Fenn, Bill Paxton, Kurtwood Smith, Art Garfunkel, Betsy Clark. Main Line Pictures. Colour.

Humiliated by his mother as a child, voyeuristic surgeon Dr Nick Cavanaugh (Sands) is obsessed with the beautiful Helena (Fenn), whom he worships. When she rejects his advances, he imprisons her and amputates her limbs, turning her into a living torso subject to his power and fantasies. In astute career moves, Madonna and Kim Basinger both turned down the titular role, and despite Sands' compulsively neurotic mad doctor, the film doesn't have the courage of its convictions and cops out with an 'it was all a dream' ending. S.J.

SHERILYN FENN · JULIAN SANDS
BILL PAXTON

Boxing Helena

A JENNIFER LYNCH FILM

Beyond love, beyond obsession, there hides something beyond reason.

'We're all Peeping Toms at heart. Some people, regardless of my attempts to make it *not* a horror film, are going to find it horrifying.'
Jennifer Chambers Lynch

Left: Jennifer Chambers Lynch behind-the-scenes on the set of *Boxing Helena*.

Above: David Cronenberg (left) and Clive Barker behind-the-scenes on *Nightbreed* (1990).

dissect or figure out women,' she says, 'it is ultimately impossible for them to exclude the physicalities of what the women are and their initial drive to be inside them, to fill them up, to encircle them and keep them.'

Nineteenth century medical paintings reveal a repressed eroticism as the scalpel-wielding surgeon peers into the bodily recesses of passive nude females. The all-powerful male voyaged into the hitherto unknown female interior. The new disciplines of dissection and gynaecology cast surgeons as colonizing and conquering heroes.

Within contemporary horror, nobody explores the theme of bodily violation more incisively than the Canadian director David Cronenberg.

Cronenberg's *Dead Ringers* (1988) delves into the lives

T

'David Cronenberg's public persona, struck me as being perfect for the role of a psychopathic analyst! He's so witty, he's so erudite, he's so urbane, and yet the movies he makes are visceral and dark and gut-wrenching.'

Clive Barker

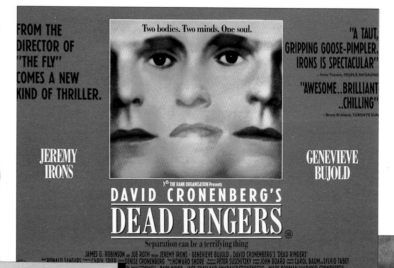

DEAD RINGERS

Canada, 1988. Dir: David Cronenberg. With: Jeremy Irons, Genevieve Bujold, Heidi von Palleske, Barbara Gordon, Shirley Douglas, Stephen Lack. Twentieth Century Fox/Rank. Colour.

In Cronenberg's dark, disturbing psychological thriller, Irons gives a remarkably powerful performance in the dual roles of twin gynaecologists Beverly and Elliot Mantle who are obsessed with the mysteries of sex and anatomy. When they begin to share the affections of an ageing actress, Claire Niveau (Bujold), their self-control begins to slip away and they discover that brothers who share everything must also share madness. Lee Wilson's seamless optical effects are incredible to watch. Based on the book *Twins* by Bari Wood and Jack Geasland, it has the offbeat Cronenberg touches – such as the bizarre 'surgical instruments for mutant women' – and remains one of the director's most disturbing works to date. *S.J.*

Above right:
Dead Ringers.

of identical twin gynaecologists. It's a contemporary take on that most familiar of horror motifs: the mad scientist and his female victim.

'I think of *Dead Ringers* as a real departure,' says Cronenberg. '*Dead Ringers* is not science fiction, and the fantasy element, which is in most of my films, is not there. The film is much more naturalistic.'

Addicted to barbiturates, Cronenberg's gynaecologists sink into madness, a madness reflected in their terrifying surgical instruments.

'The art of *The Fly* (1986) was to make the fantasy seem absolutely real. The challenge of *Dead Ringers* is the reverse – to make the realistic seem fantastic. I've always wanted to do a picture about twins, but I did not want any part of the standard twin premise – the psychotic twin versus the virtuous one.'

Banned from practising as gynaecologists, Cronenberg's fictional twins begin to regress back to childhood. Finally, in a chilling parody of a Caesarean section, one of the twins operates on the other, for the first time turning their instruments on a male torso.

'The image I keep seeing when I think of *Dead Ringers* is all of those tools,' says Chambers Lynch. 'I think that there is a fascination with how it all works, why it all works that way.'

'Gynaecology is such a beautiful metaphor for the mind/body split,' says Cronenberg. 'I think the movie is disturbing because it's all existential fear and terror: the evanescence of our lives and the fragility of our own mental states, and therefore the fragility of reality.

'One of our touchstones for reality is our bodies. And yet they are by definition ephemeral. So to whatever degree we centre our reality – and our understanding of reality – in our bodies, we are surrendering that sense of reality in our bodies' ephemerality. By affecting the body – whether it's with TV, drugs (invented or otherwise) – you alter your reality.

'What makes gynaecology icky for people is the formality of it,' continues Cronenberg. 'The woman is paying the gynaecologist – let's say it's a man – and allowing him to have intimate knowledge of her sexual organs, which are normally reserved for lovers and husbands. Everyone agrees to suppress any element of eroticism, emotion, passion, intimacy.'

David Cronenberg loosely based *Dead Ringers* on a magazine article he had read in which journalist Ron Rosenbaum reported on the true-life story of Cyril and Stewart Marcus. These twin gynaecologists killed themselves with a drug overdose in July 1975, and were found dead in their New York apartment in bizarre circumstances.

'It was front page news when it first happened,' says Rosenbaum, 'and I think what made it a distinctive kind of story was these were extremely highly respected doctors at one of the most prestigious teaching hospitals in America, and basically they were found dead and naked amid junk food wrappers, garbage that had been there for a couple of weeks.'

As Cronenberg recalls, 'I first heard about the Marcus twins through a blurb in the paper: "Twin

> 'A woman's parts could indeed become perfect. He believed this or he wouldn't have become an Ob-gyn. Once, just once, he saw the perfectly formed part of a virginal female. In medical school. A cadaver. She was seventeen. Not an attractive girl in death. But her parts were without comparison. Almost too painful to dissect, he considered removing the entire area and saving it in a jar of formaldehyde, but there would have been repercussions.'
>
> FROM 'PRECIOUS' BY ROBERTA LANNES

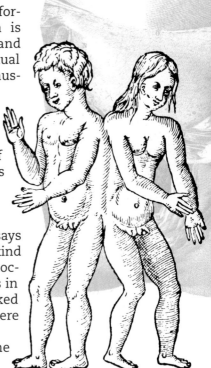

T

Below: *The Brood.*

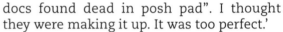
docs found dead in posh pad". I thought they were making it up. It was too perfect.'

'They were widely considered to be quite brilliant doctors,' says Rosenbaum. 'They had Park Avenue offices, very prestigious New York hospital connections. They were at the very top of their profession and they were doing work that was really the beginning of the baby boom fertility craze, which became very big in the 1980s. They were on the cutting edge of that. It was science and it was magic and what was almost a kind of cult surrounded them.

'We were able to reconstruct the basic pattern of their final days,' Rosenbaum continues. 'One twin, Cyril, was failing toward the end, and Stewart would show up and take his appointments. One woman, whose pregnancy they had helped nurse along, had a miscarriage and one of the twins called her up and shouted at her, abused her, almost as if it were her fault for losing the baby.

'Stewart eventually began to earn money by doing abortions, which was lucrative and called for less skill and less patient contact. It was in a way ironic because their lives had been devoted to fertility and now they were aborting babies.'

'I can imagine a world in which identical twins are only a concept, like mermaids,' says Cronenberg. 'The fact that Elliot and Beverly are identical twins is their evolution into something monstrous. They are creatures as exotic as *The Fly*.'

U For Unborn

BIRTH AND SEX HAVE this in common: a system of ruthless biological machinery that has absolute control of us. In a moment we are reduced to the status of slaves, which is part of the joy and part of the horror. Sex or birth, either they function according to plan, which is awesome, or they go wrong, which is the stuff of nightmares. When human flesh reproduces itself, horror is always waiting by the bed...

In the past, over a third of women died in hospital in vain attempts to give birth. A woman might well fear as much for herself as for her unborn child. And there were other fears. In a more religious age, devils and demons were the stuff of real belief. Could a woman deliver the spawn of the supernatural? The nightmare of the incubus was never far away, nor were its monstrous children. Today there are new fears: the reproductive process is haunted by genetic engineering and pharmaceutical disasters.

Modern anxieties combine with fears that are much more ancient in Ira Levin's 1967 novel, *Rosemary's Baby*, subsequently made into a classic movie by Roman Polanski.

'I thought, well I want this woman to have a child that the reader knows is not what she's expecting,' explains Levin, 'but I didn't want to get into a realistic situation with birth defects and all because that is not the stuff of entertainment as I see it. So the choices seemed to be either something from outer space or from Satan.'

'I think when a woman chooses to have a child,' says Californian horror writer Roberta Lannes, 'and she really thinks about who she is mating with: "Who is this man? Where does he come from? When his sperm meets my egg, what's going to happen?", she really doesn't know. There is a moment of very old, dark fear. Something that is as huge as the universe, as vast and mysterious and, at the same time, it's very simple and frightening.'

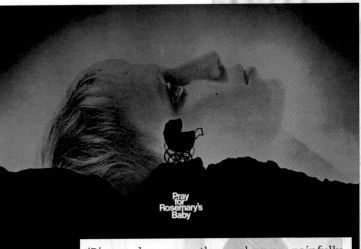

Pray for Rosemary's Baby

> 'Levin's books are constructed as neatly as an elegant house of cards; pull one plot twist, and everything comes tumbling down.'
>
> Stephen King

'Bigger he was than always; painfully, wonderfully big. He lay forward upon her, his other arm sliding under her back to hold her, his broad chest crushing her breasts. (He was wearing, because it was to be a costume party, a suit of coarse leathery armour.) Brutally, rhythmically, he drove his new hugeness. She opened her eyes and looked into yellow furnace-eyes, smelled sulphur and tannis root, felt wet breath on her mouth, heard lust-grunts and the breathing of onlookers. *This is no dream*, she thought. *This is real, this is happening.*'

FROM *ROSEMARY'S BABY* BY IRA LEVIN

Opposite: Mia Farrow in
Rosemary's Baby.

ROSEMARY'S BABY

USA, 1968. Dir: Roman Polanski. With: Mia Farrow, John Cassavetes, Ruth Gordon, Sidney Blackmer, Maurice Evans, Ralph Bellamy. Paramount. Colour.

Classic contemporary witchcraft chiller based on Ira Levin's bestselling novel. Polanski's direction plays down some of the supernatural elements of the book and replaces them with subtle menace, as Rosemary and Guy Woodhouse (Farrow and Cassavetes) move into a rambling apartment building in central Manhattan. But as their lives increasingly revolve around the flamboyant old couple next door, Minnie and Roman Castevet (Gordon and Blackmer in his last film), Rosemary begins to suspect that they want the baby she is carrying. The fine supporting cast includes veteran Bellamy as a menacing doctor, Elisha Cook Jr as the apartment manager, plus Maurice Evans, Patsy Kelly, Victoria Vetri (here billed as Angela Dorian), Charles Grodin, the voice of Tony Curtis and a nice cameo by producer William Castle. The dream sequence in which Rosemary is raped by the Devil was originally cut for the UK release, but was restored in later TV prints. The downbeat ending has the witches winning. S.J.

Sequel: *Look What's Happened to Rosemary's Baby* (TV, Dir: Sam O'Steen, 1976).

Right: Ira Levin, author of *Rosemary's Baby* and its sequel *Son of Rosemary*.

In Levin's novel, the love-making between Rosemary and her husband Guy, sanctioned by God in their marriage, becomes the channel for the Devil to plant his satanic seed.

'She was brought up in a strict Catholic household,' says Levin about his character, 'a large family with many sisters and brothers, and she was brought up to be a good, obedient girl.'

'During the time that the book came out,' continues Lannes, 'people were questioning religious values, and they were asking themselves politically, too, where they stood. And the book shocked a lot of people who wouldn't have connected religion in the same ways Ira Levin did.

'He made us think about how religion ties us, binds us to certain values – even if we question them, even if we are forced to look at them in ways we never have before. It becomes part of us. It is as archaic as our fears and our anxieties.'

'Rosemary's Baby was written and published at

the time the God-is-dead tempest was whirling around in the teapot of the 1960s,' says Stephen King, 'and the book deals with questions of faith in an unpretentious but thoughtful and intriguing way.'

At the novel's end, Rosemary gives birth to the Devil's child, a moment of horror that is also one of revelation.

'Basically, Rosemary has given birth to the comic-book version of Satan,' says King, 'the L'il Imp we were all familiar with as children and who sometimes put in an appearance in the motion picture cartoons, arguing with a L'il Angel over the main character's head. Levin broadens the satire by giving us a satanist coven comprised almost entirely of old people; they argue constantly in their waspy voices about how the baby should be cared for.'

'Pregnancy is the ultimate creative act,' says Levin. 'Having come through it, I think it gave her a great strength and courage. It's kind of like the maternal instinct takes over and she is going to defend that child and make that child as healthy as she possibly can.'

'She now looks at this baby and all of her Catholic beliefs come into fashion,' Lannes explains. 'In the beginning it made her frightened, but she doesn't question anything any more. What gave her faith to carry this child to term, and ultimately to look at this child and want to care for it, was that Catholicism, was that link to spirit. So it created a kind of circle that closed itself, but it made a lot of people uncomfortable because you have to ask yourself, "What will you do in the name of religion?"'

'My wife, raised in the Catholic Church, claims that the book is also a religious comedy with its own shaggy-dog punchline,' says King. '*Rosemary's Baby*, she claims, only proves what the Catholic Church has said about mixed marriages all along – they just don't work.' *It's Alive* was one of the top-grossing movies in America in 1974. It told the story of a man-eating baby, the pitiful result of a poorly-tested pharmaceutical drug.

'The difference

'As a writer of fantasy, I cannot conceive of any way in which *Rosemary's Baby* could be improved. It is, for this reviewer, one of the very finest fantasy films ever made.'

Harlan Ellison

'She reached out to him, her knife turning away; his lips pouted and he opened his eyes and looked at her. His eyes were golden-yellow, all golden-yellow, with neither whites nor irises; all golden-yellow, with vertical black-slit pupils.'

FROM *ROSEMARY'S BABY* BY IRA LEVIN

'"How many mothers have died at the birth of their children? How many have suckled strange little improbabilities who cause death one way or another? Strange, red little creatures with brains that work in a bloody darkness we can't even guess at. Elemental little brains, aswarm with racial memory, hatred, and raw cruelty, with no more thought than self-preservation. And self-preservation in this case consisted of eliminating a mother who realized what a horror she had birthed. I ask you, doctor, what is there in the world more selfish than a baby? Nothing!"'

FROM 'THE SMALL ASSASSIN' BY RAY BRADBURY

193

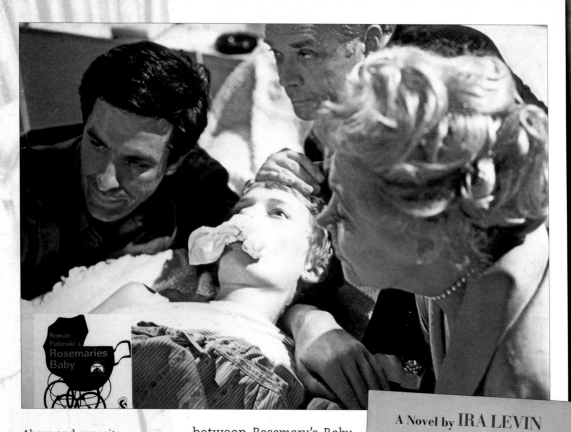

Above and opposite:
Rosemary's Baby.

A Novel by IRA LEVIN

"A darkly brilliant tale of modern deviltry that, like James'
TURN OF THE SCREW, induces the reader to believe the
unbelievable. I believed it and was altogether enthralled."

— TRUMAN CAPOTE

Rosemary's Baby

BY THE AUTHOR OF
A KISS BEFORE
DYING

between *Rosemary's Baby* and *It's Alive* is that *Rosemary's Baby* is a pure fantasy,' says *It's Alive* director Larry Cohen. 'I mean, who is really going to give birth to the Devil's child? It's one of my favourite movies and I watch it all the time, but *It's Alive* was trying to deal with something that people really do come up against. Many people do have children with defects, and in their hearts they may wish this child had never been born.

'Now they are starting to talk about being able to identify a murder gene that makes someone potentially a killer, so you could actually predict your child was going to be a potential murderer. Then do you want to have that child or not?'

Roman Polanski's **Rosemaries Baby**

SELECTED FILMS OF LARRY COHEN (b 1938)

Dial Rat for Terror (1972), *It's Alive* (1973), *God Told Me To* (aka *Demon*; 1977), *The Private Files of J. Edgar Hoover* (1978), *It Lives Again* (aka *It's Alive II*; 1978), *Full Moon High* (1981), *Q* (aka *Q – The Winged Serpent*; 1982), *Special Effects* (1984), *The Stuff* (1985), *It's Alive III Island of the Alive* (1986), *A Return to Salem's Lot* (1987), *Maniac Cop* (writer only, 1988), *The Wicked Stepmother* (1988), *Maniac Cop 2* (writer only, 1990), *The Ambulance* (1990), *Maniac Cop 3: Badge of Silence* (writer only, 1992), *Body Snatchers* (co-story only, 1993).

'Cohen's movies can still not be mistaken for anyone else's. He is still a developing, surprising talent, and it is unlikely that he will restrict himself to the horror genre in the future, but the Messianic monsters of his films are too strong to be entirely deserted.'

Kim Newman

In *It's Alive* we see the ultimate wayward child. 'Where did we go wrong?' becomes an understatement, as the delinquent baby leaves a trail of mayhem and murder wherever he crawls.

It's Alive

USA, 1973. Dir: Larry Cohen. With: John Ryan, Sharon Farrell, Andrew Duggan, Guy Stockwell, James Dixon, Michael Ansara. Warner Bros/Larco Productions. Colour.

After taking a new drug, Lenore Davies (Farrell) gives bloody birth to a murderous mutant baby (created by make-up effects designer Rick Baker) which quickly slaughters all the medical staff in the delivery room before making its escape. While her husband Frank (Ryan) tries to hold his family together and stop the police from killing his misunderstood offspring, the City of Los Angeles finds itself battling a new breed of terrifying toddlers. Cohen's witty and subversive screenplay lifts this low-budget chiller above the level of its monster movie origins. Music score by the great Bernard Herrmann.

Sequels: *It Lives Again* (aka *It's Alive II*; Dir: Larry Cohen, 1978); *It's Alive III Island of the Alive* (Dir: Larry Cohen, 1986).

'At the time that we made the picture,' continues Cohen, 'it was the drug era and parents were looking at their kids who were suddenly coming home with long hair, smoking grass, taking LSD and talking strangely, listening to music that the parents didn't understand. The parents didn't understand who was in their house, how this person came about. This wasn't the child they raised. And in a number of cases fathers actually killed their children, shot their teenage sons who came home stoned and the parents were terrified. So when I saw parents actually killing their own children, I said "Well, you know, you wake up one morning and you get the impression that you have a monster living in your home, and it was your child and it's changed into something else that you don't know, a stranger that you're afraid of."

'So these were the things that were happening in America at the time when I took this idea that I first cooked up at the age of ten, and added all the other elements together, and this is what we ended up with.'

'I figure, if people read about a picture with a monster baby or a big bird in the Chrysler Building or an ice cream that's eating people, they say, "That sounds like a Larry Cohen picture." That's what we want.'

Larry Cohen

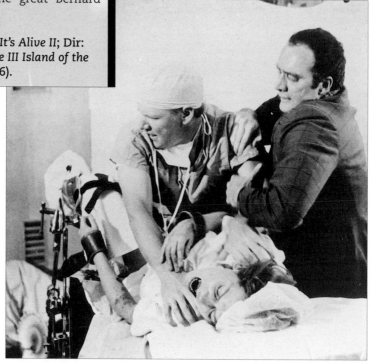

V For Vice Versa

V

'To be able to fly? To be smoke, or a wolf; to know the night, and live in it forever? That's not so bad. You call us monsters but when you dream it's of flying and changing, and living without death...'

Rachel in *Nightbreed*

HELLBOUND HELLRAISER II

UK/USA, 1988. Dir: Tony Randel. With: Clare Higgins, Ashley Laurence, Kenneth Cranham, Imogen Boorman, Sean Chapman, Doug Bradley. New World Pictures/ Cinemarque/Film Futures. Colour.

Uneven sequel to Clive Barker's box office hit *Hellraiser* (1987), helped by some impressive special effects, including some striking matte paintings of an Escher-like Hell. Most of the cast from the first film return, and the story picks up a couple of hours after the end of the original. Following her encounters with the demonic Cenobites, Kirsty Cotton (Laurence) is a patient at the Channard Institute, a hospital for the mentally disturbed. But Dr Channard (Cranham) is prepared to go to any lengths to unlock the secrets of the Outer Darkness. He succeeds in releasing the flayed remains of Julia Cooton (Higgins), Kirsty's hammer-wielding stepmother, and together they travel to Hell to confront the awesome powers of its omnipotent master, Leviathan. Higgins is as coldly menacing as ever, and Cranham is a welcome addition as the mad doctor who gets even more than he expected. Director Randel ensures that it all looks good, but post-production tinkering only confuses Peter Atkins's carefully constructed script (based on a story by Barker). *S.J.*

Sequels: *Hellraiser III Hell on Earth* (Dir: Anthony Hickox, 1992); *Hellraiser: Bloodline* (Dir: Alan Smithee [Kevin Yagher and Joe Chappelle], 1996).

Opposite: The inimitable Pinhead in *Hellbound Hellraiser II*.

ONE OF THE THINGS we are most afraid of is spawning a monster. But for some of us, monsters are welcome opportunities to be different, to act in anti-normal ways, hideous and beautiful at the same time...

Everything is in flux, everything changes. The body changes. The soul changes. We are capable of extraordinary change, internal self-transformation, which is manifested very often in my stories as physical shape-shifting.

The fiction of the fantastic brims with metaphors for this condition: tales of people whose cells are protean and souls migrant, people called by mysterious forces to a place they've visited in other lives or states; a place never understood – at least until the moment of crisis – as their real home.

If you'll forgive me, I thought I might say a little about some of my own work and its sequels – a small indulgence perhaps. In my early works, the *Books of Blood* (1984–85), I tried to address a number of issues, and there were some that kept cropping up again and again. The issues of transformation, of paradox and gender ambiguity. Sex and transformation can go nicely together. The reconfiguring of the virginal woman into lustful vampire contains more than just the seeds of eroticism.

The looks of a beautiful woman don't keep for ever in spite of make-up and plastic surgery. In our culture, becoming old is synonymous with being monstrous. But why should becoming monstrous be any less fun? Is the life of the vampire so bad? A life that offers new worlds, new pleasures, new experiences and, above all – immortality. In the sequel to my film *Hellraiser* (1987), screen-

writer Peter Atkins has our protagonist, Julia, come back from Hell, immortal, erotic and filled with new power – the woman with everything, except her skin.

'*Hellraiser* is about a hedonist achieving what he desired and finding out that it wasn't what he wanted,' explains Atkins, 'and the sequel is about a voyeur who is also disappointed when he achieves what he thinks he wants.

'Julia undergoes both a physical transformation and, if you like, a spiritual transformation. The most striking thing obviously is that she spends the first portion of the movie in which she appears without her skin. But what

THE FILMS OF CLIVE BARKER (b 1952)

Salome (8mm short, 1973/95), *The Forbidden* (16mm short, 1975-1978/95), *Underworld* (aka *Transmutations;* co-scriptwriter, 1985), *Rawhead Rex* (scriptwriter, 1986), *Hellraiser* (1987), *Hellbound Hellraiser II* (exec prod, 1988), *Nightbreed* (1990), *Candyman* (exec prod, 1992), *Hellraiser III Hell on Earth* (exec prod, 1992), *Sleepwalkers* (actor only, 1992), *Lord of Illusions* (1995), *Candyman: Farewell to the Flesh* (exec prod, 1996), *Hellraiser: Bloodline* (exec prod, 1996), *The Shining* (actor only, 1997), *Quicksilver Highway* (orig story/actor, 1997), *The Thief of Always* (exec prod, 1997).

Above: David Cronenberg (left) and Clive Barker behind-the-scenes on *Nightbreed*.
Opposite: *Hellraiser*.

> 'Much of the sex in horror fiction is deeply involved in power tripping, it's sex based upon relationships where one partner is largely under the control of the other; sex that almost inevitably leads to some bad end.'
>
> Stephen King

is also happening in terms of her character, is that she's very much embracing her altered state. Not as somebody who has been merely a victim of this stuff, but as somebody who has, in a very real way, been fulfilled by it.'

'In Barker's tales the easy mutability of the human form opens up the possibility of rebirth,' says critic Michael A. Morrison, 'at least for those willing to face his myriad marvels, mysteries and monsters. The final state of Barker's transformed is often one of certain identity but uncertain form.

'In story after story, Barker transfigures, re-sexes,

Below: *Hellbound
Hellraiser II.*
Opposite: Clive Barker's
cover painting for *Books
of Blood Volume 5.*

de-evolves, or reintegrates the corporeal form into
bizarre post-human configurations that are often barely
recognizable as once having been a man or woman.
Character after character willingly – sometimes jubi-
lantly – sheds the familiar contours of the human for the
shapes of nightmare and so gains entry to a new life and,
perhaps, a new community.'

To men, women can be both the object of fear and

**'Clive's original wish
was that Julia from
Hellraiser would be
the monster. She'd be
the Freddy Krueger of
the *Hellraiser* series
and Pinhead and the
Cenobites would sort
of be background
monsters... What
happened, of course,
was the public got in
the way. They fell in
love with Pinhead.'**

Peter Atkins

desire. Their beauty, their sexuality attracts. But their
power over us when we are at our most vulnerable can
create fear. It's paradox – and I love paradox. Most horror
fiction presents deviation from the human form as
frightening and aberrant. But what if a character does
not deviate from the human form, but merely flips it, say
from a man to a woman? Sexual transformation is both
the stuff of our fantasies and of terror. In my short story
'The Madonna' (1985) I wanted to look at sexual paradox
and transformation.

'The Madonna' is a story of another species of
women, high priestesses to an ancient goddess of fecun-
dity. These women have made their home in an urban
environment, a disused public swimming pool.

From here they seduce men, entice them for sex,
which is performed ritually before their goddess. The

V

Madonna in turn gives birth from her strange glutinous body to monstrous children, whom the priestesses feed from blood-stained breasts. The men, the ex-lovers, leave with little memory of the event, a memory that is re-awakened later, however, when they find themselves turning into women.

There are two characters to whom this transformation happens. One invites the paradox and is prepared to follow it into new realms, new worlds of experience. The other, Garvey, is a man who always loved women but cannot face the notion of being one. It's an assault on more than his manliness – it's an assault on his very being.

'The Madonna was giving birth. The swollen flesh was opening; liquid light gushing; the smell of smoke and blood filled the shower-room. A girl gave a cry, as in sympathy with the Madonna. The applause mounted, and suddenly the slit spasmed and delivered the child – something between a squid and a shorn lamb – onto the tiles. The water from the pipes slapped it into consciousness immediately, and it threw back its head to look about it; its single eye vast and perfectly lucid. It squirmed on the tiles for a few moments before the girl at Jerry's side stepped forward into the veil of water and picked it up. Its toothless mouth sought out her breast immediately. The girl delivered it to her tit.'

FROM 'THE MADONNA' BY CLIVE BARKER

'Sexuality is all too often the territory of the sentimentalist or the pornographer, too seldom that of the visionary. Yet it's a transforming act, literally. It remakes our bodies, for a time; and our minds, too. For a little space we know obsession intimately; we are at the call of chemical instructions which sharpen our senses while at the same time narrowing our focus, so that our perceptions are heightened and refined.'

Clive Barker

What does he do? How does he deal with that transformation? Now there's the metaphor, there's the problem. But he does have a solution. So those metaphors are about sexuality, they are about old age, they are about loneliness, they are about disease. They are about all the things that have always haunted horror stories.

According to Michael Morrison, many of my characters 'must at one time or another confront the monstrous, either in themselves or in someone they know well. Those who survive respond with curiosity, fascination, sometimes even joy – and always with a willingness to look horror in the face; to see, to *know*, even the most terrible of marvels, and through knowing, to become. For some the transformative journey resolves the chronic uncertainty of their precarious identity – often by simply allowing the (monstrous) buried true self to emerge.

'The journey to "a new kind of life", with death or

Above: The mutants of *Underworld*.
Opposite: The shape-changing Boone in *Nightbreed*.

'Once upon a time the Bad Place was seen by critics as symbolic of the womb – a primarily sexual symbol which perhaps allowed the Gothic to become a safe way of talking about sexual fears.'
Stephen King

EVIL COMES WHEN YOU CALL HIS NAME

CANDYMAN

FAREWELL TO THE FLESH

'Let's put subtext aside for a moment and consider the creature that cavorts at the centre of any horror movie: the monster. The leader of Hell's Sadean order of Cenobites, ol' Pinhead himself. But where, I am regularly asked, does this nightmare come from? Well, I've already made mention of the sado-masochistic elements, which reflect my own long-standing interest in such taboo areas. Associated with that milieu is the punkish influence, which makes Pinhead the Patron Saint of Piercing. But there's also a streak of priestly deportment and high-flown rhetoric in him that suggests this is a monster who knows his Milton as well as he knows his de Sade, and can probably recite the Mass in Latin (albeit backwards).'

Clive Barker

reconfiguration of the body as a common rite of passage, ends in post-human states of being that are clearly preferable to the desolate banality of twentieth-century middle-class society, at least as rendered by Clive Barker. For his protagonists, as for few in contemporary horror, the status quo of that society is neither re-established nor reaffirmed. Freed from constraints, connections and commitments, they flee into worlds of monsters, miracles and revelations.'

W For Window

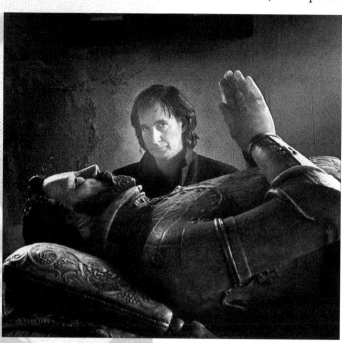

Above: Simon Marsden. Opposite: Edgar Allan Poe.

ORROR RETURNS AGAIN AND again to the torments of time – an unbearable present, an unpredictable future, an inescapable past. Every second of our lives it pulls on us like gravity, claiming us for death. But it also promises something much worse – hope, the feeling that in time we may cheat the inevitable...

When Edgar Allan Poe (1809–49) died of drink and despair in Baltimore, there was little left of him but an old coat, some unpaid bills and some of the most feverish, compelling and horrific literature in the English language. His writing has inspired movies, poetry, theatre, painting – and the photographer Simon Marsden.

In 1980, Marsden published his book of photographs, *In Ruins: The Once Great Houses of Ireland*. He followed it up with such volumes as *The Haunted Realm: Ghosts, Witches and Other Strange Tales*, *Phantom of the Isles: Further Tales from The Haunted Realm*, *The Journal of a Ghost Hunter* and, most recently, *Visions of Poe*.

The photographer's family owned a large fishing fleet in Grimsby, on England's east coast. Along with his elder brother and sister, he spent his childhood living in two archaic houses, both of them reputed to be haunted. Both his father and brother were avid readers of ghost stories, and he acquired his family's library of books about the supernatural.

'From the time I first read Poe,' says the photographer, 'which was at ten or eleven years old, I was immediately excited by his work. I was brought up in old crumbling mansions with vast parklands and overgrown graveyards, grinning gargoyles – all this imagery that I now photograph has always been with me. So Poe has somehow stuck with me as a fellow traveller. In the books I've done, travelling, photographing such Gothic mansions and graveyards, I've always kept him somewhere in my memory.

'The strange thing was that when I was asked to illustrate a book of Poe's works, I found that I already had most of the pictures. I already had grotesque gargoyles

and crumbling mansions and overgrown graveyards. I only really had to take maybe four or five more to complete the book, and it was at this point that I saw the affinity that was there.

'I identified with his tortured imagination, his romantic view of the world. My own particular way of dealing with these internal ghosts is to photograph such places and to make books out of them, to exhibit the photographs. I feel that perhaps I am exorcizing myself by doing this. I suppose I want other people to know just what it is that I am feeling and why I should be so alienated from this world.'

On his twenty-first birthday, Marsden's father, himself a keen amateur photographer, gave his son a camera. 'I instantly became "hooked" on photography,' he admits. 'What intrigued me was the magic of time and light and the enigma of "reality" that these elements conjured up. The first roll of film that I shot was of cardboard cut-outs of ghosts that I arranged in tableaux in the gardens.'

After a lengthy stay in America, he decided to return to the British Isles and subsequently embarked on an ambitious project, photographing haunted locations and ancient ruins. In the course of more than twenty years he has photographed many thousands of old buildings. Using mostly infra-red film, his pictures wreathe the haunted houses, castles, chapels and ruins of Britain and Ireland in an almost supernatural patina.

'In my photographs it's like having a canvas,' explains Marsden. 'Then back in the darkroom I begin to fantasize on the negative or on the print and I make these houses even more fantastic, even more mysterious, even more frightening. I'm really getting my ghosts out of myself and putting them into the photographs.

'Through my photographs, I hope that the viewer will experience a feeling of timelessness, and hopefully this might make them see that not everything is as it seems; that our so-called reality is not really reality at all, and that life can be anything they want to make it.

'I now realize that I am obsessed by the search for the perfect ruin, always the one that is more fantastic than the next. I also know that I will never find it. But I must go on searching, it's there within me. These houses, for me anyway, are vast tombs. Man comes and goes, but

Opposite: Whitby Abbey, North Yorkshire by Simon Marsden.

'During the whole of a dull, dark, and soundless day in the autumn of the year, when the clouds hung oppressively low in the heavens, I had been passing alone, on horseback, through a singularly dreary tract of country, and at length found myself, as the shades of the evening drew on, within view of the melancholy House of Usher. I know not how it was – but, with the first glimpse of the building, a sense of insufferable gloom pervaded my spirit... I looked upon the scene before me – upon the mere house, and the simple landscape features of the domain – upon the bleak walls – upon the vacant eye-like windows – upon a few rank sedges – and upon a few white trunks of decayed trees – with an utter depression of soul.'

FROM 'THE FALL OF THE HOUSE OF USHER' BY EDGAR ALLAN POE

'These bizarre conceptions, so awkward in unskilful hands, become under Poe's spell living and convincing terrors to haunt our nights, and all because the author understood so perfectly the very mechanics and physiology of fear and strangeness – the essential details to emphasize, the precise incongruities and conceits to select as preliminaries or concomitants to horror.'

H.P. Lovecraft

> 'Shaking off from my spirit what *must* have been a dream, I scanned more narrowly the real aspect of the building. Its principal feature seemed to be that of an excessive antiquity. The discoloration of ages had been great. Minute fungi overspread the whole exterior, hanging in a fine tangled web-work from the eaves. Yet all this was apart from any extraordinary dilapidation. No portion of the masonry had fallen; and there appeared to be a wild inconsistency between its still perfect adaptation of parts, and the crumbling condition of the individual stones. In this there was much that reminded me of the specious totality of old wood-work which has rotted for long years in some neglected vault, with no disturbance from the breath of the external air.'
>
> FROM 'THE FALL OF THE HOUSE OF USHER' BY EDGAR ALLAN POE

'One of the first books of *fantastique* fiction I purchased was Poe's *Tales of Mystery and Imagination*, in a paperback edition with a lurid cover. It cost, if memory serves, 2/6d. I was ten or so and this seemed a fortune. But then treasure houses are seldom cheap. And I thought, "My god! There are adults out there who have the same kind of dreams that I have. This is marvellous!"'

Clive Barker

these houses remain. Perhaps the only peace I will ever have will be within one of these houses or within the tomb.'

Author and critic Colin Wilson describes Simon Marsden as 'an explorer of the haunted realm of the human soul. His work is an attempt to capture a certain "strangeness" in the external world, which can make us suddenly aware of the strangeness of the world inside ourselves.'

'At almost exactly the same time as I first read Poe,' Marsden recalls, 'I was sent to a monastic boarding school in Yorkshire and I distinctly remember I would always pass by Allerton Park – this dark, forbidding house in the distance, with its tall towers and its air of mystery and doom. When I asked my father if he knew anything about this house, he would nonchalantly tell me it was a madhouse. As I looked at this gaunt building, so he would fire my imagination with all kinds of stories.

'It was with great excitement that I learned the history of Allerton. That it was indeed haunted, and that it had been exorcized. But the biggest chill of all was that the bodies of the ancestral family who had built the house and lived there for so long, lay buried within the crypt beneath the chapel. And that the house had recently been sold on condition that the bodies would remain there for ever more.'

Edgar Allan Poe has been called 'the father of modern horror'. He was born in Boston to parents who were itinerant actors. But the death of his mother and the desertion of his father resulted in Poe, aged three, being made the ward of a Virginia merchant, who later disowned him.

Expelled from the University of Virginia for not paying his gambling debts, and dismissed from the West Point military academy for neglect of duty, Poe finally embarked on a literary career. He

> 'I purchased and put in some repair an abbey, which I shall not name, in one of the wildest and least frequented portions of fair England. The gloomy and dreary grandeur of the building, the almost savage aspect of the domain, the many melancholy and time-honored memories connected with both, had much in unison with the feelings of utter abandonment which had driven me into that remote and unsocial region of the country.'
>
> FROM 'LIGEIA' BY EDGAR ALLAN POE

married his thirteen-year-old cousin Virginia Clemm in 1836, but she burst a blood vessel in 1842 and remained a virtual invalid until her death from tuberculosis five years later.

Poe suffered from bouts of depression and madness, and he attempted suicide in 1848. In September the following year, on his way to visit his new fiancée in Richmond, he vanished for three days and inexplicably turned up in a delirious condition in Baltimore, where he died a few days later.

'Poe's work was his life,' says Simon Marsden, 'and he never holds back anything from the reader. He lays bare his soul. Like Poe, I have been attracted to crumbling Gothic mansions and eerie graveyards – I suppose anywhere that one could say looked haunted. Haunted, of course, by the past. I personally believe that the past is so much better than the present or the future. Poe was perhaps looking to a past he'd never had. The present was certainly bleak, the future for him seemed bleak, and so the past was the only place he could look, and this decaying imagery was representative of his life.

'Poe had a particularly miserable life. Every woman he ever loved, from his mother to the cousin he was madly in love with, all died tragically. He lived in poverty for most of his life, his work was never recognized as he would have liked it to be, and this is, I think, why he revered death so much and made it into such a beautiful thing.

'The most striking thing about Poe's work is his fascination with death. Death was all around him, but he romanticized it. It was his fantasy, it was a release for him, but it was also a cry for help. I would say that Poe, in his own way, in his writing, was delving into his own darkest fears. His way of getting them out of his mind was to put them on paper, and I suppose in my photographs I'm doing very much the same.

'Macabre death images are perhaps the most shock-

Above: Frontispiece from *The Raven*.

Above: Funerary Statue,
Germany, by Simon
Marsden.

'Invention, creation,
imagination,
originality – a trait
which, in the
literature of fiction,
is positively worth
all the rest. But
the nature of the
originality, so far
as regards its
manifestation in
letters, is but
imperfectly under-
stood. '

Edgar Allan Poe

'Man doth not yield
him to the angels,
nor unto death
utterly, save only
through the
weakness of his
feeble will.'

from *Ligeia*
by Edgar Allan Poe

SELECTED WORKS BY EDGAR ALLAN POE
(1809–1849)

Tamerlane and Other Poems, By a Bostonian (1827), *Al Aaraaf, Tamerlane, and Minor Poems* (1838), *Poems* (1831), 'Metzengerstein' (1832), 'MS. Found in a Bottle' (1833), 'Morella' (1835), 'Shadow' (1835), 'Berenice' (1835), 'Loss of Breath' (1835), 'Bon-Bon' (1835), 'King Pest' (1835), 'Metzengerstein' (1836), *The Narrative of A. Gordon Pym* (unfinished, 1837), 'Ligeia' (1838), *The Conchologist's First Book* (editor, 1839), 'The Fall of the House of Usher' (1839), 'William Wilson' (1839), 'Silence' (1839), 'The Conversation of Eiros and Charmion' (1839), 'The Devil in the Belfrey' (1839), *Tales of the Grotesque and Arabesque* (1840), 'The Man of the Crowd' (1840), 'A Descent into the Maelström' (1841), 'The Murders in the Rue Morgue' (1841), 'The Island of the Fay' (1841), 'The Colloquy of Monos and Una' (1841), 'The Masque of the Red Death' (1842), 'The Mystery of Marie Rogêt' (1842–1843), 'Eleonara' (1842), 'The Oval Portrait' (1842), 'The Black Cat' (1843), 'The Gold Bug' (1843), 'The Pit and the Pendulum' (1843), *The Prose Poems of Edgar A. Poe* (1843), 'The Tell-Tale Heart' (1843), 'The Oblong Box' (1844), 'A Tale of the Ragged Mountains' (1844), 'The Balloon Hoax' (1844), 'The Elk' (1844), 'The Assignation' (aka 'The Visionary'; 1844), 'Thou Art the Man' (1844), 'The Spectacles' (1844), 'The Facts in the Case of M. Valdemar' (1845), 'The Premature Burial' (1845), 'The Purloined Letter' (1845), 'The Thousand-and-Second Tale of Scheherazade' (1845), 'The Imp of the Perverse' (1845), *The Raven and Other Poems* (1845), *Tales* (1845), 'The Cask of Amontillado' (1846), 'The Domain of Arnheim' (1847), *Eureka: A Prose Poem* (1848), 'Hop-Frog' (1849), 'Mellonta Tauta' (1849), *The Complete Works of Edgar Allan Poe* (1902), *The Letters of Edgar Allan Poe* (1948).

ing sort of images one can use,' says Marsden, 'because death is something that will come to all of us. We have no escape, and yet we have to survive before it happens. We put it to the back of our minds, but perhaps we should embrace it more as a beautiful thing, and this is something I think Poe did.

'For me, nobody makes death and decay more beautiful than Poe, and I suppose in the same sort of way, surrounded by these houses, I am somehow abandoning myself to death and the mystery and beauty of death.'

X For Xploitation

X

Opposite: Bath-time in *The Tingler*.

HORROR HAS ALWAYS DELIGHTED in its maverick status. The term 'low budget' might have been invented for the horror movie, and the same fevered imaginations that dream up these celluloid fantasies can be equally creative in getting them seen…

'The period of the fifties and sixties was a golden age for me,' says director Joe Dante. 'I was a kid in the fifties and a teenager in the sixties, when movies were still a little reticent about showing really horrible visuals. I remember going to see *The Crawling Eye* (1958), and there was a scene where all the characters were looking down at some dissolving piece of flesh or something. I remember all the kids chanting, "Show us, show us, show us!" and then they would show it and everyone went, "Ooh…" I thought, yeah, this is what movies are all about.

'It was a more innocent era, and I think of Roger Corman and William Castle and the exploitation, very low-budget, interactive kind of movies that had gimmicks – movies that had tricks, movies that kids could go to and expect the unexpected…'

Director John Landis remembers that 'the William Castle product and Roger Corman's Edgar Allan Poe films scared the shit out of me. I remember seeing *The Pit and the Pendulum* (1961) with Vincent Price and wanting to leave.'

'When I first started out,' says director Ray Dennis Steckler, 'I was trying to figure out some sort of gimmick to get the movie in the theatre, so I came up with the longest title in the world – *The Incredibly Strange Creatures Who Stopped Living and Became Mixed-Up Zombies!!?* (1963).'

'A title to a movie is everything,' agrees cinematographer turned director Ted V. Mikels, whose own films include *The Astro-Zombies* (1968) and *Blood Orgy of the She-Devils* (1973). 'Without the title, don't make the movie.'

For John Landis, classic titles include, '*I Was a Teenage*, whatever…*Frankenstein, Werewolf* and *How to Make a Monster*. That was very important with the horror movie – if you wanted to get the teenagers, use a teenage thing. In the fifties, television was keeping people home, so what they had to do was figure out how to get these young people away from that tube.'

One of Joe Dante's favourite films is *Attack of the 50 Foot Woman* (1958). 'You can't really get a much more absurd title, but in my estimation it is a nearly perfect film.

'There was a real sense of fun going to the movies in the fifties,' continues Dante, 'and it was partly because of

the rather flamboyant way in which the pictures were advertised. Movie advertising has always been a lot less sophisticated than the actual contents of movies.'

'There was a time when, if you didn't play a trailer,' says Mikels, 'you wouldn't book the film, you wouldn't play it.' To sell his 1971 movie *The Corpse Grinders,* Mikels came up with the concept, 'Cat food made from human ingredients for cats who like people. It's that simple.'

'I used to make trailers for Roger Corman,' says Dante, 'and even then I think the art of trailer making had pretty much died. The wipes and the lettering and the hyperbole and the promises and the swearing that you've never seen anything as good as this.'

Steckler agrees: 'Many times people would say the trailer's ten times better than the movie.'

'We went to the lengths of actually falsifying the plots and doing all kinds of tricks that really weren't very kosher,' continues Dante, 'but they would allow the picture to be successful for the three or four days that it was booked.'

'No matter what movie you make,' says Mikels, 'if you don't promote it and you don't tell the world about it, nobody's going to see it and you're not going to sell it.'

'I think hucksterism was part and parcel of the way these pictures were sold,' Dante agrees. 'If you just look at a press book from a popular movie of the 1950s – many, many pages, many different designs, many different ad lines, many different approaches depending on who the exhibitor felt the audience was. Now you get one ad for one movie. Unfortunately that ad, like the movie, has to appeal to the most number of people.'

A number of cinemas went out of their way

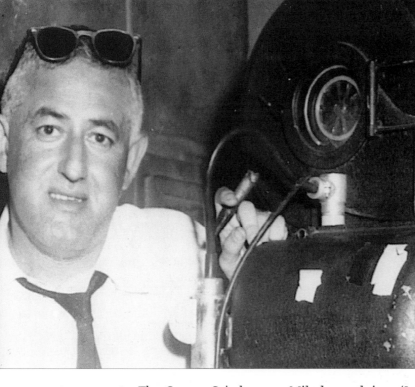

Opposite: *The She-Creature* (1956).
Left: William Castle behind-the-scenes.

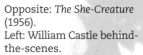

' Showmanship is an integral part of the entertainment world – you must have it. Of course, as Mr Shakespeare said, "The play is the thing" – you must have a story and a fine cast, but you have to sell and merchandise a picture and this is why I started my gimmicks. I had no cast and no money so I had to do something else to compel audiences to come into the theatre. Not having stars or a high budget I had to do something different and I became, in effect, the king of the gimmicks. I know I'm a darned good showman; no one could top my gimmicks.'

William Castle

to promote *The Corpse Grinders*, as Mikels explains: 'In some of the theatres, the managers actually constructed a makeshift corpse grinding machine and that caused a lot of attention.

'Promoting *The Worm Eaters* (1977) was one of the more real fun things we've ever done,' he continues. 'We had to steal the show. We had no budget to do it with, so I told star Herb Robins that if he would eat a worm for the press, I would eat a worm for the press, and we got news coverage you couldn't buy at any price. Gimmicks, I love gimmicks.'

The undisputed King of the Gimmicks was producer William Castle (1914–77), who raised movie showmanship to a new level. Born William Schloss, he started out directing Hollywood 'B' movies, but in the late 1950s and 1960s he produced and directed a string of successes which he promoted with cheap yet effective schemes and introduced with his ever-present cigar in the Alfred Hitchcock manner. He ended up producing such films as *Rosemary's Baby* (1968), and his 1976 autobiography was aptly entitled *Step Right Up!... I'm Gonna Scare the Pants off America*.

'I think it was William Castle who came up with a great gimmick,' says Ray Steckler, recalling Castle's 1957 movie *Macabre*. 'He was the first one to take out an insurance policy with Lloyds of London for $1000 if you died of fright.'

John Landis also fondly remembers Castle's *House on Haunted Hill* (1959), 'Where they had something called "Emergo!" and it was the tackiest thing. It was a paper skeleton on a string that came out over the audience.'

'Mine was one of the few theatres that actually had a real skeleton,' says Joe Dante. 'It came down out of the corner of the screen when Vincent Price brought out his skeleton on the screen. There were apparently very few theatres in which the skeleton survived, because once kids found out that it was happening, they would come back with slingshots and popcorn boxes. That was a pretty expensive gimmick.'

For *13 Ghosts* (1960), Castle came up with the idea of 'Illusion-O!', which involved a set of red and blue transparent plastic squares. 'I remember 3-D ghosts,' Dante continues, 'where you had Ghost-Viewers. The idea was that when the people on the screen saw the ghosts, you could put on your Ghost-Viewer.'

Ray Dennis Steckler starred in many of his own films under the name 'Cash Flagg' and soon earned his own following. 'People said, "Cash, he's that guy with those weird eyes" and "He's that guy with the hood" or whatever. So all of a sudden people started knowing Cash and they said, "Okay, Cash Flagg means this type of film."'

To promote his own films, Steckler made masks of

himself as Cash Flagg. 'We sent people out looking like me,' he explains. 'When they ran down into the audience you would see this illuminated figure coming at you.

'People would shoot you with pellet guns right in the theatre. I had to duck for my life, but it was fun. But after the pellet guns started hitting me a little bit, I said it was time to retire.'

'It's wonderful when it's so silly,' says Landis. 'The gimmick of William Castle's film *The Tingler* (1959) was to convince the audience that fear is a tangible beast. So when you are frightened, this thing grows at the base of your spine. It gets larger and larger and will kill you unless you scream.

'There's a wonderful moment when Vincent Price comes on camera and says, "The Tingler is loose in the theatre. For God's sake scream, scream for your lives!"'

'He wired every other seat with war surplus buzzers,' explains Dante, whose movie *Matinee* (1993) paid tribute to Castle's showmanship, 'and turned them on at various points in the movie.'

'So in certain first-run houses that had wired the seats,' laughs Landis, 'every fifth seat got zapped. My favourite, though, was *Mr Sardonicus* (1961).'

'*Mr Sardonicus*,' recalls Dante, 'was the first interactive motion picture where, as you came into the theatre, you

'Castle was the king of the gimmicks; he originated the $1000 "fright insurance" policy, for instance. If you dropped dead during the film, your heirs got the money. Then there was the great "Nurse on Duty at All Performances" gimmick; there was the "You *Must* Have Your Blood Pressure Taken in the Lobby Before Viewing This Horrifying Film" gimmick (that one was used as part of the *House on Haunted Hill* promo), and all sorts of other gimmicks.'

Stephen King

223

Opposite: Guy Rolfe hides behind his mask in *Mr. Sardonicus.*

MATINEE

USA, 1993. Dir: Joe Dante. With: John Goodman, Cathy Moriarty, Simon Fenton, Omri Katz, Kellie Martin, Lisa Jakub. Renfield/Universal. Colour.

Ex-*Castle of Frankenstein* contributor Dante's affectionate coming-of-age comedy, set during a Saturday matinée in Florida at the time of the 1962 Cuban Missile Crisis. With Goodman as William Castle-like showman Lawrence Woolsey premiering his film-within-a-film, *Mant!*, a parody of the monster movies of the 1950s, with its hero slowly transforming into a giant ant. With cameos by genre veterans Jesse White, Dick Miller, John Sayles, Kevin McCarthy, William Schallert, Robert Cornthwaite and Luke Halpin. S.J.

'When you play *Homicidal* at your theatre you have the greatest exploitation promotion to get you away to record business – The Fright Break. Occurring exactly 8½ minutes before the end of the picture, this sensational interlude will afford patrons who are too timid to take the climax, an opportunity of leaving the theatre.'

Homicidal campaign book

were given these fluorescent cards. There was a "Punishment Poll" at the end of *Mr Sardonicus,* and William Castle would come out on the screen and say to the audience, "At a certain point in the picture you will vote thumbs up or thumbs down," depending on whether they felt that the villain had been suitably punished. Castle would count the cards and then he'd say that Mr Sardonicus was going to die.'

'And we were morons,' Landis adds. 'We were all going thumbs down, thumbs down and, sure enough, he died.'

'Of course, there was only one ending,' laughs Dante, 'and only one piece of film with William Castle counting. They always ran the same footage at the end!'

'There are many great, wonderful horror films that were made in the fifties and sixties,' says John Landis. 'The vast majority though are dreck, and there's great enjoyment in that, too.'

Joe Dante agrees that a film does not always have to be good to be enjoyable. 'There were two different styles of monster – one was bargain basement, which you usually found at American International Pictures, where a guy named Paul Blaisdell

SELECTED FILMS OF WILLIAM CASTLE (1914–1977)

The Whistler (1944), *The Mark of the Whistler* (1944), *When Strangers Marry* (1944), *Voice of the Whistler* (1946), *Macabre* ('Insured for $1000'; 1958), *House on Haunted Hill* ('Emergo!'; 1959), *The Tingler* ('Percepto!'; 1959), *13 Ghosts* ('Illusion-O!'; 1960), *Homicidal* ('Fright Break'; 1961), *Mr Sardonicus* ('Punishment Poll'; 1961), *Zotz!* (1962), *The Old Dark House* (1962), *Thirteen Frightened Girls* (1963), *Strait-Jacket* (1964), *The Night Walker* (1964), *I Saw What You Did* (1965), *Let's Kill Uncle* (1966), *The Busy Body* (1967), *The Spirit Is Willing* (1967), *Rosemary's Baby* (producer only, 1968), *Project X* (1967), *Shanks* (1974), *Bug* (1975), *Day of the Locust* (actor only, 1975).

A MAN
SO EVIL...
HIS FACE
COULD STOP
A HEART!

COLUMBIA
PICTURES
presents

Mr.
Sardonicus

"X"

starring OSCAR HOMOLKA · RONALD LEWIS · AUDREY DALTON
and GUY ROLFE as Sardonicus

Written by RAY RUSSELL · Produced and Directed by WILLIAM CASTLE

A WILLIAM CASTLE PRODUCTION

A BLC RELEASE

HOUSE ON HAUNTED HILL

staring VINCENT PRICE · CAROL OHMART · RICHARD LONG · ALAN MARSHAL

AN ALLIED ARTISTS PICTURE · Produced and Directed by WILLIAM CASTLE · Written by ROBB WHITE

'He had a great sense of showmanship, and he was fun to work with. He had wonderful, wild ideas. I liked Bill – he was a very nice man.'

Vincent Price

'Please don't reveal the ending of *Homicidal* or your friends will kill you – if they don't, I will.'

Signed, *William Castle*

used to build them in his garage. And then there would be recycled monsters like *The She-Creature* (1956), which was used again in a movie called *Voodoo Woman* (1957), where they simply took the same suit and put a stupid wig on it.

'One of the nice things about horror movies was that they were wonderful proving grounds for people who wanted to make their early pictures. There was an adventurous spirit to monster making then, though of course now it's all computers and technology. When you look back at movies you thought were real when you were a kid, you are kind of amazed at how you forgave so many things that are very obvious – how much you wanted to be drawn into the fantasy and how much you wanted to believe it.

'Horror, as a genre, is about what really scares you,' continues Dante. 'There was a wonderful catchline, I remember, for Wes Craven's *Last House on the Left* (1972), where it said in big, bold type: "To avoid fainting keep repeating: It's only a movie... It's only a movie!" I mean, that's great. What a way to sell.'

In fact, William Castle had already used the same line eight years earlier to sell his film *Strait-Jacket* (1964). Once again, horror's consummate showman had got there first.

Y for YearZero

Above: David Britton.
Opposite: *Lord Horror* by
John Coulthart.

W E LOVE TO SCARE ourselves by talking about the Apocalypse, or the advent of the Millennium, or the Global Rapture. Ready or not, the sky might be falling in. But the best thing about the year 2000 is the way it presses panic buttons in our imagination...

Britain's new wave of horror comics provokes and shocks. The works of both Savoy Books and Alan Moore have been branded obscene and seized by police. But their comic book heroes attract as strongly as they repel.

'Almost all subjects could perhaps be expressed more coherently in the comic book form,' says writer Alan Moore. 'I believe history is one subject that responds particularly well to a comic book treatment.'

Best known for his graphic novels *Swamp Thing, Marvelman* (aka *Miracleman*), *V for Vendetta* and *Watchmen,* the multiple award-winning Moore is perhaps Britain's most iconoclastic comics writer.

Beginning in 1988, he teamed up with artist Eddie Campbell to create a sixteen-part melodrama entitled *From Hell.* A meticulous dissection of the Jack the Ripper murders and the theories and conspiracies that still surround the case, the series is described by Moore as 'a post-mortem of an historical occurrence, using fiction as a scalpel'. It was finally published as a part-work between 1991 and 1995.

'It's my belief that if you cut into a thing deeply enough,' says Moore, 'if your incisions are precise and persistent and conducted methodically, then you may reveal not only that thing's inner workings, but also the meaning behind those workings. The conviction was shared by the historical personage whose life is central to *From Hell*, although perhaps his beliefs were expressed somewhat more broadly than mine. For my part, I am concerned with cutting into and examining the still-warm corpse of history itself. In some of my chilliest moments, I suspect that this was his foremost preoccupation also, albeit in pursuit of different ends...'

If *From Hell* is a narrative journey into the dark heart of Victorian England, then David Britton's *Lord Horror* is a revisionist account of the rise of Nazism as seen through the eyes of a madman. The character first appeared in 1989 in a satirical novel written by Britton, co-founder of Savoy Books, and was later adapted into graphic format in Savoy's *Lord Horror* and *Hard Core Horror* comics.

'I don't think anyone would disagree that the

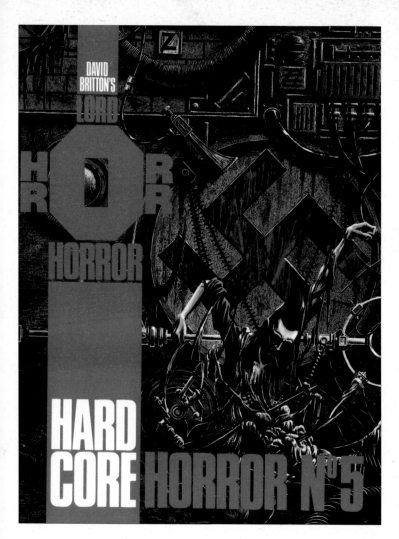

Opposite and left: Cover illustration by John Coulthart for *Hard Core Horror No 5*.

'David Britton's *Hard Core Horror* is an extraordinary work that simultaneously indicts and explodes the presumed conventions of the comic medium.'

Speakeasy, Issue 116, December 1990/ January 1991

'Soon after the appearance of *Lord Horror*, a Manchester magistrate ruled the book obscene. Since then, both Britton and Savoy Books have been involved in police raids, court cases, and the threat of destruction for a number of their publications, including a comic based on Lord Horror. A 1992 court ruling calling for the destruction of impounded copies of the novel was overturned after Savoy and international free-speech group Article 19 filed a successful appeal.'

Locus, Issue 388, May 1993

twentieth century has, in many ways, been the worst that humanity has seen so far,' says *Lord Horror* artist John Coulthart. 'And it is our belief that that demands a new form of horror.

'On the one hand you've got the glamour of violence and the glamour of the characters themselves, but on the other hand you've got them being involved in events that are totally beyond the pale. As far as the fascism and the racism goes, they're really unacceptable.

'Lord Horror is based on William Joyce, the Nazi propagandist of the Second World War. He did broadcasts to England for the Nazis under the nickname Lord Haw Haw.'

Savoy Books editor and co-founder Mike Butterworth describes the character as 'a right-wing radical, and not many people have chosen right-wing radicals as sympathetic heroes in comics'.

'The reader has to step back,' continues Coulthart,

Opposite: *Lord Horror* by John Coulthart.

'especially if it is the central character, and examine what it is they are actually being shown and what they might be identifying with. And if they identify with it, what does that say about them?'

'I always see Lord Horror as being a very Byronic character,' says Savoy artist Kris Guidio. 'The man is a metropolitan Hamlet. He was a fashion violator to be honest, so I like to think that I gave him his look. The man's a hairdresser's nightmare – you couldn't look like that and not be romantic to some extent.'

According to Coulthart, Lord Horror has a direct lineage to some other historical villains: 'His character builds on some of the horror characters of the nineteenth century,' he explains. 'You've got Sweeney Todd – madness and razor blades. You've got Jack the Ripper, you've got Count Dracula stalking through the streets, and that leads to Nosferatu, which is a kind of visual influence on some of Horror's character. I think what we've added is an extra edge of darkness which suits the extra edge of darkness that's in our century but wasn't in the previous one.'

'The numerous characters who populate the story all existed once,' says Alan Moore of his series *From Hell*. 'The motivations I have attributed to them and the words I have placed in their mouths are based, wherever possible, upon exacting historical research. Beyond that point I have relied upon guesswork and conjecture, which, while it cannot hope to be accurate, is at least, I hope, informed.

'In the course of *From Hell*, we link up a number of historical sites around London into a fascinating magical pattern, but of course if you take a large enough magic marker and a small enough map, it is possible to make any pattern that you care to make.

'One of the initial impetuses behind *From Hell* was probably born from the statement made by Margaret Thatcher, when she suggested that we should return to Victorian values. With *From Hell*, I thought it would be a good idea, perhaps instructive, if we found out what those Victorian values actually were.

'Jack the Ripper is, even among serial killers, a special figure. He was never caught. He escaped, not only into history, but into legend. What I wanted to do was to come up with a story that didn't solve the murders so much as try to solve the entire society surrounding that murder. There is no cheap melodrama, there are no shots of people running amok with bloody knives and snarling. It's all very quiet. If we show people going into a sweetshop, that's believable. If we show them walking down the street, that's believable. If we show them

Above: Alan Moore.

'There is no hanging at the end of *From Hell*. The verdict remained open, the history books silent, the noose empty.'

Alan Moore (above)

cutting a prostitute's kidney out and hanging her entrails over her shoulder, that's believable.

'Now,' continues Moore, 'if you had lived in the Whitechapel region during this period, in some way that would have had an effect upon the way your life worked. We are not just talking about architecture here. We are talking about something that I suppose you could call psycho-tecture – the fact that buildings have a massive effect upon our minds. In fact, Hawksmoor churches were designed to have a massive effect upon our minds.

'All of the forces that shape our lives now seem to have had their beginning then, whether you are talking about art or science or politics. For example, the machine gun was invented in the 1880s. The motor car. In my researches, I found out that at more or less the same time that the Ripper murders happened here, Adolf Hitler was being conceived in Austria.'

In *Lord Horror*, David Britton uses his character as a metaphor for the events that occurred during the period 1933–45, from Hitler's investiture as Reichkanzeller to the appalling horror of the Holocaust.

But not everybody was happy with Britton's unflinching depiction of the Nazi atrocities. In 1991, two years after the original novel was seized in a police raid at the Savoy offices, a Manchester magistrates' court judged the book obscene because of its title character's malignant anti-Semitism. Although author Michael Moorcock called the novel, 'one of the most authoritative indictments of the Holocaust and our moral responsibility to it', Manchester police subsequently seized copies of *Lord Horror* and *Hard Core Horror* as well, and on 19 July 1995, magistrate Janet Howard ruled the comics obscene and without any literary or artistic merit that might justify a 'public good' defence. However, Savoy maintains that the comics have been targeted because of their less than flattering portrait of Manchester's ex-Chief Police Constable, James Anderton, who initiated the original raid in 1991.

'What I was trying to portray with the Holocaust illustrations was a kind of lateral view of the real events,' explains artist John Coulthart, 'and it is what I call a metaphysical portrait of the death camps, not a realistic one. In a sense, we had to try to invent our own vocabulary. There is no story. It is just a succession of images. It is just the still shots of buildings, pipes, brickwork, schools, things like that. And so you're left with the pictures, which are worth a thousand words as far as I'm concerned.'

'It is deliberately provocative in certain ways,' admits Kris Guidio. 'There are sequences in it where I've

'There's nothing I can say about the absurdities of censorship that hasn't been said better by other people. It's self-evident in a way. You're not dealing with rational thought processes.'

Clive Barker

'Fortunately, *From Hell* is also a horror story... It is a horror story about the fateful patterns that exist in time; in human enterprise; even in the stones of the cities wherein we conduct our lives. It's the horror story buried at the roots of the twentieth century, and it just might conceivably be true.'

Alan Moore

'I cannot reveal anything except this: of course, we knew who [the Ripper] was, one of the highest in the land.'

Inspector Abberlaine, quoted by Nigel Morland, Editor, in *The Criminologist*, 1979

submitted drawings to David [Britton] and he's actually said to me, "Oh, there can be much more blood on this page," or whatever, and there is always the desire to go one stage beyond what the last person did. And of course it has worth – you know that approach has worth. We're now in a position where there is nothing like it. For better or for worse, good and bad, people use Savoy comics as a yardstick.'

Alan Moore has also not shied away from showing graphic violence in his work: 'For me, the key scene in the entire *From Hell* is the murder and butchery of Marie Kelly, where he spent two hours in a room cutting her up. He had time to be, shall we say – creative.

'You have thirty pages of a man in a room with a dead body. There are snatches of dialogue when he imagines that he is talking to somebody who isn't in fact there. But there are also long, *excruciating* silent sequences which feel very nerve shredding; these long silences where you just wish he'd say something or do anything other than keep cutting pieces off this woman. It becomes appalling. Hopefully, the reaction of the audience is a long way removed from the general arousal that these scenes seem usually to elicit. I want them actually to be in that room with me and with him.

'What *From Hell* can tell us about our own lives, is that those same ancient destructive forces, that same misogyny, that same darkness, is still with us and, for all our veneer of technology, we've not managed to banish those shadows even slightly.'

Both *From Hell* and *Lord Horror* are damning reflections of horrific historical events. As long as writers like Alan Moore and David Britton have the courage to continue to detail the atrocities that mankind is capable of, then comic books and graphic novels will continue to remain a viable form of creative expression well into the new millennium.

'As the century draws to its end,' Moore says, 'we find that our entire culture seems to be boiling and bubbling and erupting into strange new forms. I think that it is the job of artists to help us to understand the new shapes that our world is blossoming into.'

Below: *From Hell* by Eddie Campbell.

'One of the things that Alan Moore and I have in common is a kind of social contexting. The distress that we feel about the status quo, about the current English cultural condition, finds its way into the fiction.'

Clive Barker

Z For Zombie

'And death shall be no more; death thou shalt die.'

From Hymn to Christ, at the author's last going into Germany by John Donne

PHOTOGRAPHER SIMON MARSDEN HAS described images of death as 'perhaps the most shocking sort of image one can use'. Yet death is something that comes to us all – or does it? Perhaps by embracing these macabre *memento mori* and feeding our morbid fascination, we somehow hope to cheat the Grim Reaper when he comes calling...

For opthalmologist and photo historian Dr Stanley B. Burns MD, that fascination takes the form of collecting photographs of the dead. 'It's sometimes hard to admit the beauty in these photographs,' he says. 'You have a dichotomy – a wonderfully composed picture that is also a picture of a dead person.

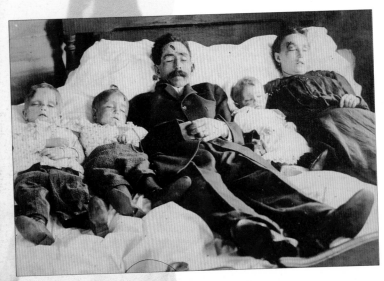

Above: The murdered Parsons family.
Opposite: *Day of the Dead.*

'As an eye surgeon I became interested in how people see, how they understand the world, in their visual perception – recognizing that perception has to do with the pictures we make in our brain as well as what we see. As a collector, one of the things that soon astounded me was the realization that the second most common type of photograph in the nineteenth century was that of a dead person.

'Now what would happen if you had never had a picture of your child and the child died? If your only opportunity was to take a picture of the deceased child, or your dead wife, then that was what was done.'

In one example, a mother holds not her child, but a daguerreotype of her dead child. 'It was a novel way to solve the contradiction,' Burns explains. 'The need to push the dead away and the need to keep the dead alive.'

Dr Burns' collection also includes pictures of murder victims, such as that of the Parsons family. 'Five members of one family who were killed by a Mr Hamilton,' he explains. 'That picture is not a documentary photograph as proof of their murder, but a memorial photograph, to be sent to family, friends and loved ones.

'You could be cleaned up,' he continues. 'Your tissues could be filled. You could be beautified. Cosmeticology became important and, as time went on, the person became more lifelike in death. Some of the comments at the time referred to how "lifelike" the person looked. How the person looked as if they were still alive, how

'Now zombies are a different kettle of rotted flesh entirely, aren't they? Because, for one thing, they're mindless – and mindlessness terrifies the wits out of me. Joke.'

Clive Barker

Z

'Zombies are about dealing with death. They represent a specific face of death. And the fact that we can even talk like this about a horror movie creation puts down the theory that the genre can't be taken seriously.'

Clive Barker

they never looked any better.

'By the end of the nineteenth century, beautification of death created an image of a person lying in a silken or satin casket, surrounded by flowers in a beautiful, comfortable setting. In another photograph we have a typical sleeping beauty. We have a woman who is lying just at rest as if a kiss would wake her up.

'You could look at that picture as long as you wanted. Some person will look at it for a fraction of a second. Another will stare at it or come back to it again, and again, and again, as if maybe there is some information about death in the photograph, something they've learned about passing that barrier between the living and the dead.'

Face to face with a monster, most of us could probably handle ourselves pretty well – charm a vapire, side-step a werewolf. But of all the horror archetypes, zombies have

always scared us witless. Maybe it is because they are so unreasonable, so unemotional. Maybe it is because there are just so damn many of them. Many people yearn for immortality – for themselves or a loved one – but, as the sages say, be careful what you wish for, it might just come true...

One of the most successful and influential horror films ever made, *Night of the Living Dead*, was filmed in Pittsburgh in 1968 by a group of commercial film-makers who had never made a feature-length production before.

'I think there are a lot of people in Pittsburgh who have been zombies in my zombie films,' says director George Romero, 'and maybe they have gone on to be zombies in other people's zombie films. People seem to enjoy doing that.'

Bill Burchinal worked for a Pittsburgh advertising agency as a television producer. 'I hired George Romero and his company to film my commercials for me,' he explains. 'That's how

Z

'There is also a great fascination with death – not so much with death itself, but what happens after. In a weird kind of way you are giving people encouragement that when they die it is not the end.'
James Herbert

Below: *Night of the Living Dead* (1968).

Below: George Remero
behind the scenes on
Dawn of the Dead.

I knew George. When I found out that he was going to do a feature film and was looking for help from all his friends to be extras, I volunteered. I spent a weekend at this abandoned farmhouse and that's how I became a zombie.'

With its stark, monochromatic photography, graphic gore and uncompromising ending, the film has spawned many sequels, copies and even a remake, and is widely regarded as a touchstone for the modern horror movie.

Romero wrote the original story and also directed, photographed and edited the film. But *Night of the Living Dead* is not the work of only one man. As screenwriter John Russo recalls, 'George Romero, Richard Ricci and I were sitting in a bar eating grilled sandwiches and drinking beer. We were kind of dissatisfied with the fickleness of our commercial clients and we were waiting for a chance to make a feature movie anyway. So I said, 'What if ten of us got together and each of us put up maybe six hundred bucks, we'd have six thousand dollars. Could we make any kind of feature movie on that?'

A corporation called Image Ten was formed to secure the investment and produce the film. Because of the low budget, *Night of the Living Dead* was shot in thirty days, with cast and crew working twenty-hour shifts. Many of the film-makers slept at the house where they were shooting, which had no running water, and friends and family would visit and cook food.

Russell Streiner was co-producer of the film and also played the role of Johnny, one of the first victims of the living dead. 'There was a local television station running an exceptionally poor package of horror films – *Attack of the Crab Monsters* or whatever – and our feeling was that if we couldn't do something that was at least as good as that, we might as well stick to TV commercials.'

According to Romero, 'The scenes that make *Night of the Living Dead* work and sort of pull you in, are the opening sequences up until Barbara arrives at the house. First you're completely disorientated, you have no idea what's going on. There is somebody out there, and then it turns out to be more than one somebody. They look very normal but they are hostile. If *Night of the Living Dead* taps into fundamental fears that have nothing to do with society or the times, I think they are probably fears of the afterlife. Fears of being isolated and alone, even in the community. Probably that's the biggest fear. You know,

BELA LUGOSI in "VOODOO MAN"
A MONOGRAM PICTURE   JOHN CARRADINE   featuring GEORGE ZUCCO

I've often joked that the most frightening thing to me is the neighbours.

'Night of the Living Dead is specifically saying that you're not talking to each other, electronic media doesn't work, people don't communicate. If they only pulled together and decided to do one thing – even if it was the wrong thing. But no one ever talks about anything, they just think they're right.

'In the film, Harry Cooper thinks he's right but he's coming from a different place, so we are all rooting for Ben because he seems to be more like us. But really Ben is wrong about the physical situation and Harry is right. I love to play with those kinds of ironies because what you find as you go through life is that there are no guarantees, no clear-cut situations. It is very rare that you meet a really evil person, and also very rare that you meet a saint.'

'One of the investors in our project was a man who had a food purveying company,' reveals Streiner, 'and one of his businesses was a butcher's shop. So we got beef bones and entrails from him which ended up in the scene that we referred to in the movie as The Last Supper.'

'The good horror director must have a clear sense of where the taboo line lies, if he is not to lapse into unconscious absurdity, and a gut understanding of what the countryside is like on the far side of it. In Night of the Living Dead, George Romero plays a number of instruments, and he plays them like a virtuoso.'

Stephen King

'Before that time,' Russo says, 'zombies weren't what I'd call heavyweight fright material like Frankenstein or the Wolf Man. But when we made them flesh-eaters it gave them a whole new dimension. And then the fact that they didn't die, it was like having a kind of eternal life that nobody really wants.'

NIGHT OF THE LIVING DEAD

USA, 1968. Dir: George Romero. With: Judith O'Dea, Russell Streiner, Duane Jones, Karl Hardman, Keith Wayne, Judith Ridley. Image Ten. B&W.

This gruesome, low-budget zombie film has acquired a cult reputation since its original release, thanks to the stark black and white photography, bleak locations and a cast of unknowns, all of which give the picture a disturbing, documentary-like feel. A Venus probe returning to Earth brings with it an alien contamination that revives the newly dead. A small band of survivors barricade themselves in a farmhouse and attempt to repel the flesh-eating ghouls who lay siege to the building. The opening graveyard sequence is a minor masterpiece of atmospheric horror and, despite repeated viewings, the surprise ending still has the power to shock. *S.J.*

Sequels: *Dawn of the Dead* (aka *Zombies*, Dir: George A. Romero, 1978); *Day of the Dead* (Dir: George A. Romero, 1985). Remake: *Night of the Living Dead* (Dir: Tom Savini, 1990).

Calling upon their friends and associates in the advertising business, the film-makers used around 250 extras, many of whom played pasty-faced, living dead ghouls.

Bill Hinzman was one of them, and he recalls his motivation for the role: 'Subconsciously, I remembered a Boris Karloff movie where he had been electrocuted and was dragging one leg and one arm was limp and groping and he was contorted. I tried to do that, though it became quite sore after a while, doing it for all that time. And then I just tried to think what it would be like to be very hungry.'

Marilyn Eastman, who played Helen Cooper in the film, was one of the original backers and also supervised the make-up. 'Everybody wants to believe in life after death,' she says, 'and I think the living dead is the closest thing to that idea. Except people do come back – so you get your wish for immortality – they come back as horrifying things.'

Co-producer Karl Hardman, who played the cowardly conservative Harry Cooper, agrees. 'It makes you not want to come back.'

'Yes,' continues Eastman. 'That's very difficult for people to handle because they do want to believe that there is life after death, but they don't want to believe that it's monstrous.'

One of the film's most disturbing scenes is when

'In 1968, the year that popularized rebelliousness and non-conformity, *Night of the Living Dead* did its bit for the Age of Aquarius by ignoring decades of cinema convention.'

Kim Newman

Harry and Helen's daughter Karen, who has been bitten by a ghoul, dies in the basement and returns as one of the cannibalistic dead.

'I thought it would be very nice if Karl's daughter Kyra could work with him,' explains Eastman, 'and I suggested that she be used, and I think it was very nice for her and for him.'

Kyra Schon, who portrayed Karen Cooper, recalls that 'My father told me that I would be playing a zombie or a ghoul, and that I'd be eating my father's arm and killing my mother. And I thought, great. That sounds great.'

'There was no rating system at the time in America,' explains Romero, 'and so basically the film went out unrated. It was one of probably half a dozen films that made people complain and insist that the industry control itself.'

Marilyn Eastman reveals there is one question she is always asked about her involvement in the film: 'Everybody always wants to know what the blood is splattering on the wall in my death scene. What did you use? And it was Bosco chocolate syrup, which gave us the best look, the best texture, and I don't know why we thought it was better than Hershey, but at the time that's the decision we made.'

George Romero admits that much of the film's attraction is its gore and violence. 'I know that for anyone who loves horror, that's the stuff you love. It doesn't gross you out, it makes you giggle. That's when you munch your candies or your pretzels, or whatever, even more vigorously – when there is bleeding going on.'

Russell Streiner says, 'One of the key scenes in *Night of the Living Dead* is the scene where Johnny, the character that I play, comes back. It's the real signal that everything is lost. The people in the house are really done for.'

'The initial thought is, "My brother's back,"' explains actress Judy O'Dea, who portrayed the film's nominal heroine, Barbara. 'You know that first thought: "He's back, he's alive." Because I will him alive. I want him to be alive, yet I see the dead in his eyes, and I know that there's no saving me. Because not only am I going to die, but I am going to die at the hand of the brother I loved.'

'Horror is radical,' says Romero. 'It can take you into a completely new world, new place, and just rattle your cage and say, wait a minute – look at things differently. That shock of horror is what horror's all about. But in most cases, at the end of the story, people try to bring everything back – the girl gets the guy and everything's fine and things go on just the way they were. Which is

'I think the film is an attempt to make money. And it's an attempt to tell a good, honest, emotionally involving story. A lot of critics have jumped off the deep end in likening the ghouls to the silent majority and finding all sorts of implications that none of us ever intended. I think George wants to encourage that kind of thinking on the part of some critics. But I'd rather tell them they're full of shit.'

John Russo

WE ARE GOING TO EAT YOU!

ZOMBIE

...THE DEAD ARE AMONG US!

'There are no boundaries between good and evil where love is concerned.'

James O'Barr

'People once believed
that when a person
died, a crow carried
their soul to the land
of the dead. But
sometimes,
something so bad
happens that a
terrible sadness is
carried with it; and
the soul can't rest.
Then sometimes, just
sometimes, the crow
can bring that soul
back to make the
wrong things right.'

From *The Crow* (1994)

Above: James O'Barr.

really why we are doing this in the first place. We don't want things the way they are or we wouldn't be trying to shock you into an alternative place.'

In the film's unexpected ending, after surviving a long night of horror defending the farmhouse against the marauding dead, black hero Ben (Duane Jones) is callously shot and killed by a posse of redneck zombie hunters. His body is then added to a pyre of burning corpses.

'We always had that ending,' says Romero. 'It seemed like the only fitting end. And even though the posse goes rolling across the countryside leaving our hero dead, we get the feeling that they are not going to win either. There's this new society coming. In the end, none of this is going to work guys.'

James O'Barr was born in 1960. He grew up in the Detroit area and was raised in institutional and foster care. A self-taught artist since his early teens, O'Barr studied Renaissance sculpture and the work of such comics artists as Frank Frazetta, Barry Smith and especially Will Eisner.

'God had had His elbow on my neck my whole life,' says O'Barr, 'like I was being tested to see how much I could put up with.'

In the early 1980s, someone very close to the artist was killed. 'To me at the time she was an angel,' he recalls. 'It was like the sunshine came into my life for the first time. I finally had something to live for. Then when her father called me on the phone from the hospital, I thought it was an incredibly poor joke to tell me. But when he started to cry I knew it wasn't a joke any longer. A drunk driver came down her street and killed her. I wanted some kind of retribution for it. I wanted someone to pay for all this anger and pain that I was going through, and that was essentially where the story of *The Crow* came from. That was the genesis of it.'

O'Barr joined the Marines and, while stationed in Berlin, he began drawing *The Crow*. 'It came pouring out,' he says. The first issue was published in February 1989 by Caliber Press. It was dedicated to Ian Curtis, the lead singer of the band Joy Division, who hung himself at the age of twenty-five.

'*The Crow* is a love story fuelled by a horror story,' explains O'Barr, 'and it concerns Eric and Shelly who are madly in love and who are atrociously killed by a gang of young thugs. Eric returns from the grave to mete out vengeance against these characters.'

Four issues appeared before the series was put on hold because of financial difficulties. In 1991, Tundra Publishing began repackaging the out-of-print Caliber issues in two volumes, and published a third issue

ZOMBIES IN THE MOVIES

White Zombie (1932), The Ghoul (1933), Ouanga (1934), Revolt of the Zombies (aka Revolt of the Demons; 1936), The Walking Dead (1936), Condemned Men (1940), The Ghost Breakers (1940), King of the Zombies (1941), Bowery at Midnight (1942), I Walked with a Zombie (1943), Revenge of the Zombies (aka The Corpse Vanished; 1943), The Soul of a Monster (1944), Voodoo Man (1944), Zombies on Broadway (aka Loonies on Broadway; 1945), Scared Stiff (1953), Creature with the Atom Brain (1955), The Gamma People (1955), Teenage Zombies (1957), Voodoo Island (aka Silent Death; 1957), The Zombies of Mora Tau (aka The Dead that Walk; 1957), Invisible Invaders (1959), Plan 9 from Outer Space (1959), Night of the Ghouls (aka Revenge of the Dead; 1959), The Dead One (1960), Doctor Blood's Coffin (1961), Invasion of the Zombies (aka Santo contra los Zombies/Santo vs the Zombies; 1961), Tales of Terror (1962), The Atomic Brain (aka Monstrosity; 1963), War of the Zombies (aka Roma contra Roma/Night Star, Goddess of Electra; 1963), The Earth Dies Screaming (1964), The Last Man on Earth (aka L'Ultimo Uomo della Terra; 1961/64), Terror Creatures from the Grave (aka Cinque Tombe per un Medium/Cemetery of the Living Dead; 1965), The Plague of the Zombies (1966), The Astro-Zombies (1968), Night of the Living Dead (1968), I Eat Your Skin (1964/71), Virgin Among the Living Dead (aka Christina, Princesse de L'Erotisme/I Desideri Erotici di Christine; 1971), Bracula – The Terror of the Living Dead (aka La Orgia de los Muertos/La Orgia dei Morti/Return of the Zombies/Beyond the Living Dead/The Hanging Woman; 1972), Children Shouldn't Play with Dead Things (aka Revenge of the Living Dead; 1972), Horror Rises from the Tomb (aka El Espanto Surge de la Tumba; 1972), Horror Express (aka Panico en el Transiberiano; 1972), La Invasion de los Muertos (aka Blue Demon y Zovek el la Invasion de los Muertos; 1972), Neither the Sea nor the Sand (1972), Tombs of the Undead (aka Garden of the Dead; 1972), The House of Seven Corpses (1973), Psychomania (aka The Death Wheelers; 1972), Vengeance of the Zombies (aka La Rebellion de las Muertas; 1972), Messiah of Evil (aka Dead People/Return of the Living Dead/Revenge of the Screaming Dead; 1973), Night of the Sorcerers (aka La Noche de los Brujos; 1973), Return of the Evil Dead (aka El Ataque de los Muertos Sin Ojos/Attack of the Blind Dead; 1973), The Living Dead at the Manchester Morgue (aka No Profanar el Sueno de los Muertos/Breakfast at the Manchester Morgue/Don't Open the Window/The Living Dead; 1974), The Dead Don't Die (TV, 1974), Horror of the Zombies (aka El Buque Maldito; 1974), The Legend of the 7 Golden Vampires (1974), Shanks (1974), Sugar Hill (aka Voodoo Girl; 1974), Night of the Seagulls

Left: The Beyond.
Middle: Boris Karloff in The Ghoul (1933).
Opposite: The Evil Dead.

(aka *La Noche de las Gaviotas/Terror Beach/Night of the Death Cult*; 1975), *Shock Waves* (aka *Almost Human/Death Corps*; 1976), *The Child* (aka *Kill and Go Hide!*; 1977), *Dawn of the Dead* (aka *Zombies*; 1978), *Les Raisins de la Mort* (1978), *The Day it Came to Earth* (1979), *It Came from the Sky* (aka *The Alien Dead*; 1979), *Zombie Flesh-Eaters* (aka *Zombi 2/The Island of the Living Dead/Zombie*; 1979), *Zombie Holocaust* (aka *La Regina dei Cannibali/Doctor Butcher MD (Medical Deviate)/Queen of the Cannibals/Island of the Last Zombies*; 1979), *The Bloodeaters* (aka *Forest of Fear/Toxic Zombies*; 1980), *The Children* (1980), *City of the Living Dead* (aka *La Paura nella Citta dei Morti/Gates of Hell*; 1980), *Nightmare City* (aka *Incubo Sulla Citta Contaminata/City of the Walking Dead*; 1980), *Zombie Lake* (aka *Le Lac des Morts Vivants/El Lago de los Muertos Vivientos*; 1980), *Zombie 3* (aka *Le Notti del Terrore/Nights of Terror/Zombie Horror*; 1980), *The Beyond* (aka *E tu Vivrai nel Terrore... L'Aldila/Seven Doors to Death*; 1981), *Dawn of the Mummy* (1981), *Dead & Buried* (1981), *Kung-Fu Zombie* (1981), *Night of the Zombies* (aka

Gamma 693; 1981), *Revenge of the Zombies* (aka *Black Magic II*; 1981), *Zombie Creeping Flesh* (aka *Inferno dei Mort-Viventi* 1981), *The Evil Dead* (1982), *I Was a Zombie for the FBI* (1982), *La Morte Vivante*; (1982), *Conquest* (aka *Mace il Fuorilegge*; 1983), *Thriller* (1983), *The Trail* (aka *Pao Dan Fie Che*; 1983), *Zombie Island Massacre* (1983), *Bloodsuckers from Outer Space* (1984), *Death Warmed Up* (1984), *Hard Rock Zombies* (1984), *The House* (1984), *Killing Time* (1984), *Night Shadows* (aka *Mutant*; 1984), *Night of the Comet* (1984), *Ragewar* (aka *The Dungeonmaster*; 1984), *The Return of the Living Dead* (1984), *Suffer Little Children* (1984), *Surf II* (1984), *The Dark Power* (1985), *Day of the Dead* (1985), *Lifeforce* (1985), *The Supernaturals* (1985), *Warning Sign* (1985), *Deadly Friend* (1986), *From a Whisper to a Scream* (aka *The Offspring*; 1986), *I Was a Teenage Zombie* (1986), *Redneck Zombies* (1986), *Zombie Nightmare* (1986), *Evil Dead II* (1987), *Graveyard Disturbance* (aka *Dentro il Cimitrio*; 1987), *House II: The Second Story* (1987), *Raiders of the Living Dead* (1987), *Return of the Living Dead Part II* (1987), *The Serpent and the Rainbow* (1987), *The Video Dead* (1987), *C.H.U.D. II Bud the Chud* (1988), *Dead Heat* (1988), *Ghost Town* (1988), *Howl of the Devil* (aka *El Aullido del Diablo*; 1988), *Magic Cop* (aka *Mr Vampire V*; 1989), *Night Life* (aka *Grave Misdemeanours*; 1989), *Pet Sematary* (1989), *Two Evil Eyes* (1989), *The Vineyard* (1989), *Voodoo Dawn* (1989), *Crazy Safari* (1990), *Dead Men Don't Die* (1990), *Night of the Living Dead* (1990), *Cast a Deadly Spell* (TV, 1991), *Chopper Chicks in Zombietown* (1991), *Waxwork II: Lost in Time* (aka *Lost in Time*; 1991), *Zombie '90: Extreme Pestilence* (1991), *Army of Darkness* (aka *Evil Dead III: Army of Darkness*; 1992), *Braindead* (aka *Dead Alive*; 1992), *Cthulhu Mansion* (aka *Black Magic Mansion*; 1992), *Pet Sematary II* (1992), *Weekend at Bernie's II* (1992), *Death Becomes Her* (1993), *Return of the Living Dead 3* (1993), *Dellamorte Dellamore* (aka *Cemetary Man* 1994), *Ed and His Dead Mother* (TV, 1994), *Shrunken Heads* (1994), *Witch Hunt* (TV, 1994).

THE CROW

USA, 1994. Dir: Alex Proyas. With: Brandon Lee, Ernie Hudson, Michael Wincott, David Patrick Kelly, Angel David, Rochelle Davis. Crowvision/Miramax/Dimension Films. Colour.

Billed as 'an urban fantasy of love and revenge', this loud, flashy and very violent supernatural thriller is based on the cult comic book series by James O'Barr. Set in a dark, dreary, rain-soaked near-future, where murder victim Eric Draven (Lee) is resurrected by the titular bird to avenge himself on the quartet of psycho-thugs who raped and killed his wife. Hudson stands out as Albrecht, the tough but tender chain-smoking cop, but Lee (to whom the film is dedicated) never manages to make much of an impression as the indestructible avenger under the theatrical make-up. Ultimately, the film is derivative and empty, but that didn't stop it becoming a box office hit. *S.J.*

Sequel: *The Crow: City of Angels* (Dir: Tim Pope, 1996).

containing the conclusion to the story. 'Death', the final chapter of *The Crow*, appeared in May 1992 and became the bestselling single issue in Tundra's history.

In February 1993, Australian rock video and commercials director Alex Proyas began shooting a movie version of *The Crow* for independent producer Edward R. Pressman. Action star Brandon Lee, the son of martial arts legend Bruce Lee, was chosen to play Eric Draven.

'Because we do not know when we will die, we get to think of life as an inexhaustible well,' said Lee, 'and yet everything happens only a certain number of times. How many more times will you remember a certain afternoon of your childhood, an afternoon that is so deeply a part of your being that you can't even conceive of your life without it? Perhaps four, five times more. Perhaps not even that. How many more times will you watch the full moon rise? Perhaps twenty, and yet it all seems limitless.'

'I don't believe Eric is a hero,' says O'Barr. 'He can be absolutely cold-blooded and ruthless at times. When he goes into a room to get one person, everyone else in the room is going to die as well. I think what he's doing is terribly romantic, but I wouldn't call him a hero.'

'He's a Victorian hero in some ways,' says author and critic John Shirley, who co-scripted the film version with David J. Schow, 'because he's extremely romantic and he's very tragic. But his whole style, the way he chooses to dress and his look and just his little bit of flirtation with androgyny, is very late twentieth century and very rock 'n' roll. That's what makes him post-modern. He's a post-modern zombie.'

Filming progressed smoothly on *The Crow* at the Carolco Studios in Wilmington, North Carolina, and Brandon Lee felt that he was destined to play the part. 'This is the best role that I've ever had the opportunity to get my hands on in film,' he said.

The final scenes set in Eric and Shelly's apartment had been saved for the last week of filming, allowing Lee to work without the theatrical make-up he wore as the avenging hero. Then, on the night of 31 March, the actor was injured when a blank cartridge was fired from a prop gun.

'There were a number of bizarre accidents on the set,'

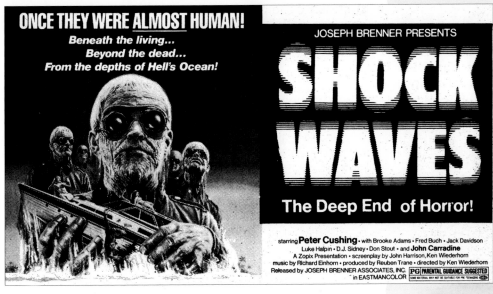

ONCE THEY WERE ALMOST HUMAN!

Beneath the living...
Beyond the dead...
From the depths of Hell's Ocean!

JOSEPH BRENNER PRESENTS

SHOCK WAVES

The Deep End of Horror!

starring **Peter Cushing** · with Brooke Adams · Fred Buch · Jack Davidson
Luke Halpin · D.J. Sidney · Don Stout · and **John Carradine**
A Zopix Presentation · screenplay by John Harrison, Ken Wiederhorn
music by Richard Einhorn · produced by Reuben Trane · directed by Ken Wiederhorn
Released by JOSEPH BRENNER ASSOCIATES, INC. PG PARENTAL GUIDANCE SUGGESTED
in EASTMANCOLOR

reveals Shirley. 'For instance, there was an electrician who was hurt very badly. There was a man who ran amok on the set at one point. There was another man who was apparently chased by the police on to the set. Then Brandon was killed.'

Brandon Lee died a few hours later at the Wilmington Hospital. He was twenty-eight years old.

'I'm not exactly sure how his death resolved all the turmoil in me,' says O'Barr, 'but it just kind of brought it full circle to where I could see everything in perspective. You know, you may wake up next to your wife or your lover a thousand times, or you may only wake up to her twenty times. So think about that every time. Don't take anything for granted. Standing there at his gravestone I realized that. I'm not nearly as angry as I used to be. There is still some in there, but that's me.'

Filming was immediately shut down with only eight days of shooting left, and *The Crow* was finally completed using a live-action double and digital compositing.

Tragically, Brandon Lee's premature death mirrored the theme of O'Barr's allegory about love, loss and retribution. When asked for his own views about his character's return from the grave, the actor replied: 'If I were given the opportunity after a year of having been dead to come back, who would I want to share it with? Who would I want to see? The person I would want to see would be my fiancée, Eliza, because I'm getting married after the film. And the thing about Eric is that the one person he would want to try and share this with isn't there any more, and that's the tragic element, the haunted element of this character.'

She's
ALIVE–YET DEAD!
DEAD–YET ALIVE!

The Strangest Case In All Mysteria!

Darkest Voodoo Secrets Revealed In—

I WALKED WITH A ZOMBIE

with JAMES ELLISON
FRANCES DEE
TOM CONWAY

RKO RADIO PICTURES

'For in that sleep of death what dreams may come.'

From *Hamlet* by
William Shakespeare

INDEX

Page numbers in *italic* refer to the illustrations.